CENTENNIAL

MERCER
UNIVERSITY PRESS

*Endowed by*
TOM WATSON BROWN
*and*
THE WATSON-BROWN FOUNDATION, INC.

# CENTENNIAL

## A HISTORY OF THE HENRY W. GRADY COLLEGE OF JOURNALISM AND MASS COMMUNICATION AT THE UNIVERSITY OF GEORGIA

E. CULPEPPER CLARK

*Mercer University Press / Macon, Georgia*

MUP/H910



Published by Mercer University Press
1400 Coleman Avenue
Macon, Georgia 31207


9 8 7 6 5 4 3 2 1

Books published by Mercer University Press are
printed on acid-free paper that meets the requirements
of the American National Standard for Information Sciences—
Permanence of Paper for Printed Library Materials.

Book design by Jim Burt / Burt&Burt

ISBN 978-0-88146-551-2

Cataloging-in-Publication Data is available from the Library of Congress

# FOREWORD

*Namesake*

THE HENRY W. GRADY COLLEGE OF JOURNALISM AND MASS COMMUNICATION IS BOTH A TRADITION AND A TRUST. At its centennial, approximately 65 faculty members, 35 professional staff members, 1,400 students, and over 23,000 alumni hold it. Named for the New South's chief journalist and publicist, his life and career continue to inspire. Born in Athens, Georgia, on May 24, 1850, he was too young to fight in the Civil War, although it swirled about his youth and took his father at Petersburg. As Sherman marched through Georgia, Grady was fourteen years of age. He graduated from the University of Georgia in 1872 and immediately after studied at the University of Virginia. At Georgia he was an artful orator and debater, joining Phi Kappa, the younger of the two literary societies, and successfully took on competition from the older Demosthenian Society. At Virginia he wanted desperately to be named senior orator and, when narrowly missing that prize, asked his mother for another year in Charlottesville to make good, which under depression-era circumstances was not affordable.

Grady also showed a flair for journalism and upon returning to Georgia made his way to Rome, about sixty miles west and slightly north of Atlanta. He displayed a gift for engaging the community and for writing about its people and

Henry Grady, second from left back row, and Chi Phi brothers, including future Chancellor Walter B. Hill, at left of Grady. *Hargrett Rare Books and Manuscript Library, University of Georgia*

events. Yet he was not equally skilled at business and his ventures there eventually failed. By the late seventies, he had made his way to Atlanta, where he soon linked up with Evan P. Howell and William A. Hemphill, the owners and managers of *The Atlanta Constitution*. They instantly saw the value he might add. On a trip to New York, Grady borrowed $20,000 from Cyrus W. Field, the financier who had backed the laying of the Atlantic cable, and bought a third interest in the *Constitution*. That investment and those partners provided a platform that would make the name Henry Woodfin Grady synonymous with the New South and famous in Atlanta, the region, and the nation. At his untimely death in 1889, a nation would mourn.

Grady was a tireless promoter of all things Atlanta. During the eighties he organized and executed three major expositions. The Cotton States Exposition in 1881, the Piedmont Expositions in 1887 and 1889, opened Atlanta for the world to see and transformed it into a destination point for commerce and investment. But his lasting fame was made in the course of three years. On the night of August 31, 1886, Grady's home shook, crystal tumbled and lights danced and swayed as tremors shook the city. Grady knew something big was happening and headed to his office. He and staff quickly discerned that telegraphic traffic was coming from all points but Charleston. Sensing correctly a natural disaster of epic proportions, in fact an earthquake of 7.6 magnitude, Grady made his way to Charleston with great difficulty, arranging for wagons and buggies when rail would not reach the city by the sea. Still, he was there by late September 2 and filing stories that evening, stories picked up by many newspapers, but most notably Joseph Pulitzer's *New York World.*

Those stories cemented Grady's reputation, not simply as a regional journalist, but as a national figure. When later that year the New England Society of New York looked about for a speaker for its December gathering at Delmonico's, Grady was their choice. The great men of commerce, finance, war, and religion were there, almost all Republicans, both the architects and scions of victory in a Civil War now only two decades past. Grady knew his opportunity and seized it. That speech, acknowledged by Missouri Senator Champ Clark a generation later as "the most famous after-dinner speech within the memory of living man," established Grady as spokesperson of the New South spirit of progress and good will.

Grady, New South's chief journalist and publicist. *Hargrett Rare Books and Manuscript Library, University of Georgia*

Grady eased into his speech with compliments to the platform party, which included William Tecumseh Sherman, whom he characterized as a man "a little careless with fire." The audience loved it, but Grady was driving toward his main point, lines attributed to an earlier distinguished Georgian, Benjamin Harvey Hill, a member of both the Confederate and later U.S. Congress. Grady proclaimed, "There was a South of slavery and secession—that South is dead. There is a South of union and freedom—that South, thank God is living, growing every hour." Yet Grady had been given his main opportunity when earlier in the ceremonies Dewitt Talmadge, one of the great preachers of the day, said that the nation was yet to identify a "typical American," an individual who personified the virtues of the nation. Being a great extemporizer, Grady took exception, the nation had produced a "typical American," a man who embodied the virtue of a diverse people and united what stern custom parted wide. That man, "the first typical American, the first who comprehended within himself all the strength and gentleness, all the majesty and grace of the republic, [was] Abraham Lincoln." The audience burst into unabashed applause.

As the host committee congratulated itself on such a superb choice for the postprandial speech, Henry Grady had three years and one day to live. In that time, he traveled throughout his region and from Dallas to Boston preaching the gospel of a New South, emerging phoenix-like from the ashes of defeat and destruction. If Grady oversold the South's accomplishments, he won sufficient converts to make it the dominant theme for progress and prosperity that would finally be realized in the mid-twentieth century, when during the civil rights era Atlanta billed itself as the city "too busy to hate." In that time Atlanta would come to embrace another of its favorite sons, Martin Luther King, Jr., who like Grady would not live beyond age thirty-nine. King took the South, however resisting, the rest of the way.

Indeed, it was while Grady was in Boston addressing the subject of race and the South's future that he contracted pneumonia. Upon his return to Atlanta, he collapsed on the station platform and died two days before Christmas, plunging Atlanta into mourning at a time of high celebration. Grady did not have the keys or yet the vision that would unlock the shackles of segregation and open the South to all its potential, but that night in Boston he was groping with the most difficult issue of the South's, indeed the nation's, past and in a city that had led the charge for abolition and the possibilities of freedom, even if those possibilities would not be realized for another century.

So, for the first time since the Civil War, Atlanta and the South found itself building a monument to someone other than a soldier or commander or statesman of the Lost Cause. At the corner of Marietta and Forsyth, Grady's statue, in oratorical pose, shouts his vision above the din and tumult of Atlanta traffic. Atlanta's charity hospital, a high school, a county in Georgia and one in Oklahoma, even an elementary school in Dallas have all been named for him, and so too this college. The New South's foremost publicist and journalist, the man who made a name for himself in three years of earnest endeavor, lives on in the generations of students who proudly proclaim themselves as Grady grads. When we say that Grady College is both "a tradition and a trust," the college holds the trust for "democracy's next generation." Although he could not have envisioned its entailments, Henry W. Grady would have liked that most of all.

A word on Liberalism. In Chapter 2 you will find Georgians primarily but with links to Chapel Hill as well talking about liberalism as the nation sought new definitions about a founding term. Only in recent history has the term liberal become one of disparagement from the political right in American politics—the "L" word. In its eighteenth-century incarnation, it was coterminous with enlightenment thought. In that century it was in fact revolutionary, the American and French revolutions specifically. The road

Unveiling of Grady statue, October 1891. *Courtesy* ***Atlanta Journal-Constitution***

forked in the 19th century with Federalists and Anti-federalists, Washingtonians and Jeffersonians, Lincoln and Douglas divided over its implications for government. Still, most parties and factions appropriated the term for their own purposes. Republican reformers in the late nineteenth century who fought corruption in government and allied with progressives in the South like Grady, called themselves Liberal Republicans, practicing what today is called Classical Liberalism. In the early twentieth century, progressive Republicans who identified with Teddy Roosevelt differed with progressive Democrats who supported Woodrow Wilson along lines resembling the split between Washington and Jefferson.

The New Deal, with its ideas of social and economic reform, along with expanded citizenship and the role of government, changed all that. For many on the right in American politics, liberalism would become a term of opprobrium. The explanation has relevance for this story, because our notions of journalism and its role in society are embedded in the First Amendment to the Constitution, a document of the eighteenth century, when liberalism was a compelling, even revolutionary thought. So in this account of the emergence of journalism education generally and the Grady College specifically, educators, politicians and concerned citizens debate and discuss the term "liberal" in ways that differ in some respects from its common usage now. When today some say the media, or journalists specifically, are all liberal, they are right in that journalism's role is to speak truth to power, especially in the public sector but also in the private sector where government enables the accumulation of great wealth and power. Conservative columnist Thomas Sowell thinks he is doing it in the traditional sense, as does liberal columnist Thomas Friedman. They are both liberals in that respect. More strikingly, the so-called revolution ushered in by Ronald Reagan and Margaret Thatcher in the 1970's grew out of a movement in the 1930's known to pundits, theorists, and historians who embraced it as "neoliberalism" or the "third way."

A recent historian of liberalism, Edmund Fawcett, says it is a "practice" not an ideology. He dates its origins to the 1830s, although acknowledges its intellectual debt to earlier Enlightenment thought. As a practice, or what rhetorical scholars call "praxis," meaning process, liberalism is an approach to government that believes it should be "non-obstructive, non-obtrusive, and non-exclusive." Not until the 20th century did the non-exclusive feature emerge, meaning individuals should not be excluded from government by virtue of class, race, gender, and so on—in brief, equality. Although Lincoln articulated an idea of equality in his later considerations of why a great Civil War was necessary, it would not flower for another hundred years to motivate current political practice and debate. Having triumphed over fascism and dealt a blow to communism in World War II, liberalism, as understood in modern political discourse, now finds only about twenty percent of American voters identifying with it. Its shrinkage parallels the equation between the "non-exclusion" of minorities with use of "entitlements"—the unearned dividend, by conservative lights. Those identifying as conservatives own forty-five percent of the current electorate. It is a fundamental debate and national divide.

The conversation about liberalism as back-story picks up in chapter two and is echoed throughout, especially as Gradyites who held prominent roles in the Atlanta newspapers of the twentieth century challenged readers toward the new way forward. From the fifties through the eighties, chapters four and five, the debate over who is or is not progressive enough rends and tears at the fabric of the "two Georgias," Atlanta and the rest of the state, and indeed inner and outer Atlanta, as the politics of race and culture define them.

This story, then, matters. It is about journalism, media, and communication as fundamentals of American democracy. It is also about how the

University of Georgia came to accept that charge as fundamental to its mission. And while journalism cannot escape its political edge, a College of Journalism and Mass Communication is also about its allied disciplines that range from advertising and public relations to entertainment and documentary film-making in the digital age, the storytelling disciplines that capture who we are in both nonfiction and fiction alike. In this account each emerges separate and distinct, if from a common starting point.

## A NOTE ON SOURCES AND ACKNOWLEDGEMENTS

I have been talking about the Grady College for nine years, seven as dean. This book is but the tip of conversations, books, articles, papers, manuscripts and the online e-verse that has transformed historical research. My previous books arose from thousands of hours in the bowels of libraries and their appropriately named special collections. I loved every minute of it as I leafed the pages touched by the principals who had produced them, even to the detritus of filing cabinets. In those moments I made physical contact with the authors of my stories. The same is true of this story. Every day in the Journalism Building, in meetings on and off campus, and in thousands of miles visiting friends and alumni, I was in my element, talking about what the Grady College does and, more importantly, what it means. Each and every person I have engaged about the college and their relationship to it and their own lives and families know me to draw energy from them.

So in acknowledging sources, I begin with students, colleagues, friends, and the greater Grady family. They were and remain my inspiration, and each knows it. In the chapters that follow there are profiles of a few among the many. Had I acknowledged all in that way, this book would have had no ending. Indeed, it does not, other than its arbitrary cut off, because each and all are in my memory forever. In the pages that follow you will find notes to secondary and primary sources that show where I found facts and interpretations of the day to day. I have tried to be spare in the noting, so as not to burden the reader, with the result that not every factoid from an annual report has an endnote. For example, facts that obviously come from a particular year will not have a note. Also, I have made liberal use of parenthetical comments to amplify the text without forcing the reader to endnotes. A list of sources appears at the end.

The online universe changes everything. Literally, almost no impulse or thought fails to get an answer. Reliability, for example the crowd-sourced

Wikipedia, has been much discussed and vetted. Of course, the online universe contains much more: links to obituaries, articles, curriculum vitae, and so on. So that universe has also been a rich source. I will walk through but one example as lead-in to the story I am about to tell.

One of the enduring friendships I acquired as dean is with Steve Oney (ABJ 79), a former Nieman Fellow at Harvard and a writer who lives in California. Only this year, he spent six months as a Shorenstein Fellow at Harvard. A year ago, I was with Steve and his equally accomplished wife Madeline Stuart in their Hollywood Hills home, and did we drill down! Fact checking yesterday, I came across reviews and commentary on his highly acclaimed book *And the Dead Shall Rise: The Murder of Mary Phagan and the Lynching of Leo Frank*, a story that serves as backdrop to the beginnings of the Grady College. Someone murdered thirteen year-old Mary Phagan in 1913 (the year the University of Georgia offered its first course in journalism.) She was found in an Atlanta pencil factory where she worked and under circumstances that suggested rape. Leo Frank, a Cornell-educated engineer, was manager there and in the building at the time the murder likely occurred.

Steve Oney. *Courtesy Steve Oney, photo by Kristen Buckingham*

Frank was accused and convicted. Subsequent trials upheld the conviction but admitted of doubt as to his guilt, so much so that the governor of Georgia commuted his sentence to life in prison in 1915 (the year the Journalism School was founded at UGA.) Because Frank was a Jew and a northerner, passions were inflamed. Twenty-eight white men, among them a minister, at least two judges, and a former governor, seized Frank from his prison cell in Middle Georgia, drove him 120 miles through the night to a site just outside Marietta, near where little Mary Phagan had grown up the daughter of a tenant farmer, and lynched him at 7:00 am on August 17, 1915. The state of Georgia pardoned Frank in 1987.

I tell this story here in part as evidence of the dark side in the era of the college's origins, 1913-1915, but more as a note on sources. If one Googles Oney, one will find all sorts of commentary on his book, including a screed from a far right, anti-Semitic source that not only lambastes the book's findings and conclusions, but also Wikipedia itself, not only for its much discussed error-rate (about the same as *Britannica*) but also for its, as they descried, "well-known" Jewish ownership. The point is that sourcing in the digital age admits of any and everything and requires of readers today a certain trust in an author's discernment. I ask it here.

This book can and will be read at a number of levels: a straightforward history of a college as it interacts with its university, state, national and global environments; a collection of essays about its achievements and the individuals whose lives and careers are emblematic; another collection of photographs that move us from sepia-toned days to Technicolor to digitally scanned sunrises. It is both a full-blown intellectual, cultural, and political history and a moving set of features. Most will skip about for familiar faces and events, a few I hope will indulge or enjoy its digressions into journalism as an essential tool of democracy, and its back stories of intrigue and adventure in Atlanta. Perhaps no college of journalism and mass communication is as blessed as is Grady to have an idyllic setting, Athens, and a tumultuous urban and media landscape, Atlanta, as its backyard. In any event, I invite the reader to have at it.

This study is also auto-ethnographic, meaning personal. I have been engaged in senior academic administration for twenty-three years, seventeen as a dean and six as executive assistant to a president, and before that, eleven as a department head or chair. So I know how personality complicates as well as enables leadership. When this story reveals the foibles and frailties of deans and presidents it is not to detract from their successes. It is simply what our founder Steadman Sanford called "the personal equation." One faculty review of my own leadership as a dean resulted in twenty-five percent wanting me to go and seventy-five percent thinking it would be alright if I stayed on. I agreed with both groups.

I have listed works cited at the end but pay special thanks to the beloved George Abney for a remarkable master's thesis, completed in 1959 and covering the first forty years of the college. Supervised by the legendary Dean John Drewry, it is a faithful account of "who, what, and when." Also valuable is Dr. Frank N. Hawkins's unpublished manuscript, intended as a university bicentennial (1985) history of the college. Because I began my career as a historian of Henry Grady and the New South movement, I trust the reader will find this account of the college named for Grady both informed and enriched by my life of scholarship, which includes Reconstruction and Civil Rights. I do believe strongly that the mission of this college is about the First Amendment and democracy. Thus, any centennial accounting of the college is a reckoning of the evolution of democracy's first principles in the United States and the American South.

As with the hundreds of conversations I have enjoyed, interviews improve the story. The first began in the home of the fourth Henry Grady, arranged by his son, the fifth (now III), on a hot August afternoon in 2013. I had known Henry from my first year as dean. Although a scholar of the original Grady, I had not yet met a member of the family until suddenly, having concluded a civic club speech in my home county, Grady, I got a buzz on my Blackberry. The caller-ID showed "Henry Grady." I punched "on" and there he was, the fifth descendant. Telling him he could never guess where I was, a friendship began that led to his becoming co-chair of the Centennial Campaign and a Fellow of the Grady College. All of the original Henry Grady's direct descendants went into banking, a wise choice. Still, as a business student at UGA, Henry III, developed a fondness for the Grady College, attending its annual birthday parties for his great, great grandfather each May 24. For this writer, Henry has been a fount of wisdom and knowledge, which he has given equally to my grandchildren. Watching him walk back from the Oyster Bar at Grand Central, up Lexington to the Waldorf, with my namesake grandson in tow, explaining the streets of New York, I could not hear him, but I knew it was Henry Grady.

Henry W. Grady III, convocation speaker, December 2013. *Grady College Archives*

Finally, my appreciation goes to my successor, Dean Charles Nelson Davis, and to Dr. J. Parker Middleton, Senior Director of Development and Alumni Relations, for their encouragement and for reading the manuscript, to former deans J. Thomas Russell and John Soloski for their input and recollections, to faculty emeriti for their reminiscences, to the Centennial Editorial Board for its input. In all over twenty have read this manuscript, a few would have done it differently, most were favorable. As always, a huge debt goes to the librarians at Russell Special Collections. Caroline Killen was resourceful in reaching even beyond Hargrett Rare Book & Manuscript Library to find what I needed, and Steven Brown, whose knowledge of Athens and the university made him a most valued counselor and friend as I searched for explanations. His introducing me to Charlotte Thomas Marshall has made it all the richer. She too is a historian of the Classic City and its university, who generously shared information about events and characters that populate this book. Thanks to Mary Linneman who processed the photographs that Cindi Johnson, Steven, and Caroline located. To work in Hargrett Rare Books & Manuscript Library is to be blessed.

Dr. Kay Loveland, debater on a team I coached at Chapel Hill and a nucleus of those wonderful days, placed her expertise as a clinical psychologist in understanding the most dramatic moment in this account, the shooting on the night of December 23, 1949, of Dean John Drewry and his fiancée, Miriam Thurmond, by his ex-wife Kathleen Merry Drewry. Also on that debate team were Joe Loveland and Joe McGuire who provided good counsel and encouragement. Paul Kurtz, former associate dean of the Law School, improved my understanding of the Georgia Code as it applied in the 1950s. Steven C. Jones, Judge of the United States District Court, Northern District of Georgia, and past president of the UGA National Alumni Association, also shared valuable insight into the Drewry Case. Beverly Logan, Clerk of Athens-Clarke Superior Court, was invaluable in locating remnant records of the Drewry trial. Grady's own Mark Johnson, photojournalist of exceptional talent and consummate teacher, advised and helped process photographs for this book. Among Mark's many contributions to the college, he recently engineered a move of the headquarters of the National Press Photographers Association to the Grady College—a real coup. From the dean's office, Gabrielle Mason and Sean Polite facilitated the workflow. Brooke Rooks, Terri Baker, and Denise Mattox have kept accounts, fact checked, and provided the necessary hugs.

A most special thanks to my executive assistant as dean, Cindi Johnson, who served as project assistant. She expedited all its features and entailments, photographs to be sure. Her institutional knowledge of the college and its friends and alumni, built from twenty-one years of service, eleven of which were in the dean's office, was invaluable. Then Mary Grace Griffin, my student assistant, researched the college's international reach through its Cox Center. Oh, Mary Grace, and also Meredith Dean, how special you have been in my last year as dean and in this year of writing. Of course and as you both know, I have filed adoption papers and expect custody fights with your parents, but as you also know, when it comes to custody fights, with me it is a class action for all Grady's wonderful students. The names and faces are always there: Lauren, Cylla, Emily, Davis, Zach, Mary Boyce, Jeffrey, David,

Caroline, Baron, Katie (and one Katie Dean), Lizzie, Alexis, Julia, Carolyn, Mandy, Cayce . . . .

Finally, to Stephen, who saved his dad from the toils and snares of technology, and to Mary, who allowed and enabled this last shot at being a dean, and who has through the years been the best reader and advisor this writer could have asked for. Together we dedicate this book to the Grady Family and to our grandchildren (in birth order):

*Stephen (né Archie)*

*Cully*

*Beau*

*Will*

*Jack*

*Maggie*

# CENTENNIAL

# 1 BEGINNINGS: STEADMAN VINCENT SANFORD

Steadman Vincent Sanford, 1871–1945. *Hargrett Rare Books and Manuscript Library, University of Georgia*

NO NAME IN THE HISTORY OF THE UNIVERSITY OF GEORGIA HAS BEEN MORE CONSEQUENTIAL THAN THAT OF STEADMAN SANFORD. Of course Augustus Baldwin, like George Washington, must receive his due as the founding father, but Sanford founded the modern university, the evolution of which shapes today. Born in Covington, Georgia, in 1871, he received his undergraduate degree from Mercer in 1890. He spent the next thirteen years in Marietta where he was successively a teacher, principal of the Male Academy, and later superintendent of schools. In 1903 he sought and accepted appointment as an English instructor at the University of Georgia. He received a master's degree at the University of Chicago and studied at Oxford University and the University of Berlin. It was from a sabbatical to Berlin in 1913 that he returned resolved to establish journalism education in the English Department. Receiving the green light, he taught UGA's first course in journalism that fall.

Sanford was truly a student of the Progressive Era, an era of muckrakers, enterprising journalists who exposed the ills of capitalism, such as in the meat-packing industry that in turn led to reforms, especially in Theodore Roosevelt's administration. In fact it was TR who first called them "muckrakers," a term he derived from *Pilgrim's Progress* and applied at first negatively to describe journalists who kept their heads down to rake muck rather than look up for the inspirational. (Media always blamed.) It soon became a badge of honor. It was also an era that found abuses in journalism. "Yellow Journalism" prodded the nation into war with Spain and a protracted war in the Philippines, thereby foreshadowing the type of warfare that would emerge following World War II to the present day. It was in that environment that calls went out to higher education to prepare students for responsible careers in journalism. Missouri was first in 1908, but Georgia was not long in answering the call when Sanford offered its first course five years later. Within another two years, 1915, the University of Georgia would establish a School of Journalism with Sanford as its director and first professor.

To understand Sanford better one must begin with the fact that he was only twenty-one years Henry Grady's junior; thus his growing-up years were cast in the spell Grady created. His grandfather, a highly regarded mathematician, was on the faculty of Mercer College when it was located in Penfield, just south of Athens in Greene County. His grandfather would move to Macon when the college relocated there in 1879. Sanford received his undergraduate education there, beginning in 1886, the year of Grady's famous "New South" address, with Sanford's senior year marked by the editor's tragic death and the public mourning it occasioned. Sanford's 1890 graduating class of ten students emerged onto a social landscape of profound change, change that in turn had profound implications for journalism.

One of Grady's more famous speeches, "The Farmer and the Cities," sought to address the growing tension caused by the shift toward an urban future, which he championed. By the 1890's various farmer movements had coalesced around the Populist Party, which raged against discriminatory freight rates, bankers, industrialists, and urbanism in general. It also harbored a particularly dark side of nativism and racism. In the South it gave rise to disenfranchisement of African Americans and segregation ordinances that lynch law enforced. In truth, and on the issue of race, farmers found solidarity among merchants, bankers, industrialists, and journalists. In the four decades that followed, whites lynched almost 4,000 African Americans in order to establish "white supremacy," a hideously ironic defense for a race that already considered itself supreme.

Recent historians argue that the New South movement itself and Grady in particular were racists. Grady did believe with the vast majority of white Americans that people of African descent were inherently inferior. No more than a handful of white southerners advocated for racial equality, and Grady rebuked them.[1] As one historian noted, what the North defeated at Appomattox was the Confederate nation "state," not the Confederate nation.[2] It lived on, albeit with a New South imprimatur. Grady devoted his last speech, the one in Boston, to the subject of the South and race. While Grady wanted to believe that white southerners should and would concede humane treatment to a subordinate black population, he did not believe it should be on the basis of equality but on *noblesse oblige*.[3] But Grady's pronouncements about African Americans were often less patrician than vernacular.

Grady's successors, even educators like Sanford and Drewry, would treat race, as Grady had, for the most part with silence, silence being the preferred tool of power. Even in the social ferment of the 1950's and 60's, with major events affecting the Grady College, the annual reports remained silent on the university's and the college's transformation. To be sure, the New South movement championed urbanization, industrialization, and agricultural diversification—factors that militated against a future of discrimination and injustice. Yet, in the first half of the twentieth century, the racial order in the American South meant that journalism, the fourth estate, was not and could not be equated with democracy, much less practice it, certainly not as it had come to be understood in the South. As Lillian Smith, whose Laurel Falls Camp for Girls in North Georgia became base for her advocacy of human rights, observed, "The newspapers had worked out a system of leaving out everything they thought might 'upset the people.'"[4]

Perhaps the most eminent scholarly elaboration of Grady's position came from LaGrange, Georgia native, UGA graduate, and Columbia-trained historian, Ulrich Bonnell Phillips, who by the time of his death in 1934 was regarded as America's preeminent historian. In a famous essay, titled "The Central Theme of Southern History," he concluded that theme to be a "settled determination to maintain white supremacy,"[5] a theme that even to this day gerrymanders its way through southern and indeed national politics. Interestingly, Steadman Sanford's chosen fraternity at Mercer was Kappa Alpha, the order that among all southern fraternities is most dedicated to maintaining a Confederate heritage; in that day, all fraternities with southern chapters were. Mercer gave him one other thing, a nickname. Ever after he would be known as "Steadie" Steadman Sanford.

Most importantly, Sanford wanted to be a teacher. Marietta, Georgia, needed one, so he set his sights on the Male Academy there. It was in a living and boarding arrangement with the McClatchey family, that he met his future wife, Grace McClatchey. In 1894, Grace temporarily broke their engagement, citing his "likes, among which she enumerated 'card parties, dances, the punch bowl,' and 'other amusements.'"[6] Indeed, Sanford was so well liked in Marietta that he became superintendent of its public schools. Smitten equally by the era's *élan*, he enlisted for the Spanish-American War, which gave him a uniform, a rank, and an encampment no farther away than Griffin, Georgia, but forever after made him a proud veteran. Already, he had been instrumental in establishing the Marietta Rifle Association, becoming captain of "The Rifles," a group that primarily paraded and provided a social outlet for scions of the Confederacy.

The summers of 1898 and 1899 following his active duty found Sanford at the University of Chicago, earning graduate credits, though never an advanced degree. Still, it was evidence that he had more in mind than staying in Marietta. John D. Rockefeller had only recently established the University of Chicago; but its mid-western progressive spirit reflected its founding president, William Rainey Harper, far more than the dour, fundamental Baptist Rockefeller. Sanford's biographer believes that Sanford absorbed Rainey's enthusiasm for progressive education and embrace of students.[7] In truth, it was an outward disposition Sanford already had. As an instance, he started a Chautauqua movement in Marietta that proved highly successful, mirroring the adult-education and self-improvement movement popularized on the shores of Chautauqua Lake in southwestern New York.

William Barnard Hill, Chancellor, 1900–1905. *Hargrett Rare Books and Manuscript Library, University of Georgia*

By the turn of the century, Sanford had introduced himself to William Barnard Hill, the University of Georgia's progressive new chancellor, and let his interest in a position there be known. (It certainly would have helped that Sanford's grandfather, prominent on the faculty at Mercer, almost certainly knew Hill as a prominent Macon attorney and vice versa.) in the summer of 1903, Steadman, Grace, and their children packed for Athens. On Hill's recommendation the trustees named Sanford an Instructor of Rhetoric and Literature at a salary of $1,200 a year. The Athens campus had approximately 300 students, including sub-freshmen, and 25 members of the faculty. Sanford was instantly successful among colleagues and admired by students for his manifest interest in their lives, qualities that would mark his career for the next forty-two years.

What inclined Sanford toward journalism is not clear, but on his return from a sabbatical to Berlin and Oxford during the 1912-13 academic year, he offered the first course that fall. He had applied originally for leave during the 1908-09 academic year. It could be that the tragic death of their ten year-old daughter, Grace Deveraux, from typhoid fever in 1907, made it too soon to go. (Grace was the second of four children and the only daughter.) In any event, he spent June 1912 packing the family for a year's stay in Europe and acquiring letters of introduction. In that same month the Tsar and Kaiser, Nicky and Willie as they were known to each other, moored their royal yachts side-by-side off the Baltic coast and saw each other for the last time. As cousins and grandsons of Queen Victoria, they always used the affectionate address, although neither liked the other very much.

1913 would be Europe's last summer before catastrophe struck in 1914. In all, six empires went into a war that only two would survive. There would be 37 million military and civilian casualties of which 17 million died, almost half of those civilian. These figures include only a fraction of those who died in the great influenza epidemic of 1918, widely believed to be at least 50 million, some historians think more nearly 100 million worldwide. F. Scott Fitzgerald, one of those writers who, although he did not fight, tumbled out the back end of the Great War, lamented: "the silver cord is cut and the golden bowl is broken," his "beautiful lovely safe world blew itself up."[8] Still, in 1913 Europeans felt good about themselves. Science, music, and arts reigned supreme. Berlin seemed the epicenter of intellectual advances, among them, the graduate seminar that anticipated the future of graduate education in America by merging teaching and research. No one expected war, even as the Kaiser and his Grand General Staff planned for it. Retrospectively, 1913 would feel more like Europe's Indian Summer. In many ways it was.

Sanford and his family enjoyed the time in Berlin and London immensely. He returned with a "Certificate in German Study." In a nod to accountability and at the request of the trustees, he supplied a list of the graduate courses he had taken, accompanied by the name and institution of each instructor. He listed: "Anglo Saxon, Dr. Brandl, University of Berlin;

Middle English, Dr. Spies, University of Berlin; Schiller, Dr. Schmidt, University of Berlin; Beowulf, Dr. Napier, University of Oxford; Shakespeare's Predecessors, Sir Walter Raleigh, Oxford, England." On his return to Athens in late July, he learned of his promotion to a full professorship in English. In 1914, the trustees cured the absence of an advanced degree by recommending him for an honorary doctorate (Litt.D.). Interestingly, Sanford never used the title, and when an appointment called for it, he would answer, "no advanced degree." Such was his admirable modesty and honesty.

So where did the interest in journalism come in? Apparently not on sabbatical and the record is silent on what motivated him. We do know he considered journalism a literary genre; and because of its practical and immediate applications would draw more students to English and the study of literature, composition and critical thinking. He was a professor of rhetoric as well as literature and therefore appreciated the role of persuasion in public discourse. He was a devotee of Henry Grady, himself a pioneer in journalism, and like Grady, a promoter: witness for example the Chautauqua movement in Marietta. Sanford was a public man.

Moreover, as Doris Kearns Goodwin observed, the 1890s launched the golden age of journalism.[9] For the next thirty years, journalists exposed corruption in government and malfeasance among the titans of finance, industry, and corporate monopoly. As noted, Teddy Roosevelt styled them "muckrakers" for exposing the "muck" made by the malefactors of wealth. Roosevelt nonetheless used these journalists to promote his own progressive program. Ray Stannard Baker, Ida Tarbell, Jacob Riis, and Lincoln Steffens exposed meatpacking scandals, Standard Oil's iron-fisted monopoly, the shame of cities where corrupt urban bosses held sway, and more. As national journalists, not southern, they fueled a new era of corporate regulation and government reform under Roosevelt's New Nationalism and to a lesser extent Woodrow Wilson's New Freedom. Moreover, calls had gone out promoting professional education for new journalists. Before his death in 1909, Joseph Pulitzer had been a leading proponent, establishing the journalism program at Columbia University. Even a national association for amateur journalists emerged. Most of its members were the sons and a few daughters of successful editors and publishers, but who could not find jobs in their parents' discipline,[10] much like bloggers today.

James Middleton Cox figured in here too. In 1898 he bought the *Dayton* (Ohio) *Evening News*, styling it "the people's paper." A two-term congressman, he was elected as a Progressive Democrat to three terms as governor of Ohio. Although non-consecutive, he was the first three-termer in that state. Nominated by the Democratic Party in 1920 for president, his running mate was Franklin Delano Roosevelt. Cox lost the election to fellow Ohioan, Warren G. Harding, largely because of Cox's strong support for the League of Nations. Cox was already establishing a publishing empire. By 1939 he acquired the *Atlanta Georgian* (Hearst) and *The Atlanta Journal* and with it WSB Radio. Because the purchase was sealed the week before the Atlanta premiere of "Gone with the Wind," people joked that it was to get tickets. Cox immediately shut down the *Georgian*. In 1948 he added television to the WSB portfolio and in 1950 he bought *The Atlanta Constitution*. His progressivism characterized the best in journalism of the early twentieth century, which in turn furthered the call for journalism education.[11]

.mes Middleton Cox, emocratic presidential ndidate, 1920, and founder of hat would become the *Atlanta urnal-Constitution*. *Courtesy* ***Atlanta urnal-Constitution***

Whatever the influence, it is clear that Steadie Steadman Sanford wanted to start something new at Georgia. Journalism education had already taken root in the Midwest and East, Missouri (first in 1908) and then Columbia, had taken first steps. Georgia would be among the first in the South, excepting Robert E. Lee's experiment at Washington and Lee (formerly Washington College) in the late 1860's and a recent start-up at Louisiana State University. Emory College, while still at Oxford, Georgia, taught a course in 1912, as had Georgia in 1913. One other thing helped: UGA was becoming increasingly aware of the need for an Alumni and Publicity Bureau and thus authorized one in 1913, anticipating public relations. The trustees also resolved on June 14, 1913, while Sanford was still in Oxford and London, "that the Committee on Laws and Discipline be instructed to inquire into the propriety and expediency of establishing in the University at an early date a School of Journalism in which shall be taught the branches required for editing and publishing newspapers and like periodicals."

One other factor was that the *Red & Black* in those days reported to the Athletic Association and given Sanford's close ties to Athletics, it may have been another way of tying athletics to academics. Although speculative, it is interesting.[12] With all the other factors, it is a given that journalism education was emerging in twentieth-century America's earliest years.

Enter David Crenshaw Barrow, who succeeded Chancellor Hill on his untimely death in December 1905. Interestingly, Barrow's succession occurred simultaneously with the establishment of Grady County, Georgia, January 1, 1906, made all the more interesting because Barrow with some 3,000 acres was the largest landholder in the newly established county, named of course for Henry Grady. Barrow's father and namesake acquired the land in 1849 in what was then Decatur County, on the Georgia-Florida border, just above Tallahassee, and developed it as a slave plantation with over 90 slaves. It stood out because it was the largest slave plantation in an area of mostly small, yeoman farmers. It survived the war and reconstruction as slaves became tenants. Chancellor Barrow was also the largest landowner in Oglethorpe County, bordering Clarke County, Athens.[13]

David "Uncle Dave" C. Barrow, Chancellor, 1906–25. *Hargrett Rare Books and Manuscript Library, University of Georgia*

Fortunately, Barrow turned out to be as progressive as had William Barnard Hill, whose foreshortened five-year chancellorship inaugurated UGA's march to its twentieth-century future. For the next twenty years of Barrow's leadership, UGA would define itself as an important player in the state. Barrow had been university dean in Hill's administration. He and Sanford hit it off. In one lengthy conversation just before leaving for Europe, Sanford convinced Barrow completely that a journalism school was essential; and Barrow in his 1913-14 report to the trustees commended Sanford's fall term class in journalism as a viable course. Sanford offered the course again the following year with the class being highly praised by the *Athens Banner* for putting out a May 27, 1915 edition of the paper. Barrow then took it to the Board of Visitors (advisory to the chancellor) in 1913, which in turn recommended that Georgia establish a journalism school. They saw "a great movement . . . sweeping the West and East," and it seemed to them that the training of journalists was "one of the vital demands of modern education."[14]

Nathaniel E. Harris, a future governor of the state and a friend of Henry Grady himself, wrote the resolution in hand. When, as a student in 1870 and editor of the *Collegian*, young Mr. Harris had fallen on hard times, it was the aspiring journalist Grady who encouraged none other than Alexander H. Stephens (Vice President of the Confederacy, soon-to-be member of the U.S. House of Representatives, and later governor, 1883-84) to lend the young

Civil War veteran enough money to complete his education. Harris went on to Sparta, Georgia, where he purchased an interest in the *Hancock Sentinel* before launching a successful career in Georgia politics.[15] Such was the interconnectedness between Grady, the journalist, and the advent of journalism education at UGA. Harris was also a law partner in Macon of future Chancellor Hill, Hill being the first Georgia alumnus and non-clergyman to preside over the institution.[16]

Nathaniel E. Harris. *Courtesy Library of Congress*

Harris also sponsored legislation in 1885 that established the Georgia School of Technology, which would become the Georgia Institute of Technology. Grady was a huge backer of this development, seeing it as an instrumental part of his New South program. As a reform governor of the state, 1915-17, Harris sponsored compulsory public education and favored improved funding for higher education, although neither took hold because of a hopelessly archaic tax system and general legislative intransigence. Many legislators thought of the university as godless and elitist, and many if not most favored denominational schools that dotted the state. Still Harris's grateful alma mater conferred on him an honorary degree for trying, and Georgia Tech still considers him a key figure in its founding.[17]

## 1915, BIRTH OF A COLLEGE

As war raged in Europe, the founding of journalism education at the University of Georgia provided some comic relief. Sanford got what he prayed for. On the strength of Harris's resolution and recommendation of the Board of Visitors, the trustees authorized a School of Journalism and a bachelor's degree in journalism with the proviso that Sanford would "carry this on for the next four years, without additional cost. . . ." The school was to be ancillary to the English Department with the further recommendation that "this school should not change Professor Sanford's relations to his classes" or "relieve him of any duties in connection with his work."[18]

On further thought and on the recommendation of influential board member Hamilton McWhorter, the trustees made Sanford's "duties" ancillary to the English Department, not the "school," and gave Sanford the title Professor of Journalism. In truth, not much changed for Sanford as he had already been teaching journalism for two years, and it was viewed as integral to the English Department's mission. What changed was the creation of a vessel for journalism education that would start in name first and eventually in function as an independent, freestanding school and later college. Sanford was tireless, teaching most often 24 hours a week, occasionally 27 and never less than 18 (the norm was 15). He continued a substantial load when he became Dean of the University and President of Franklin College in 1926. Further, when he became president of the university in 1932 and later chancellor of the system in 1935, he continued to teach a course each term.[19]

By 1917 Sanford had elaborated seven courses, including "Newspaper Reporting and Correspondence," "Newspaper Editing," "Special Articles," "Editorial Writing," "History and Principles of Journalism," "Psychology of Business Procedure," and "Newspaper Advertising." These were listed separately from English as they now (1917) supported a separate degree program, a bachelor's degree in journalism. In that same year Sanford organized a program approved by the United States Army in supply and logistics, in effect quartermaster training, a critical need given entry into WWI. Students who felt the Sanford touch in that program would write thank you notes. At a personal level, he and Grace worried about their eldest son, Shelton Palmer, who was "over there" as a second lieutenant. Parents and son kept up a steady flow of letters and packages. All this was in addition to everything else. Sanford allowed no moss to grow.

It is a stretch now to think how intimate the university was then. In 1915 it had grown to about 500 students ( a relatively small high school today) and held at that level through 1917 despite predictions that falling cotton prices would make it difficult for many students to return. Students knew their president much as they know their department heads and deans today. Barrow was known as "Uncle Dave" by students, denoting the familiarity he enjoyed. Sanford was the same, always available. When asked what a university was, Nicholas Murray Butler, the long-serving Columbia University president during the first half of the twentieth century, replied, "It is a log, with a student seated at one end and a professor on the other with a book in between." And so it was.

It was also a campus that certainly, compared to today, had a down-at-heel look. There was a reason. Beginning in 1917, despite some fits and starts, agriculture, the mainstay of the Georgia economy, began a downward slide from a position that was not that robust to begin with. In 1920, UGA received an $85,000 state appropriation for a budget that neared $250,000

Old College, fixed up in 1908 but barely adequate for housing and teaching UGA students. *Hargrett Rare Books and Manuscript Library, University of Georgia*

while Georgia Tech received a more generous $150,000. A first casualty was maintenance, although it had for some years depended on convict labor with unpredictable results. Faculty complained especially about Old College, which smelled bad, looked worse, had electrical wiring that threatened to burn it down, and had no heating so that classes frequently had to be canceled, all that despite a 1908 remake of Old College that included replacement of its original brick.[20]

Even with funding woes and a worsening economy, students continued to show up, some 1,000 by the early twenties, including women in Franklin College by 1918. Of course, women had been present at some distance from campus in the State Normal School since 1890, but none in Franklin until the American Association of University Women brought pressure and more progressive thinkers stuck a finger in the air and found a wind blowing. The only dorm on campus for women could house at most 70, and the space for men was not much better. The result was that students lived in boarding houses and private residences that took them in. Still, and as today, young men and women liked to be in Athens.

Much of the reason lay with something that "Steadie" Sanford remains known for in particular: athletics. The football stadium bears his name for a reason. Shortly after arriving at the university, he was asked to serve as faculty adviser to athletics. He was tireless in that role too. He got to know faculty advisers at other schools, and by 1921 he was instrumental in forming the Southern Conference that would become the Southeastern Conference in 1932. In fact some refer to him as the godfather of the nation's most storied and successful football conference. Students in particular and colleagues in general liked him for that reason too, although the usual assortment of complainers, faculty especially, thought he had overdone it.

That sentiment reached a boiling point when in 1927 it became more than rumor that a new stadium was to be built along Tanyard Creek, the dividing line between North and South Campus. The whopping cost was to be $200,000, not far off the university's budget for an entire year. Sanford got around howls of robbing Peter to pay Paul, by creating a Georgia Athletic Association, which borrowed $150,000 against gate receipts and got the contractor to advance another $50,000. Still, there were over-runs, fairly modest, and a suit by the contractor for payment that was settled. When done, UGA had the handsomest stadium anywhere, in the most beautiful setting, and the rest is history.[21] The first game was against Yale in 1929, which Georgia won (our bulldog is better than yours), and Yale's generous president allowed Georgia to keep its share of the receipts, $45,000, for a true win-win.

1921 was the year Sanford persuaded Barrow and the trustees to name the college for Henry W. Grady, who continued to enjoy an unsurpassed reputation among southern journalists and whose words inspired school boys to proclaim his New South Address, or portions thereof, in countless declamation contests. Only later would the general acclaim be tempered, as when Lillian Smith conceded in 1949 that Grady was rightly known as "the 'conciliator,' who talked a good kind of common sense that seemed lucid and statesmanlike in comparison with most, though he showed little awareness of the moral problems of human relations so completely unsolved or the economic and social needs of the eighty percent of whites who were not in the dominant group."[22] That view would have sounded ill-tempered in 1921.

1921 also saw the Grady School's first newly minted graduate, Lamar Jefferson Trotti from Decatur, Georgia. Following a stint in Georgia newspapers, he made his way to Hollywood where he found his métier in screenwriting. From 1933 until his untimely death at age 52 in 1952, Trotti wrote or produced, sometimes both, a major motion picture every year for Twentieth Century Fox, including "The Oxbow Incident," "Cheaper by the Dozen," "Young Mister Lincoln" and "I'd Climb the Highest Mountain,"

Dr. Craig Barrow, president of the Alumni Association, presents Sanford with "cup full of gold" at dedication of Sanford Stadium. *Hargrett Rare Books and Manuscript Library*

1929 Georgia Bulldogs score first touchdown in first game in Sanford Stadium on blocked punt recovered behind Yale Bulldogs' goal line. Georgia won. Another step forward for southern football. *Hargrett Rare Books and Manuscript Library, University of Georgia*

Trotti as Hollywood success story. Dean John Drewry on left and Thomas W. Reid on right. *Hargrett Rare Books and Manuscript Library, University of Georgia*

Lamar Jefferson Trotti, Grady's first graduate. *1921* ***Pandora***

which was set and filmed in Georgia and based on a book written by Georgia author Corra Harris. Nominated twice before, he received an Oscar in 1945 for best original screenplay for the movie "Wilson." President Wilson, being another Georgian and later president of Princeton University, who in Trotti's college days was acclaimed as a great reformer, but his reputation would later be tarnished for reasons similar to those that detracted from Grady's. Among other things, Wilson entertained at the White House with a showing of D. W. Griffith's "Birth of a Nation," a technically celebrated motion picture in 1915, based on Thomas Dixon's novel *The Clansman*, which in turn celebrated the South's efforts to re-establish white supremacy by force, which of course it did.

Then in 1922 came the Grady School's second graduate and arguably its most influential, John Drewry. A native of Griffin, Georgia, Drewry received a Bachelor of Arts degree in 1921 but returned in 1922 to receive a Bachelor of Journalism the following year. (His Bachelor of Journalism was the last of its kind, after which the Bachelor of Arts in Journalism became the ABJ.) Like his mentor, Sanford, he was Phi Beta Kappa, member of Phi Kappa literary society and a member of the Kappa Alpha Order fraternity, a neo-Confederate bulwark. Also like his mentor, he believed the university needed to get on with representing itself to the state. One of Sanford's original attractions to journalism was the state's press, small and large. His personal attention to them attracted them to him. He had not yet gotten the exact formula, but Drewry would. The state's press loved Sanford. Even when Sanford would no longer be related directly to the press by virtue of the school he founded, he still attended all the Georgia Press Association gatherings and what would eventually become a collateral Georgia Press Institute, an academic/professional meeting of minds. Sanford understood the importance of these relations when he became top dog.

John Drewry, the future. *Hargrett Rare Books and Manuscript Library, University of Georgia*

In these middle years of the twenties, Drewry elaborated a seven-step publicity plan for the university that catapulted it into statewide prominence, everything from media relations that included small town and big city presses, events, publications, governmental relations—the whole nine yards. He organized the first press bureau, which became the University Division of Publications with its own director. Drewry accomplished all that under the direction and support of Sanford. Sanford's wishes became Drewry's accomplishments. During the summers of 1923 and 1924, Drewry attended Columbia University, then took additional coursework at Georgia and received a master's from UGA in 1925. Thus, with two undergraduate degrees and a master's, he qualified for a fulltime instructor's position. On December 23, 1926, Drewry married Kathleen Jeannette Merry, a match that would prove near fatal twenty-three years to the day later.

Starting as Sanford's "assistant" in 1922, for the next four years Drewry would teach courses, go to school, work for the *Athens Banner-Herald* as a reporter and news editor, review books and take turns directing university publicity—multi-tasking before the term existed. Then things changed in

1926. Chancellor Barrow stepped down in 1925, and Sanford wanted his job. He had influential trustee support, but in the end that job went to Charles M. Snelling, who had been dean of the Franklin College of Arts and Sciences since 1906. Sanford was promptly given the title Dean of the University and President of Franklin College, certainly an expression of confidence. Despite the fact that he had a crushing work load, being elected to the executive committee of the National Collegiate Athletic Association, building a stadium, running a college, among much else—he retained his title as director of the Grady School.

On assuming his new duties, Sanford asked Drewry to resume directorship of the Press Bureau in 1930, and of course, Drewry also had to ramp up his work with the school. By the end of the twenties enrollment at Grady had reached about 70. The work was daunting for both men, but they proved up to it, even though Sanford's manifold duties almost cost him his health. Of course, at this juncture the Great Depression overcame everything, starting earlier in the South with the agricultural recession of the twenties and the collapse of the Miami bubble in 1927, the big Wall Street collapse coming in October of 1929. Ironically, it would have less effect in the South, because it had less to begin with, but it was still bad enough.

## REORGANIZATION

The university presented its own set of problems—chief among them, its organizational structure. Governed by trustees and a chancellor, the University was in practice three campuses: the Georgia State College of Agriculture, the Georgia State College for Teachers, and the Franklin College. Each had its own president, and although reporting to the chancellor, each steered its own course, a fragmentation that worsened in the 1920s with Agriculture the chief culprit. In part because of the Smith-Lever Act of 1917, co-authored by former Georgia governor and senator Hoke Smith, agricultural education could benefit from federal funding, and Andrew Soule, president of the Agriculture College, did not want to share its relative largesse. Although some funds passed through to Franklin, Agriculture retained most, as indeed the legislation intended. (Education for a "job" as present trends portend, not for its own sake.)

Then in the late twenties, influential trustees and alumni of the University began to push for consolidation, not only on the Athens campus but statewide as well. They saw in the proliferation of colleges and junior colleges a threat not only to cooperation but also to economies of scale. Leading the charge were Hughes Spalding and Philip Weltner, prominent Atlantans and UGA trustees. Resisting was the acerbic President Soule, liked by almost no one despite his success with the Agriculture College. He was particularly galling for Sanford in his new role as President of the Franklin College, the mother campus of UGA. It became more intense as the trustees pressed not only for consolidation in Athens but a regents system to govern the entire state.

Richard Russell, 1921, who became Georgia's most influential figure in 20th-Century national politics. *Courtesy Richard B. Russell Library for Political Research and Studies, University of Georgia*

With the election in 1932 of Richard Russell as a reform governor, change was imminent. From nearby Winder, Georgia, and a UGA alumnus himself, Russell allied with Spalding and Weltner to push the reform agenda to a successful conclusion.[23] By 1932, the UGA campus of three often warring Colleges was consolidated under one president and the legislature approved a statewide regents system under a chancellor. Although Sanford had hoped for the chancellor's job, it went to Snelling and Sanford became President of the University of Georgia. By 1935 Sanford was chancellor of the University System of Georgia, answerable to the Board of Regents. Over the next ten years, Sanford literally defined the role of Chancellor of the University System.

## DREWRY TAKES CHARGE

All these changes had direct implications for the Grady School. On assuming the presidency of UGA in 1932, Sanford knew he could no longer retain the director's portfolio for Grady, with Drewry his logical successor. For the next thirty-seven years, Drewry would serve first as Director of the Grady School of Journalism and then after 1940 as Dean, a truly phenomenal time of growth and change in journalism education. Drewry was an exemplary, indeed exceptional leader. Tom Dyer in his history of the university said that three members of the UGA faculty transformed it: 1) John Donald Wade in English, who would depart for Vanderbilt in the early thirties in order to join a literary movement that included among others Robert Penn Warren; 2)

E. Merton Coulter, a historian who wrote copiously about the American South, albeit from a neo-Confederate view point; and 3) John Eldridge Drewry. What made each transformational was the ability to create a national audience for their work, thereby moving the University itself from a parochial state school to standing among the nation's flagship universities.[24]

Indeed what Sanford and Drewry shared with Henry Grady was a well-honed instinct for, and understanding of, publicity. Each understood its value for self as well as institutional promotion, self and institution really being inseparable. In the twenties Sanford courted the Georgia press as he steadily rose within the University, but it was Drewry in the thirties who would institutionalize the relationship. The Georgia Press Association was late in forming compared with other states, but in 1887, while Grady was still living, it came together. It was one of the few things in journalism that Henry Grady did not have a direct hand in, the association being primarily oriented in the early years to weeklies.

In 1928, Emily Woodward of Vienna (pronounced Vy-anna), Georgia, became the first, and for the longest time, the only woman to head a state press association. That same year, with encouragement from Sanford and Drewry, she established the Georgia Press Institute, an academic/professional arrangement to promote the understanding and practice of journalism. In its first year, it met at Mercer University in Macon, just north of Vienna. In its second, UGA hosted the institute, while in years three and four it met at Emory in Atlanta. From 1932 on, the Georgia Press Institute was a regular feature of journalism education at Georgia, with Drewry taking the lead in arranging the Institute's workshops and panels on an annual basis. A predictable result was that journalism education at Mercer and Emory went to the margins as Athens moved to the foreground. Even as Chancellor, Sanford attended all association and institute functions. To this day, if one asks a person on Peachtree Street in Atlanta what is tops about UGA, the answer often will be journalism, followed by law, although a host of other programs now get recognition.

Emily Woodward, far right, next to Sanford with Drewry second from left, Georgia Press Institute. *Hargrett Rare Books and Manuscript Library, University of Georgia*

**LEFT:** Academic Building, first home of Grady School. *UGA Photographic Services;* **RIGHT:** the Academic Building, now the Holmes-Hunter Academic Building, named for Hamilton Holmes and Charlayne Hunter-Gault. *UGA Photographic Services*

As the school grew from a handful of students in 1920 to 70 by the end of the decade, and especially with Sanford's move up the ladder, it became increasingly clear that Grady could no longer be a one or two-person show. University historian, Tom Dyer notes that its faculty, as its student body, remained predominantly male through the twenties. Only in education and home economics could one find female faculty. That changed in 1928 when Mrs. M.H. Bryan, Nan Coughlin, "won appointment to the faculty of the School of Journalism under circumstances which indicate that she sought the appointment at least partially to establish a precedent." The sudden resignation of an unidentified assistant instructor in the summer of 1928 created the opportunity for Drewry, Sanford, and Snelling to fill the vacancy without board approval. In her application Bryan noted its precedent-setting possibility and the probable opposition of the trustees, but her qualifications were apparent, so the move was made.[25] She became the first female faculty member in Franklin College, a happy result for journalism education as the percentage of women students in Grady would outpace the percentage in the university until the present day. (It is now 80 percent female.)

In those early years, the school occupied two rooms in the Academic Building, just off the Arch on Broad Street, but a modest construction boomlet was about to take place through UGA alumni donations. The alumni association hoped the legislature would follow suit in some form of match. It did not. Still, with a New York consulting firm and over a one-month period, the alumni secured approximately $600,000 in gifts and pledges against an overall goal of $1 million. Before the decade was out, the total was thought to have reached $800,000 including a $60,000 gift from George Foster Peabody,

**LEFT:** Memorial Hall just completed in the Twenty's, and until recently, the gathering place for Grady faculty at lunch. It is still missed. *Hargrett Rare Books and Manuscript Library, University of Georgia;* **RIGHT:** Communication-Journalism Building, C-J Building, completed 1928. *Grady College Archives, UGA Photographic Services*

a Columbus, Georgia, native turned New York financier and benefactor of the university. The fund created, called the War Memorial Fund to honor those who lost their lives in WWI, resulted in the completion of Memorial Hall, begun in 1910. Discussions of what to do with remaindered funds from the campaign led to the decision to construct a facility for journalism and business education; thus developed the Commerce-Journalism Building, short-handed as C-J Building in later years. Completed by the 1928 academic year, journalism at Georgia had a handsome, new building to rival any in the burgeoning field of journalism education. Later expanded, the south wing of the C-J Building would remain journalism's home for the next 40 years. Just west of the Main Library, it was privileged. (The current Journalism Building will reach forty-six years in its centennial.)

In his survey of higher education in the South, done for a 1934 volume titled *Culture in the South*, Herman Clarence Nixon wrote, "Commerce and journalism in this section (the South) are sometimes, though not always, counted as snap courses for athletes. . . ."[26] However true that may have been, and Nixon provides no evidence even as he hedges, it certainly was not the case at Grady and UGA. Although some athletes may have taken an occasional elective, athletes did not flock to the College. Nixon's view, published in 1934 took not only a jaundiced but an elitist view of higher education generally, as when he wrote, "The southern literate whites, taken as a whole, are largely a non-reading public, and practical steps or programs toward remedying this shortcoming should prove more far-reaching in value than all the technical courses in journalism."[27] Nixon was an Alabama Polytechnic Institute (Auburn) graduate.

**ABOVE:** Robert Sherrod *1929* ***Pandora*; BELOW:** Benjamin Hill Hardy. *1928* ***Pandora***

Of the sixty-one students who graduated in the twenties with the degree Bachelor of Arts in Journalism, twenty were women, an amazing percentage in the day. Previously noted was Grady's first graduate, Lamar Jefferson Trotti of Oscar-winning fame. In the last class of the decade, 1929, was an equally promising student, Robert Sherrod, from Thomasville, Georgia. Born in 1909, he would go on to become a famous WWII correspondent. His book *Tarawa*, published a month after that famous battle in the Pacific, is a classic of war reporting, capturing the horrific experience of men in mortal combat. Later he would edit a volume in *Life Magazine*'s memorable pictorial history of WWII before eventually landing at *The Saturday Evening Post* and becoming editor before that publication collapsed in the sixties. Already in financial distress, Curtis Publishing reached the breaking point in part by the famous lawsuit brought by former Georgia football coach Wally Butts and Alabama's legendary coach Bear Bryant over a libelous charge of fixing the 1962 game. No evidence links Sherrod to the story and Curtis Publishing was on the brink before a jury handed down its costly verdict, but surely he must have known and advised as he became editor while the controversy swirled. However, Sherrod's papers at Syracuse do not reflect his involvement, as a request of a special collections' librarian there confirmed.

Special note should also be made of Benjamin Hill Hardy, Jr., (ABJ 28) (Benjamin Harvey Hill, who inspired the Hardy family given name, was a Senator in the Confederate Congress and later served in both the U.S. House and Senate. It was to Hill that Grady attributed his famous opening lines for his New South Address). Ben Jr.'s father was publisher of the Barnesville, Georgia, newspaper and along with two brothers made for a formidable publishing family in Georgia. Ben Jr., did everything at UGA. He was editor of the *Red & Black*, also the campus humor magazine, graduated Phi Beta Kappa, was nominated for a Rhodes Scholarship, and admitted to the Order of the Sphinx, UGA's most exclusive society. Interestingly, he and a best friend resigned from that society over some dispute, proof he could stand his ground.

Following stops at his father's paper, *The Atlanta Journal*, and a brief venture in Biloxi, he joined AP in Washington, D.C. and eventually New York. During WWII, he returned to Washington, D.C., which landed him an assignment at the embassy in Rio de Janeiro. In 1946 fortune smiled and put him on Defense Secretary George C. Marshall's staff as a public affairs communications officer at the Pentagon and at State when Marshall moved over as Secretary. Then came "the assignment:" Write the speech that would become Truman's "Four Points Doctrine," which in turn became the United States strategy for the Cold War that lay ahead. Originally it was to be Three Points: support for the United Nations; economic support for war torn nations, The Marshall Plan; and closer military cooperation with western governments, eventually NATO. On his own initiative Hardy added Point Four, assistance in making U.S. technology more globally available, what became the Technical Cooperation Administration. Initially some at State resisted including the fourth point in the draft, as not sufficiently vetted, but it eventually wound up in presidential advisor Clark Clifford's hands, who liked it, and got it before Truman, who embraced it.

Ben Hardy went on to become public affairs officer of the Technical Cooperation Administration and chief of its policy council. On a TCA mission from Iraq to Iran in 1951, the commercial flight he took encountered a snowstorm and crashed with no survivors. Like Grady, Hardy knew instinctively that journalism and publicity, in the form of public affairs communication, were born twins and that the power of a speech to shape public policy gives the speechwriter a unique seat at the public table. In 1954, the Grady College named its chapter of Kappa Tau Alpha, the journalism honorary society, for Benjamin Hill Hardy, Jr.[28]

Of the sixty twenties graduates, it remained for a student majoring in Home Economics to provide the best glimpse into why one should study in Grady, but first she had to get something off her chest. The instructor in her Saturday morning class, May 3, 1924, was no doubt John Drewry. The student, Matilda Callaway, was at least ten years his senior, having "for ten years . . . been a business woman engaged in the profession of child training." She stumbled onto the class in journalism when an elective in English was not available. She clearly was impatient with what she considered Drewry's condescending manner toward students, his saying "no serious minded students enter the University" and then "at the end of the scholastic term (a faculty member's) sacrifice for the ignorant and unappreciative souls has been in vain." Well, Drewry was just twenty-two years old and in only his second year of teaching, proving perhaps that the best defense for a callow teacher is a good offense. It prompted Callaway to write an essay over the weekend, titled "WHY I CAME TO THE UNIVERSITY OF GEORGIA, And Why I Registered for a Course in Journalism."[29]

Callaway said "ambition" and $300 in savings led her to UGA in 1923. She had done course work earlier at the State College for Women in Milledgeville. Finding herself in journalism, with its "first term" (term denoting first third of the course) devoted to history, her "imagination" ran to "the development of the paper industry, the evolution of type and typing machines and the gradual growth and power of the press." The "second term" would be devoted to magazines. "Why would it not be both profitable and enjoyable," she asked, to develop a "reading acquaintance . . . of the long list of magazines appearing each month at the News Stands? (This I have done and I find my new friends most fascinating)." The "third term" would be devoted to "preparing and presenting news." "Written and oral expression I reasoned." And why not? "With these reasons in mind, it was not hard (for Callaway) to decide that Journalism would make the best substitute for English." "There was never a thought in my mind that anything I should write would reach publication or bring remuneration but I did think that effort and interest would be recognized and appreciated. Little did I dream that I should be subjected even *en masse* to the criticism of the morning hour."

Matilda Callaway at her retirement. *Hargrett Rare Books and Manuscript Library, University of Georgia*

Callaway had articulated the raison d'être for the study of journalism as well as Sanford, or Drewry for that matter, could have hoped from a student. Her essay found in a jumble of papers and manuscripts in the Hargrett Library, proves that no one should underestimate a student's will, desire, and certainly not attention to an instructor's demeanor. A month later she received her Bachelor of Science in Home Economics degree and later in 1933 an M.S. in Home Economics. She had a long and memorable career as a member of the Home Economics faculty of the University of Georgia, now Family and Consumer Sciences. Students remembered her fondly. As chapter advisor to their honor society and director of one of four Home Management

Houses, her House was a nine-room laboratory and quasi-dorm. One student recalled that Callaway luxuriated in long bubble baths, interrupted once in 1957 when girls knocked to tell her of a "rumored/ threatened" panty raid. She quickly girded up to meet the threat. The twenties and the fifties indeed had a lot in common, both roaring in their own ways.[30]

# 2 THE THIRTIES AND FORTIES

THE 1930S WERE YEARS OF GROWTH, CONSOLIDATION, AND CONTINUING ELABORATION OF THE NEW DISCIPLINE OF JOURNALISM. Honor societies began organizing in 1930 and included Theta Sigma Phi (an honor society for women in journalism, now the Association for Women in Communications) and Kappa Tau Alpha (the oldest honor society in journalism). By the end of the decade, the school formed its own broadcasting honorary, DiGamma Kappa, the first known honorary in that discipline. Grady had begun instruction in radio in the 1938-39 academic year, an early entrant into that field.

In 1931 the school made another claim to lasting fame with the establishment of the nation's first Internship Program, designed to give students practical professional experience before graduation. Drewry always compared it to interning in medical education, a claim and concept that has gained renewed currency in this century with reference to the "teaching hospital" model. Also in 1931, the Georgia Press Association established a Hall of Fame and made the Grady School its official home. Not surprisingly, the first inductee was Henry W. Grady himself and the association commissioned Georgia artist, Steffen Thomas, to do a bust of Grady. They chose Thomas after visiting the University of Alabama where a year before that university unveiled a bust of its legendary president George Hutchison Denny, also sculpted by Thomas. Today the bust of Grady is in the Dean's Office, a constant companion. (Over the years Grady became home to all its disciplines' various State Halls of Fame: including Broadcasting, Advertising, and Public Relations.)

Bust of Grady by Steffen Thomas, 1932. *Grady College Archives*

The Newspaper Hall of Fame and the decision to make Grady the permanent home of the Georgia Press Institute were sure signs that Drewry was moving steadily toward making Grady and Georgia journalism coterminous. In 1933 he organized the Georgia Collegiate Press Association, which witnessed robust gatherings of college editors and staffers from all over the state. While various campuses hosted the gatherings, no one doubted where the seat of journalism resided. If all this smacked of too much professionalism, Sanford and Drewry were committed to journalism as literary genre and naturally at home both in the Department of English first, then later as a school within the Franklin College of Arts and Sciences. The early curriculum included the short story along with literary criticism, ethics, history and law; and Drewry remained a syndicated book columnist even after his retirement in 1969. The reading room named for him contained a large collection of his books with still more donated to the Main Library. (As of 2014, the books moved to the main library and the anomalous if meticulous replicas of famous ships, crafted by a member of the UGA maintenance staff, housed elsewhere. Intended originally as a reading room for journals and publications as well as a media information center, the digital transformation has rendered that purpose null. With Tom and Edwina Johnson and a generous gift from the Peyton Anderson Foundation, the Drewry Room is now re-configured as a much-needed commons area and named the Peyton Anderson Forum.)

Drewry was also active in the accreditation movement for schools of journalism, which eventually adopted the standard that 75 percent of an undergraduate's course work must be taken outside journalism. Because of Drewry's work in national associations, the Grady flag was everywhere visible and its reputation as among the elite schools of journalism secure. Still, he was determined to make the journalism school professionally relevant. That meant attention to the details of publishing; thus, the internship initiative as well as teaching the fundamentals of the business side. The school even set up a printing shop that taught the mechanics of that trade. Indeed, the first major gift to Grady came in 1922 and was a Mergenthaler Linotype machine. That "hot type" printing press served as a learning laboratory for journalists who would "have to do it all," as most community journalists did. The linotype and hot metal printing would not begin to yield to cold type and offset printing until the sixties and only gradually then. Hugh Jackson Rowe, editor of the *Athens Banner-Herald* and the Athens representative on the Board of Trustees, arranged the gift.

Hugh Jackson Rowe, Grady's first donor. *Hargrett Rare Books and Manuscript Library*

During the thirties the faculty remained small, only four added, and continued to reflect the arts and sciences emphasis. The first was Edward Cass Crouse who held two degrees from the University of Wisconsin. Crouse was a drama critic who knew theatre as well as any. In 1932 he merged the two warring theatre troupes on campus, Thalian and Blackfriars, and was so active with these thespians that when UGA decided to form a separate department of drama in 1940, he was named its first head. Another hired in the thirties was Willett Main Kempton, also with strong ties to Madison, Wisconsin. He had a long suit in international reporting, serving in Germany and with United Press in Africa. In the summers of 1937 and 1938 he took groups of students to both Berlin and Spain. Grady's first study abroad program foreshadowed the long suit Grady would develop in international studies. The 1937 brochure said that students who signed on at $488 would sail third class on the USS Bremen and spend seven weeks in Europe visiting eight countries. "News from Europe is increasingly involved. We are living again in a pre-war age. Propaganda and censorship abroad seek to color public opinion through our press."[31] One can only imagine being in Hitler's Berlin in those fateful summers.

The thirties were also the years of America's transformation from small town, Midwestern idealism to big time industrialization, urban expansion, and social engineering. Despite the Great Depression, FDR's New Deal arrived in time to save big banks from collapse and launch social programs to rescue average Americans from joblessness and the fear of living out their final years in penury. It would have huge implications for journalism, and both Sanford and Drewry identified with Roosevelt's approach. They no doubt saw it as a continuation of Woodrow Wilson's New Freedom and the

Grady faculty in 1930's: first row A. Lynne Brannen, Jr., Assistant in Journalism, Dorothy Murray, secretary, Dyar Massey, Jr., Assistant in Journalism; second row, Drewry, Director and Professor, Willett M. Kempton, Assistant Professor, Edward C. Crouse, Associate Professor. *1939* ***Pandora***

South's solid adherence to the Democratic Party. In fact, it was more like Teddy Roosevelt's New Nationalism, understanding that "bigness" was here to stay with government regulation of corporate trusts as the public's surest safeguard. Theodore and Franklin were distant cousins, a generation apart, and in different parties. Although the families did not much like each other, the policies and practical effects of their governing strategies came to the same end.

## ATHENS AND CHAPEL HILL WEIGH IN

FDR's brand of liberalism radiated out through the academy. In the South it would take root most visibly at Chapel Hill, where native Georgian (Bethlehem, near Athens) Howard Odum led the charge. After an undergraduate degree at Emory in nearby Oxford, Georgia, he received a master's in classical literature from Ole Miss before obtaining a Ph.D. in Psychology at Clark University and another in sociology at Columbia. He taught at Georgia from 1912-19 before heading to Chapel Hill. (At Georgia he taught educational sociology in its summer institutes for women teachers.) Beginning with the study of Negro folklore, Odum eventually established a school of regional sociology, funded in part by money from the Rockefeller Foundation.[32]

The journal Odum founded, *Social Forces*, would have significant influence among a small but influential cadre of southern journalists of liberal bent. Among them was Gerald Johnson, a journalism faculty member at Chapel Hill, who would go on to the *Baltimore Sun*, where he and H.L. Mencken kept up a steady critique of southern backwardness. Odum's program in turn would provide much of the core research that led to Gunnar Myrdal's *American Dilemma*, the work that in turn led directly to the Supreme Court's famous footnote 11 in Brown v. Board of Education, which declared "separate (segregation) to be an inherent denial of equality." (What Odum did for human ecology, his son, Eugene P. Odum, would do for environmental ecology at Georgia, the School of Ecology being named for him. Eugene also collaborated with his equally famous brother Howard T. Odum, another award-winning environmental ecologist at the University of Florida.) And it all started in Bethlehem—Georgia, that is.

Journalism caught the liberal drift, but not much more. In the end, journalism's opinion leaders in the South would split Wilsonian liberals into ardent supporters and opponents of the New Deal, more of the latter as the twentieth century wore on. In neither case did it win much support for African-American aspirations, certainly not from Sanford or Drewry. But also

Odum wedding party, Eugene, the groom, and his famous father, Howard, second from right.
*Hargrett Rare Books and Manuscript Library, University of Georgia*

not from William Terry Couch, celebrated head of the University of North Carolina Press, where Chapel Hill's vaunted liberalism would crash on the shoals of race, Howard Odum being a latter day, if gradual, exception. Couch had done much for the cause by publishing Odum's work and others on African-American thought, culture, and experience. Yet, Couch approached the prospect of a desegregated South as if it were a hot stove. When Couch asked Howard University's Rayford Logan, to assemble a collection of essays on *What the Negro Wants*, he was shocked at the temerity of what African-Americans truly wanted; so taken aback that he wrote a publisher's introduction to distance himself from the authors.[33]

Couch said there were three possible views of the Negro: 1) that he is naturally inferior and left to his own devices produces no civilization; 2) that the Negro's condition is produced by natural inferiority but that it can be overcome gradually and the prejudice from it cured; or 3) that the Negro is not inferior, "that he only appears to be so, that his condition is wholly and completely a product of race prejudice and the consequent disabilities inflicted on the Negro by the white man." Couch said that this latter view, with which he took exception, preferring the second, was the dominant view of the day.

Of course, Couch exaggerated when he called it dominant, but it was the view that prevailed in Myrdal's *American Dilemma*, and with it *Brown vs. Board of Education.* In what amounted to pique, if not envy, Couch was quick to say that Myrdal's work was preceded by "numerous books, pamphlets, and articles presenting the same arguments." He conceded only that it was published "under more reputable auspices (Carnegie Foundation), and was more readable than the mass of material sharing its attitude." What most offended Couch was Myrdal's insistence on "cultural relativism," the view that cultures are neither inferior nor superior, just different. Couch said that those who believed in relativism could not believe in equality because they had rejected "universal values." Couch could not shake the Victorian link that equated culture with civilization, that he defined generously as "an accumulation of universal values from various cultures"—an artful if disingenuous dodge.

If Couch felt a sea change in liberalism, it was only at the surface. Liberalism, for most who dared use the term in the South, was seldom more than skin deep, a kind of studied critique of the region's Gothic political behavior. Journalists in particular adopted this brand of liberalism as a foil against Kluxers and fundamentalists. The surest route to a Pulitzer Prize in the twenties and thirties was an editorial attack on the Klan by a southern editor, or so it was believed. Julian Harris, son of Joel Chandler Harris, received one for his paper in the mid-twenties, as a crusading editor for the *Columbus Enquirer-Sun*.[34] Harris even got praise from the splenetic Gerald Johnson, who also found a good word for W.T. Anderson of the *Macon Telegraph*.[35]

In March 1926, Drewry himself weighed in with letters to Julian Harris and Marcellus E. Foster of the *Houston Chronicle* about their forward positions in denouncing the Klan, saying that while credit must go to the *New York World* and to Hearst's *International Magazine*, the Texas and Georgia journals were "all the more courageous" for being from down South. Drewry also corresponded with the *Birmingham Age-Herald* and its sister the *Mobile Register*, as well as the *Birmingham Post* for their outspoken stands against the horrendous convict-leasing system where it persisted last in Alabama. Drewry developed a hand-written essay on journalistic courage from these exchanges.[36]

Couch knew very well this side of liberalism. Early in the thirties he asked John D. Allen, another member of the journalism faculty at North Carolina, to do an analysis of southern newspapers.[37] Allen observed that southern editors frequently expressed views on race, religion, and education at odds with their predominantly conservative cultural and economic views. The resulting chaos, Allen thought, merely reflected the fact that journalists acted "harmoniously with the society in which they functioned." Liberalism, he continued, imbued society with the concepts of Rousseau, the Physiocrats of France, Jefferson, and the frontier. Indeed, "modernity," meaning the eighteenth and nineteenth centuries, devoted itself to getting these ideas "grounded into the polities of nations." Even in the American South these ideas gained currency, though with less "conviction of their efficacy" owing to the South's "peculiar institution (slavery)." Yet after adopting it in the eighteenth century in pursuit of revolution, these liberal "concepts were shorn of their vitality." By 1830, Allen concluded, liberalism "could frighten only the most timid souls." One by one the democratic dogmas became mere cant as "the notion of 'natural rights' . . . degraded to mean the right of every man to get the better of his neighbor."

Allen understood that to employ liberal rhetoric by the 1930s was not necessarily to understand it. "It (liberalism) may be, and sometimes is merely an easy way of attracting a reputation, or satisfying the convention that a newspaper supply leadership." Liberalism in print, Allen concluded, was "simply an average journalist employing a perfectly safe stereotype to round out his daily stint. Or he may be only a conservative journalist declaiming for fair dealing, but failing or refusing to comprehend why a principle has been violated."

This notion of liberalism as patina, the gilt-edge on the pages of a book, was nowhere more evident than in the career of John Temple Graves. Born in 1892 in Rome, Georgia, Graves grew up in College Park, a suburb just south of Atlanta. His distinguished father first won general acclaim for his funeral oration on the death of Henry Grady, proclaiming the line that appears on the pedestal of Grady's statue in Atlanta: "And when he died he was literally loving a nation into peace." The younger Graves grew up secure in his father's reputation. He graduated from Princeton, obtained a law degree from George Washington University, served in World War I, and returned to Washington as an economist for the Federal Trade Commission. He made an unsuccessful swipe at becoming a novelist and thereafter settled into being a bureaucrat, where he might have remained but for his father's illness. In 1925, he joined his father in Florida as an editorialist for the *Palm Beach Post*.[38]

In 1929, an auspicious year, Graves moved to Birmingham where he assumed editorial duties with the *Age-Herald*, later the *Post-Herald*. In 1937, *Newsweek* magazine described him as the "first successfully syndicated Southern columnist." Under the heading "This Morning," he poured forth his brand of Wilsonian liberalism. He believed liberalism to be more an attitude than a set of beliefs. As an attitude it was characterized by "open-mindedness, intellectual generosity, respect for the rules of thought and for the right to think, courage to do your own thinking without the regard for either foreign or domestic prejudices."

In fact, Graves' brand of liberalism was also a set of beliefs. For him Woodrow Wilson's New Freedom with its promise of competitive individualism and refereed competition was superior to Theodore Roosevelt's New Nationalism with its vision of regulated monopolies and oligopolies. Whether rooted in beliefs or attitudes, Graves' liberalism contained within it the germ of intellectual paralysis. It was inherently a form of nineteenth-century Idealism, an approach described best by the intellectual historian, Perry Miller. "The Idealist," Miller observed, "was confident that in the climax of his argument he could resolve every contradiction, every objection, into an all-inclusive synthesis, and therefore was generously prepared, in the opening portions of his discourse, to acknowledge to the limit the seeming evils of existence." In so doing the Idealist could celebrate "the enduring verities of religion and morality."

John Templeton Graves, second from right, amidst a power-house group of Atlanta journalists. Clark Howell, Sr. who had just taken over business and news operations at the *Constitution*, is to his right, son of the Clark Howell who had succeeded Grady at helm of the paper. *Hargrett Rare Books and Manuscript Library, University of Georgia*

After 1938 Graves became archly anti-New Deal. He acknowledged that pellagra and rickets were the common lot of the common man in the South. He wrote of poor housing and other abuses heaped upon southern blacks, but in the end, he believed it was the southern white man's burden and no form of Rooseveltian statism was part of the solution. In a seeming paradox, Graves found justification for his inward turn, indeed inspiration, in the life and works of Henry Grady. Graves viewed Grady's "nationalism" and the whole theme of "reconciliation" as subordinate to the New South orator's regional loyalty. He saw Grady as moving like John C. Calhoun from an early flirtation with nationalism to a more enduring and mature regionalism. Graves called it the "centripetal" pull of the region. He saw in Grady's last speeches, especially the ones in Dallas and Boston, "not a nationalist," but "a challenging, aggressive, stand-taking man of the South." "I believe there came to him (Grady) in his last years a conviction that if Southern poverty was to be overcome and real peace of economic equity and social balance attained for the nation, the South must be permitted to express itself and its special circumstances."

Graves, scion of Georgia journalism, was right about Grady, and ironically, Graves was also right in acknowledging that the South was without the economic means of remedying its enduring poverty. He was wrong only in thinking the white South was in any danger of surrendering its regional autonomy. That said, Grady preached a gospel of materialism, couched in a regenerative language of national reconciliation that would eventually lift all boats. Moreover, journalism as imbedded, if nascent, democracy was the "still small voice" for an alternative South, and in the halls of the Grady College aspiring journalists would lead the way. So would their principal mentors, Sanford and Drewry. Enter Franklin Roosevelt.

## A NEW DEAL

As university historian Tom Dyer notes, "The most lasting effect of the New Deal programs on the campus could be seen in the extensive construction program undertaken largely with federal money. Although Governor (Eugene) Talmadge, an ardent foe of the New Deal, had initially blocked the use of federal funds on Georgia's campuses, he later relented and allowed University System officials to seek the federal monies."[39] It was a godsend. Interestingly, Roosevelt's most intimate connection to Georgia, his "Little White House" at Warm Springs, resulted from a suggestion by UGA benefactor George Foster Peabody that the president might find the location attractive and relaxing. He did. It became his "get-away" and ultimately the place of his death on April 12, 1945.

FDR also represented a difficult tightrope for Sanford to walk. Eugene Talmadge, who would win two two-year terms as governor in the thirties, 1933-37, was no fan of the president. Talmadge's small government populism was antithetical to the New Deal and its priorities. Still, with one exception, Talmadge avoided open hostilities because of the president's and the Democratic Party's popularity in the state. The exception was a meeting of the Georgia Press Association in 1935, where after an hour-long diatribe by Talmadge against the New Deal, the association "introduced [and approved] a resolution unequivocally endorsing the administration and the achievements of Franklin D. Roosevelt."[40] (Talmadge always baited the press.) Members of the GPA, by a large majority, never supported Gene Talmadge, and besides, Republicans were still the party of Lincoln and now of Hoover. In 1938, the regents approved an honorary degree for Roosevelt,

Eugene Talmadge's crude anti-New Deal populism dominated Georgia politics, especially his vitriolic racism. *Hargrett Rare Books and Manuscript Library, University of Georgia*

FDR receives honorary degree from UGA, 1938, a rebuke to Talmadge politics. *Hargrett Rare Books and Manuscript Library, University of Georgia*

which Sanford was happy to oblige, his own feelings for the president being strong. The occasion, however, proved less than fortuitous.

The day settled upon, August 11, 1938, started happily with ceremonies in Athens but ended on a sour note when FDR went to Barnesville, Georgia, and openly campaigned against Senator Walter F. George, a patrician in the Senate if Georgia ever had one. Although personally friendly with the president, George had been a reluctant New Dealer at best and openly against FDR's infamous court-packing scheme, an attempt to enlarge the Supreme Court in order to overcome its hostile conservative majority. In the end, the over-reach ended in no harm as George easily won re-election and Roosevelt would carry Georgia solidly in the '40 and '44 presidential elections. Still, it was politically awkward for Sanford and the university, as it made them more suspect among Talmedgeites, as if that were a more or less proposition.

1938 would be the high water mark for the financially strapped university, the aforementioned construction boom being one factor and Governor E. D. "Ed" Rivers, 1937-41, another. Rivers had pledged a "state New Deal." In his first two-year term he made good on his pledge of increased funding, but 1938 saw a sharp economic downturn. Roosevelt, always more conservative than most thought, decided to balance the federal budget and the resulting fiscal austerity cut into recovery. It also made the state budget equally vulnerable. So the rest of the thirties felt the effects of a continuing depression. Not until WWII's massive deficit spending would the state and nation begin to experience genuine recovery. One thing that did continue into the forties for UGA was construction, because two million dollars in federal and state funds had been set aside and seventeen new buildings sprang up to ease overcrowding.[41]

Ask students of the thirties what they remember most, and they often say "dollars," so few of them. University fees were $100 for the school year, twice that for out-of-state students. Almost none had cars. They traveled by rail or family car at 15 cents a gallon, most of that in taxes. Students walked. Bus service did not exist. Georgia Power took its trolleys off the streets in 1928, a move it would not make in Atlanta until 1946. A room off campus rented for $10 a month, meals added another $8. For a dime, a student could entertain a date in the most popular place in town, Costa's mirrored-walled soda fountain on College Avenue. Cigarettes were 15 cents a pack and many smoked, most acquiring the habit in Athens. A nickel would buy a hamburger, a hot dog, or a seven-ounce bottle of Coke and on it went.[42]

**ABOVE:** Carolyn McKenzie's (soon-to-be Carter) yearbook picture. *1940* ***Pandora;*** **BELOW:** Don Carter's yearbook picture, by far the luckier. *1938* ***Pandora***

Still, the students kept coming and Grady experienced continuous enrollment growth throughout the decade. Journalism in all its facets remained attractive. Moreover, Drewry bragged that the state's leading publishers and now broadcasters entrusted their sons and daughters to the school. With a total enrollment of 241 in the 1939-40 academic year, Drewry tallied fifty as sons, daughters, and other relatives of the fourth estate, and the daughters outnumbered the sons considerably. Of the sixty-nine students who graduated in 1940, forty-two were women, among them was Hallie Carolyn McKenzie (ABJ 40) who would go on to an award-winning career as a photojournalist, first with *The Atlanta Constitution* and later with Coca-Cola. While at the *Constitution*, she would be pursued by a 1938 graduate and cousin of future president Jimmy Carter, Donnel Earl Carter (ABJ 38), then with the rival *Journal*, and together they enjoyed highly successful careers in newspapers, he winding up as Vice President for News at Knight-Ridder. Don and Carolyn created a Chair for Journalism Excellence and together pledged and made the largest single gift to the College.

Another stellar graduate from the thirties was Lessie Bailey (ABJ 34). Following graduation, she married Charles Smithgall, a Georgia Tech grad. They met at WGST in Atlanta, she writing copy, he reading copy. His reading news so annoyed her while writing that at first she did not like him, but that changed and together they enjoyed a remarkable career in broadcasting and publishing. In their early Atlanta years, she worked as continuity secretary for Lambdin Kay, public service director for WSB, formerly titled general manager. It would be the most consequential connection for the Grady School and arguably for the University of Georgia. It started when Kay, who served on the executive committee of the National Association of Broadcasters, complained that Columbia University, home to the Pulitzer Prize, refused to jury electronic, public service journalism; i.e. radio. Wondering where to turn, Lessie knew just the person, John Drewry. Kay placed the call in 1939 and made history. (At this writing, Lessie has celebrated her 105th birthday in Grady's centennial year.)

**ABOVE:** Lessie Bailey Smithgall. *1934* ***Pandora;*** **BELOW:** Lambdin Kay made "the call" that launched the Peabody Awards. *Hargrett Rare Books and Manuscript Library, University of Georgia*

Supported by Sanford, Drewry went to work immediately. He had a series of conferences, first with Sanford, then successively Marion Smith, former Regents chairman, Harmon Caldwell, president of UGA, Mrs. Marjorie Peabody Waite, adopted daughter of George Foster Peabody, and Harry Hodgson of Athens and friend of Peabody. All agreed to serve on the planning committee. Their purpose was to have the nation's oldest chartered public university encourage social responsibility by recognizing outstanding examples of public service by the nation's youngest media, radio. They also wanted to honor a distinguished American by naming the award for Peabody.[43]

Born in Columbus, Georgia, in 1852, Peabody's family moved to Brooklyn, New York, at the end of the Civil War, where by age 28, Peabody joined his friend Spencer Trask in the investment

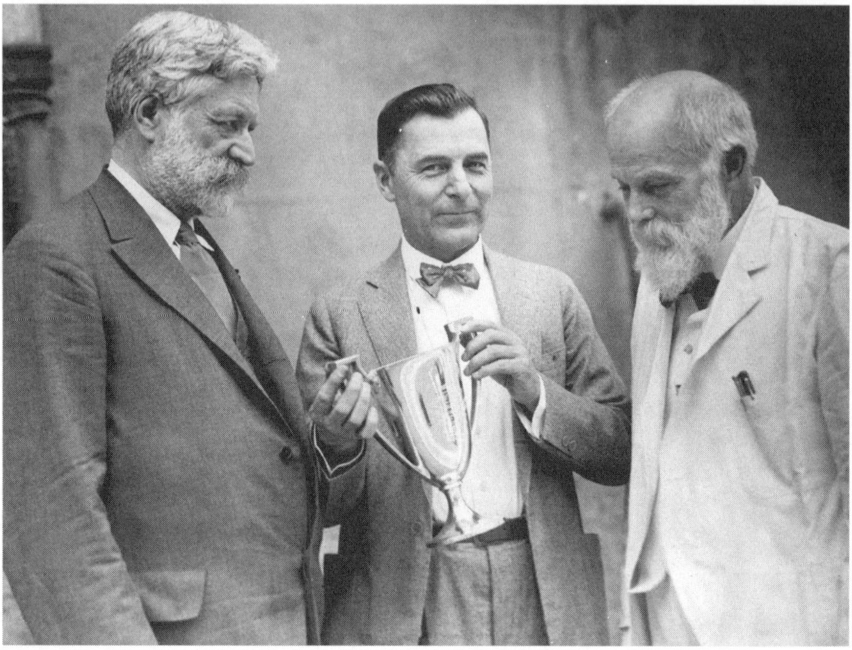

Peabody looks on as Harry Hodgson, UGA Athens Trustee, accepts accolades for a successful alumni campaign, ca 1920s. Chancellor Barrow on right. *Hargrett Rare Books and Manuscript Library, University of Georgia*

banking business. They invested in railroads (primarily out west and in Mexico and Latin America), utilities (one becoming General Electric), and sugar beets. By 1906, he retired to devote the remainder of his life to philanthropies, among which were Negro education, various peace movements, and the University of Georgia. He was close to all its chancellors from Hill to Sanford, giving a total of $250,000 to the University, an equivalency of $13.2 million in today's dollars.

Also, as a lifelong and active Democrat, he was close to Woodrow Wilson and Franklin Roosevelt. He married once, Spencer Trask's widow Katrina, he at age 69, she at 68. Already an invalid, she died eleven months later. Peabody soon thereafter adopted as his daughter Marjorie Waite, a young widow, who had come to Yaddo, the Trask estate at Saratoga Springs, to run a school for working women. At his death in 1938, Marjorie Peabody Waite would carry on his legacy of philanthropy that now included Yaddo, the famous artists and writers' colony. Among numerous other Yaddo residents were novelists of the Southern Gothic, including another Columbus, Georgia, native, Carson McCullers (née Lula Smith Carson) who in 1951 wrote *The Ballad of the Sad Café* while in residence at Yaddo.

William S. Paley, left, accepts first Peabody Award for CBS. Marjorie Peabody Waite, adopted daughter of George Foster Peabody, and Chancellor Sanford make the presentation. *Grady College Archives*

Soon the planning group had its recommendation before a committee of the Regents that included Albert S. Hardy, editor of the *Gainesville News* and soon president of the National Editors Association (NEA); Clark Howell, editor and publisher of *The Atlanta Constitution*; Abit Nix, Athens attorney; and George Hains, Augusta attorney. They reported favorably and the Regents approved the establishment of the George Foster Peabody Radio Awards in May 1940, adding television in 1948. Membership on the advisory board consisted of the chancellor and "twelve other outstanding American citizens who have demonstrated in a notable degree their interest in public affairs, and who also by position and achievement are prepared to evaluate in an impartial and detached manner the contributions of radio stations and chains in connection with this award." Recipients would receive a certificate of distinction and a medal, designed by famous sculptress, Evelyn Beatrice Longman Batchelder. The medal bears the likeness of Peabody on one side and the great seal of the State of Georgia on the other. The original inscription on the medal, "Peabody, lover of men" was thereby scratched.

UGA presented the first awards at the Commodore Hotel in New York on March 29, 1941. CBS received the first one, William S. Paley accepting. In the early years the National Association of Broadcasters participated. The Peabody Board that juried the awards drew an illustrious array of members.

Edward "Ted" Weeks of *The Atlantic Monthly* served as first chair of the Peabody Awards Board. *Hargrett Rare Books and Manuscript Library, University of Georgia*

Bennett Cerf, president of Random House, and Drewry present a Peabody to Lassie. *Grady College Archives*

Until 1968 only two people chaired the board, Ted Weeks (pronounced Wicks) editor of *The Atlantic Monthly* and Bennett Cerf, president of Random House. From the beginning, faculty and students of the Grady School actively supported the work of the board by receipting entries, doing preliminary screenings and reports, and archiving all entries, not just winners. With awards made in the spring of each year, entries were (and are) from productions and broadcasts of the previous calendar year; thus 1941 presentations were for programs that aired in 1940 and so on. In the early years, large, medium, and small stations formed categories with public service the emphasis.

The 75th anniversary comes in 2015-16. In those years the Peabody rightly claims standing as the oldest and most prestigious award for electronic media, but in the early days not everyone saw so clearly and potshots were taken, as this one from *Time Magazine*: ". . . a new type of accolade, which radio piously hopes will rank with journalism's Pulitzer Prizes and cinema's Oscars, was awarded for the first time last week. The trophies were four bronze medallions, each the size of a hockey puck. Their name: the George Foster Peabody Award for conspicuous service in broadcasting." While some sniffed, the University of Georgia had staked its claim, a most impressive hockey puck indeed.

Some original founders are still with us, Lessie Smithgall obviously being one. She and her husband, Charles, made a generous gift to establish the Lambdin Kay Chair for the Peabody Awards, the

Peabody Award Medallion. *Grady College Archives*

Fifth Annual Presentation of the George Foster Peabody Awards in New York. *Hargrett Rare Books and Manuscript Library, University of Georgia and Grady College Archives*

Warren Jones (right) as a student assistant works with faculty member Tyus Butler in assembling first Peabody Award submissions. *Courtesy Warren Lee Jones*

holder of which serves as director. Also still with us is the Reverend Warren Lee Jones (ABJ 41). While a student he served on the first screening committees, then later as a graduate assistant and, in the '43 academic year, a member of the faculty, he helped Drewry administer the program. (Because he entered military service from 1943-46, he is credited with four years on the Grady faculty, military service being credited.) He was also in the first class of DiGamma Kappa, a Delta Sigma Chi scholarship recipient, and member of Phi Beta Kappa. In recent years he has regularly attended the awards ceremonies in New York. His recall is as clear as yesterday.

Warren Jones with Phi Beta Kappa and DiGamma Kappa keys. *Grady College Archives*

Gathering clouds ended the thirties and lapped over into the new decade. In those angry days, fierce rhetoric by America Firsters, led by Germany-admiring Charles Lindbergh, gave future Gold Star mothers hope that America would stay out of war. Gene Talmadge with equal vehemence opposed the war along with anything else Roosevelt supported. (Lindbergh's fraternization with Nazis reflected a view of, or sympathy for, racial ordering not incompatible with Talmadge's. Each believing that liberal, limited

The way they were. Students in a 1941 reporting class. *Hargrett Rare Books and Manuscript Library, University of Georgia*

government could exclude others based upon race for sure, and no doubt other reasons as well; e.g., being a Jew.) Still, students knew enough to be anxious; and some were already signing up as the Axis powers, including Japan, were threatening U.S. interests, especially the Philippines. The 1941 graduating class was only slightly down from 1940, but things were teetering. Three Sundays before December 7, Grady students put out a rotogravure section for *The Atlanta Journal.* Asked to prepare a page featuring University of Georgia journalism students, complete with numerous pictures as the gravure process enabled, Bob Vanlandingham, or Bobby as he was known in Cairo, county seat of Grady County, was its editor.

Featured in two pictures is Quimby Melton, Jr., who would succeed his father as a leading Georgia publisher. In another is Dan Magill, Jr., interviewing coach Wally Butts. Magill (ABJ 42) would become Georgia's legendary tennis coach and father of intercollegiate athletics publicity at UGA. In another, Jim Tate interviews President Harmon Caldwell. Tate (ABJ 42) would go on to a pioneering career in corporate communications at Atlanta Gas Light. And in one is Bobby "Van," who would soon find himself with a Phi Beta Kappa key but on a U.S. warship in the Pacific. He would return to Cairo to teach, go into the family auto and farm implement business before returning to his first love, journalism, writing for the *Cairo*

Bobby Vanlandingham steps off on Senior Day, 1942. A few months later he would be on a warship in the Pacific. *Courtesy Vanlandingham family*

*Messenger*. A public figure with a family name that spelled leadership and service, his writing was *New York Times* quality and his vision progressive. Staffers and even the owner/publisher always referred to him as "chief," as in "editor-in-chief," although the title did not exist. The paper continues to bear his imprint ten years after his passing. "Bobby" lived and contributed in interesting times; but when he edited the rotogravure edition, he could not have known what the future held. Then December 7 came three weeks later and everyone knew. The world in which Steadman Sanford grew up and came to maturity was in its final act. Sanford himself would die in 1945, or as a recent historian has styled it: *Year Zero*.

**LEFT:** Quimby Melton, key to a family tradition in Georgia journalism, as *Red & Black* reporter. **RIGHT:** Dan Magill interviews Georgia football coach Wally Butts. *Grady College Archives*

Jim Tate interviews President Caldwell. *Grady College Archives*

## THE FORTIES BECOME THE FIFTIES

In the first thirty years of the college's existence, 87 million people would lose their lives in two world wars, intersected by a great global depression of unprecedented magnitude, not to mention the great influenza that took from

50 to 100 million lives globally, most in a six week period during 1918 and most among the healthy and strong where its viral presence was most virulent. At the university, enrollments plunged in the forties as young men answered the call and marched off to war. The difference for the United States was that the war was still "over there."[44] Of those who marched off under Old Glory's banner, 100,000 did not return in 1918 and WWII would claim another 400,000; tragic numbers, but overwhelmingly soldiers of courage in uniform who accepted the risk, and almost no civilians. Unlike in Europe and Asia, America's greatest generation came back to a place with families and friends who feared for their loved ones but who remained safe. Moreover, the fighting war would be over in three years for Americans. For the involved world, it lasted a minimum of seven.

These differences spelled opportunity for an America still recovering from its speculative economic collapse. Returning veterans found jobs and a GI bill to pay for their higher education. The government provided ballast for what the private sector had destroyed. It also provided opportunity for African-Americans to demand and assert their rights. In this democratic resurgence and optimism, the Grady School itself would be buoyed; after all, its business was democracy.

Even in the nadir of mobilization and war, Grady was graduating the future. (UGA and Grady streamlined graduation for students expecting to enter service.) In 1943 three names emerged from the 30 graduates: Willis Johnson, who became a master storyteller for banking in Atlanta and whose daughter, Betty Hudson (ABJ 71), would later be another celebrated graduate; Jesse Outlar from Omega, Georgia, who became a legendary sports journalist and whose daughter Jan (ABJ 73) established a generous scholarship in his honor; finally Eugene Patterson from Adel, Georgia, who became one of America's most distinguished and honored journalists after being a Silver Star group commander for George Patton's Tenth Armored Division. The result, he was among those first to Bastogne in the Battle of the Bulge to "plug the hole," even before the 101st arrived, then sweeping across France and into Germany to end the war.

The acceleration of graduates made for odd occurrences. George Octavius Marshall from Americus, Georgia, started at Georgia Southwestern in Americus, then on to UGA in 1941 where he became a campus leader in the short year and a half before mustering in December 1942 for the campaign to take back Europe. He did a reminiscence of that time, the frontispiece of which reveals more than words can say about who fought that war.

**LEFT:** Willis Johnson played a key role in the Industrial Editors Institute which Drewry established in partnership with the National Association of Manufacturers. **RIGHT:** Gene Patterson jumping his ROTC cavalry horse in Sanford Stadium. *Grady College Archives*

Three legendary sportswriters and each a Grady Fellow. *Courtesy* ***Atlanta Journal-Constitution***

He returned with a bronze star and, as will be seen, became an influential member of the UGA faculty in its English Department. Although a December '42 graduate, he is seen here in a 50th Anniversary photograph of Grady's Class of '43.

In 1944 two of the twenty-two graduates were male. In 1945 it would be four of twenty-three, with one of those being Aubrey Richard Morris of WSB fame, who "brought newspapers to radio." Then, with an economy amped up on government-spending and war-manufacturing steroids along with the GI bill, enrollments swelled. 1946 graduates numbered forty-three; 1947, eighty-six; 1948, 122, among them Claude L. Williams, Jr., (he already had a Franklin degree awarded in 1944). Williams was a returning veteran, who had received a Purple Heart, Bronze Star, and Silver Star—the latter an award that went to Medal of Honor-worthy soldiers who did not die. He made his stand on the

**LEFT:** George Marshall ready for war. *Courtesy Charlotte Thomas Marshall;* **RIGHT:** George Marshall, Betty Hoyt Savell, Jesse Outlar, and Willis Johnson recognized for fifty years of alumni leadership. *Grady College Archives*

Claude L. Williams, Jr., soldier. *Courtesy Claude L. Williams, Jr.*

Siegfried Line. Williams became one of the great pioneers of post-war radio and advertising in Georgia. In the early sixties he was a prime mover behind the *Athens Daily News*, which became a Grady laboratory, with Grady graduates Glenn Vaughn and Mark Smith and Grady matriculate, Lewis Grizzard, launching a new style of journalism, at least new for Athens. The immediate post-war years were heady times. 1949 would produce more than 150 graduates, while 1950 topped that. Eventually it would drop back, but for now America was growing and with it came Georgia and its underfunded university. Indeed, Georgia with its military installations and unmet human needs became a welfare state, a charge of the federal government as tax money flowed south from states that were corporate, industrial, financial, and educational powerhouses. They did not seem to mind.

## WHAT IT WAS LIKE

Two graduates and a faculty member from the '49-'50 rosters illustrate the powers of friendship through intellectual and spiritual seeking so characteristic of the Grady spirit. Harold Earl Davis grew up in Sasser, Georgia, just out from Dawson, the county seat of what in the Civil Rights Movement would become known as "Terrible Terrell" for its brutal suppression of black citizens, including a church fire-bombing and police brutality that included murder. Harold's mother was a pianist, and at her knee he learned not only the piano but also opera. He could identify arias from a mere bar or two with amazing accuracy. His friend, Arthur Bland Darwin, was born and grew up in York, South Carolina. Both had intellectual, spiritual, and musical affinities. Art flew missions as a gunner in B-24s over Europe, his odds of surviving improved because his missions were toward war's end, but in those mechanical flying behemoths, still hazardous. Harold mopped up in post-war Europe. Both would distinguish themselves as Sigma Delta Chi scholarship recipients at Grady, always reserved for the most accomplished students, and would graduate Phi Beta Kappa.[45]

They enjoyed the influence of Franklin Butler, who joined the faculty in broadcasting in 1940 when Crouse went over to head the newly formed drama department. Butler was from Norfolk, Virginia, and educated at Middlebury College in Vermont. He was at the Asheville School for Boys in North Carolina when he left for Georgia. Neither Art nor Harold cared about radio and took no classes from him, but Butler possessed a more profound asset, wide ranging interests in the arts, literature, history and religion, which resonated with these aspirants and seekers. Together and with Harry Malone from Albany, Georgia, also a veteran, and others, they formed a salon of mutual interests and inquiry, the ideal. Harold, a Baptist, and Art, an Episcopalian, both inclined to the Anglican practice for a time and inquired into Catholicism as a correlate but settled on Episcopal. (Harold, owing to another influential faculty member, explored agnosticism and atheism but came back, owing to yet another faculty member who introduced him to Thomas Aquinas.)

**LEFT:** Arthur Darwin, standing back left, with flight crew. *Courtesy Mary P. Clark;* **RIGHT:** Harold Davis in occupied Europe. *Courtesy Priscilla Arnold Davis*

Harold and Arthur competed over identifying operatic arias—Harold would win—and in the summer of 1949, they set off for Alaska in a Model T, named Agnes for an Athens barmaid at Huddle, a favorite hangout. Harold's cousin and another friend, Bill McClure (ABJ 50) made it a foursome. Only Art could get reasonable employment as a printer, so Harold returned early and started a master's degree in history, with the result that both graduated in 1950, Harold (ABJ 49) with a master's in (50) and Art (ABJ 50). The glue among these friends was what one always assumes to be the best of college life, inquiring into the nature of things. We should never forget that. Butler left in 1950 to pursue a doctoral degree in philosophy and religion but came back in the fall of 1951 to teach part-time. In 1952 he took a fulltime one-year appointment, following which he left for Aiken, South Carolina, as acting headmaster of Mead Hall. Soon thereafter he returned to The Asheville School and spent the rest of his career there teaching Latin, English, and French. As Davis noted, "He was really born to be a schoolman, not a radio man."[46]

(In 1957, Arthur Darwin would marry with a reception in the home of the author's future wife in Clover, South Carolina. Harold and his wife Priscilla Arnold (ABJ 56) attended, as would Franklin Butler, his wife and daughter. While there, Butler's daughter ran into a plate glass window, which

Art Darwin, Harold Davis, and Bill McClure huddle over sandwiches on the hood of Agnes, their ever faithful Tin Lizzie. They were off to Alaska. *Courtesy Priscilla Arnold Davis*

required stitches—fortunate that my future wife's father was a doctor and good at suturing. The author would not meet his wife at Emory for another six years, nor connect with Harold Davis until the 1980's through a mutual interest in Henry Grady. Harold would become a mentor and friend, with whom the writer came to experience a continuation of the conversations that Butler and his students shared those many years ago at Grady. Later, Harold and the author would discover the inter-familial connections. Accordingly the author and his wife endowed an award in the college in honor of Harold and Arthur's friendship as exemplary of the Grady spirit—now the Darwin-Davis Award.)

## IT'S NEVER OVER

The forties would presage the fifties in another, less attractive way. It was Gene Talmadge redux, with his racial agenda. The episode was ugly for the university, southern-styled racial politics at its gargoylish worst. The object of Talmadge's rage was Dean of the College of Education Walter Dewey Cocking, known by all as a very nice man. A native of Iowa and product of Columbia University, his progressive ideas for education convinced the Regents to commission him to study the University System of Georgia in context of all higher education in the state and resulted in a 1940 report they liked. (Earlier, he had done a study on the Negro in higher education in Georgia for the Rosenwald Fund, which led to charges by Talmadge and allies that Jews and communists were pushing it. Julius Rosenwald was part owner and for a time head of Sears, Roebuck and Company. Like George Foster Peabody, he devoted a significant part of his charities to the educational advancement of African-Americans in the South.)[47]

True to form, the best laid plans by a forward thinking academic often prove subject to caprice, in this case Sylla Hamilton, who taught in a high school operated by the College of Education and was fired. She blamed Cocking, who had very little to do with it. She had powerful connections to the Talmadgites, and she used them to cause trouble. Specifically she charged that Cocking was so "foreign," meaning not Georgian, as to suggest "social equality" in education, meaning blacks studying with whites. Moreover, rumors spread that Cocking was having an affair with his black maid, typical of all politics of race, meaning lies are always better.[48] Thus Cocking found himself caught between Scylla (Hamilton) and Charybdis (Talmadge), a rock and a hard place.

Talmadge, who did not like the regents, much less the faculties they protected, went on a purge. He began with Cocking and moved on to the popular president of Georgia Southern in Statesboro, Marvin Pittman; and before it was over, hit six more. Pittman, too, was foreign—that is, Mississippi—but more importantly, the disgruntled woman who fingered him was also well connected to Talmadge. To effect his ends, Talmadge used his appointive powers to stack the Board of Regents with his cronies (FDR court-packing in another setting) in order to fire these good men and a half dozen more. The July 14, 1941, meeting of the regents was the blood-letting, and Talmadge and his toadies were at their crudest in slurring foreigners (furriners), communists and "nigger lovers." It was appalling, a caricature of racism at its ugliest. Ironically, a year before, Cocking served as chief registrar as 700 UGA students and faculty members signed up for the draft, over a full year ahead of Pearl Harbor;[49] but then "Ole" Gene was closer to the America Firsters who opposed American involvement than to America's emerging "greatest generation" of patriots.

Sanford laid low, hoping to wait Talmadge out and let his notoriously mercurial temper turn for the better. Howard Odum was called in from Chapel Hill to advise and interestingly wound up with a similar recommendation; to wit, fire Cocking and give the worm, Talmadge, time to turn. But others, President Harmon Caldwell for instance, threatened to resign and did, with no action taken. Still, even Georgians could recognize a power grab and the Southern Conference of Universities de-listed the Georgia System's colleges and universities, while the Southern Association of Colleges and Schools, SACS, withdrew its accreditation. Now, even Talmadge could see his vulnerability, and Humpty was put back together, this time with the governor's appointing authority removed and the regents resuming control in a reformed system that remains to this day. And in the end, Talmadge lost re-election to reform-governor Ellis Arnall, who because governors could not serve consecutive terms held the office for four-years before Talmadge was back.[50] Still, it was an awful black eye for higher education in Georgia.

UGA students had taken to the streets to protest Talmadge's high-handedness. It signaled a new turn to youth in politics, which would play out through the rest of the century. Talmadge would be re-elected in the 1946 Democratic primary, the only four-time elected governor, but die before taking office, leading to the famous or infamous three-governor controversy in Georgia. The more important token was the important shift of race in American politics. Cocking's mild suggestions of education for all was but the tip of an iceberg that had broken loose when in 1934 Charles Huston and Thurgood Marshall at Howard University's Law School determined to take down segregation by targeting higher education. In 1938, they would make inroads in Missouri and Maryland and by 1950, court rulings in Oklahoma and Texas made the Brown decision inevitable. The University of Georgia was drifting as a leaf on the bosom of a broad river, neither influencing nor directing its flow; but all these things would liberate the South (whatever its persisting denials), also America, and certainly the University of Georgia. Journalism, too, would make its final turn to democracy, at least the possibility of doing journalism in service of a democratic society.

## FINALE

Global war and southern tradition clouded these inexorable events. Just as Bobby Vanlandingham could not know three weeks out what would happen on December 7, the happy returning veterans and fellow students came back to a world they still knew, or at least thought they did, but time was running out. Football, which had experienced remarkable success during the war years, still had legs. (It was the era of Sinkwich and Trippe.) Fraternities once again amassed pledges to complement sorority rush. Grady kept pace,

Students burn an effigy of Gene Talmadge at the arch. *1942 **Pandora***

First row, Drewry, Marie Caldwell (secretary), Tyus Butler, Philip Berk; second row, John Talmadge, John S. Peters, Franklin Butler; third row, Constable, Louis T. Griffith. *1952* ***Pandora***

actually over-matched it. The curriculum that Drewry had stream-lined for war, by among other things creating a one-year program for those who were subject to the draft or would be returning veterans, returned to its natural banks. Proportionately, faculty growth matched student growth, not one-to-one but nearly enough so. None of the Grady annual reports indicated an awareness of, much less a discussion of, the inevitable future of an integrated world. Surely it took place. It did in other settings; for example, religious emphasis weeks, in classrooms, over coffee, but not yet as a part of the School of Journalism's agenda. Eventually it would have to, but for now the Grady silence was that of its namesake.

## CODA

The forties had a final act. There are always three or so deans who figure in likely succession scenarios to the presidency—few ever succeed that way.

John Drewry was one of those. He was Sanford's handpicked successor as director and dean. He was the architect of UGA's publicity plan and effectively chaired its implementation. Just as Eugene Talmadge discovered the liability of taking on regent Clark Howell, publisher of the *Atlanta Constitution*, Drewry knew the value of maintaining good relations with people who bought paper by the ton and ink by the barrel. The Georgia Press Institute did it for newspapers, the Georgia Radio and Television Institute for broadcasters, the Georgia Collegiate Press Association, a Southern Writers Workshop, the Education-Industry Conference on Public Relations in alliance with the National Association of Manufacturers, the Southern Industrial Editors Institute for those who told the stories of American industries—all represented an exhaustive and exhausting effort to make Grady relevant to all the disciplines it served. Annual Reports devoted much space to all these meetings and all the distinguished conferees that attended. It was truly impressive. No dean since Drewry, despite equally exhausting endeavors, has equaled it. These connections and relationships made Drewry most likely to succeed.

(When Harmon Caldwell moved over from his presidency to become system chancellor, the surprise successor, Jonathon Clark Rogers, who had been president of North Georgia College for the last fifteen years, was appointed in January 1949. Immediately the long festering war between Agriculture and the rest of the university broke out. It would not end until Omer Clyde Aderhold was appointed president in 1950, all of which made the Rogers presidency feel provisional; thus the jockeying of various candidates, including Drewry, for the position.)

One particular instance of Drewry's prowess was his rescue of the state press association, when following WWII the demands placed on GPA outstripped its office. In 1946, when its secretary was asked to resign, Drewry drew up a charter that offered a member of the Grady faculty as secretary-manager of the GPA office. The school would assign the secretary to UGA's Atlanta Division (now Georgia State University) with teaching responsibilities and secretarial duties supported by Grady to a maximum of $5,000, with any expenses beyond that amount supported by GPA. W. Stanford Smith, a 28 year-old army veteran, Grady graduate and 1940 editor of the *Red & Black*, assumed the responsibilities. He had also been a staff member of the *Augusta Chronicle* and *Cairo Messenger*. Smith seemed to have the energy of Sanford and Drewry combined and did a phenomenal job of serving both GPA and Grady. His position also gave Drewry another window on Atlanta media

**ABOVE:** Drewry's owlish eyes. *Hargrett Rare Books and Manuscript Library, University of Georgia;* **BELOW:** Virginia Dekle Moore. Drewry asked if she could write a "pretty letter." She could and did. *1947* ***Pandora***

generally.[51] Smith's abilities led him to the American Newspaper Publishers Association in New York City in 1953 as its executive officer, a position he would hold for many years. He had done wonders in seven years for Georgia.

Drewry was also a personality. His glasses made his eyes "owlish," his precise and precious southern enunciation, his exaggerated pronunciation of Georgia place-names like Hahira, his distinctive calling of the roll—all made him memorable. His knowledge of popular and classical culture gave him ready metaphors that would sweep the yearning-to-know before him. He was a performer. As with all larger-than-life-personalities, some students would be inspired, others not so. Harold Davis admired him, Davis's wife Priscilla did not, for reasons elaborated later. Harold's friend Arthur Darwin saw him as an "unctuous little popinjay," but with qualification. "His bearing and demeanor," Arthur wrote, ". . . made him a cartoonist's dream, all of which he took in good grace. As he lectured with a gravity approaching unctuousness, there was a hint of a smile and cast of eye suggesting it was all a big put-on and we all knew it."[52] There was a mix. At a gathering in Mt. Pleasant, South Carolina, among a generation of students who had experienced Drewry's "affect," their conclusion was that while Atlanta-area students were not so taken by him, the rest of Georgia, largely rural, was. One South Georgia student, Virginia Moore (née Dekle), upon graduation in 1947, applied to be an assistant in the Dean's Office. He asked her but one question, "Can you write a pretty letter?" She took that to mean not only stylish but flawless.[53]

Drewry lectured from "yellowed" notes he wrote in hand as short lines representing single thoughts or ideas or topics, often a note about a magazine or newspaper.[54] In an article likely for the *R&B* and dated May 16, 1978, the reporter described how Drewry's lectures would begin with a fairly small point about communication or journalism history upon which he would elaborate in ever expanding gyres of knowledge and anecdotal detail from his treasure of memory. Then came a day he had to be away, and he asked a student assistant, Gene Patterson, to do his lecture in absentia. "When Drewry returned, he discovered that Patterson, not able to elaborate on fine points as eloquently as he, had delivered the entire quarter's worth of lectures in the single day he was gone."[55]

Whatever Drewry's dramatic or melodramatic persona, he mattered. Moreover, his relationships with Georgia media and command of the national media corps through Peabodys were truly impressive. So impressive that events of the night of December 23, 1949, would not derail him, except from becoming a viable candidate for university president. On that night, he had dinner with his wife of twenty-three years, Kathleen Merry Drewry (they had divorced in August) and with their eighteen year-old son, Milton. It would have been their 23rd anniversary. Accounts vary: he called it "a supper conference" to discuss a Christmas gift for Milton and a debt she owed that he might help with; she said it was a continuing effort on his part for reconciliation. In any event, hers was a fragile emotional state, as their correspondence dating to the thirties revealed a pattern of mental health issues.[56]

When they parted somewhat early that evening, she suspected he was going to visit his former secretary and now fiancée, Miriam Thurmond. He was, but as usual Miriam was with her mother and grandmother in the house they shared. When he arrived about 9:00, Miriam and her mother were making Christmas candy in the kitchen. Miriam and John later repaired to the living room. As they talked, Kathleen Drewry, who had borrowed a neighbor's car, entered through the unlatched front door and emptied five bullets from a pearl-handled .32 caliber revolver into Drewry and his wife-to-be, the first two into him, the second two into her, and the final struck him again—his wounds in the chest, hers in the stomach. A sensational trial followed in April. The state charged and convicted Kathleen Drewry with the attempted murder of Miriam Thurmond; the sentence was from two to four years. Her attorneys took it to the State Court of Appeals, which sustained the trial judge, but on a writ of cert, the State Supreme Court ordered a retrial based upon the trial judge's faulty explanation of an insanity plea. A retrial in January 1952 resulted in acquittal. One juror, on condition of anonymity, said the twelve men decided quickly and unanimously that she had "acted under stress and strain so severe it would have unbalanced the strongest man." Having posted bond throughout, Kathleen Drewry never served time. That said, Drewry and Miriam Thurmond had married on March 16, 1950 and lived happily and productively ever after until his passing thirty-three years later. He was twenty years her senior.[57]

Having been seriously but not gravely wounded, Drewry walked into his early January class with two bullets still in him and a slight limp and called the roll. (The wound in his chest was not lethal because of a wallet he wore in his vest pocket. Faculty figured that only a "dean's wallet" was thick enough to stop a bullet. The wallet also contributed to an urban legend that he had been shot in the buttocks while diving over the sofa.) To the breathless students, nothing appeared amiss. As one former student put it, "He exuded a poise that seldom wavered. He was, in fact, like a skilled actor, expertly performing his assigned role as the impeccable college dean, but seldom exposing the real personality behind the performance."[58] The worst was yet to come, as during the April trial the court allowed Kathleen Drewry to enter unsworn lurid and salacious accusations of unusual sexual demands by Drewry, forty-two pages and three hours in all, while at the same time saying that he read so much, it was like being married to a "bed lamp."[59] The event and its circumstances provided sensational news. *The Atlanta Journal* carried stories displayed across eight columns with two-line, all capital banner headlines. The paper was delivered daily to Athens, and the Athens paper did not back off either. The national press also blared it, in part owing to Drewry's high Peabody profile.

Curiously, although the *Red & Black* editors clipped the headlines and pasted them to their walls, in part to cover fading paint, they refused to cover the story, offering the following explanation: "We feel that what happens in a man's private life is primarily his own concern as long as it does not affect his public duties. The affair is in the past; President (Jonathan Clark) Rogers has quite properly announced that it will not affect the Dean's standing, and we feel that the subject should be dismissed from the wagging tongues of campus gossip mongers." When Dean Drewry finally showed up in the *Red & Black* offices, which he seldom did, he saw the clippings, chatted with the staff briefly, and as he turned to leave, amiably said, "These walls really do need painting. I'll send the painters down in a few days."[60]

The institutes and associations Drewry had formed and nurtured all moved resolutions of praise and support without ever alluding to the incident itself. Letters poured in, among them one from the dean of the Medill School at Northwestern, another from Ted Weeks of the *Atlantic Monthly*, and from twelve former students at Rich's, Inc., in Atlanta, four days after the shooting, saying "Although you 'made us what we are today,' not even you could teach us what to write on such an occasion, but you do know that this message comes from loyal and sincere hearts, troubled because trouble has come to you."[61] Drewry remained a remarkable man of admirable ability who made a college in Henry Grady's likeness. In fact, when he died, February 11, 1983, the *Atlanta Journal-Constitution* called him "the most important figure in Georgia journalism since Henry W. Grady." Ironically, as the trial ended and moved into its appellate phase, the school celebrated Grady's 100th birthday with a Grady Memorial Stamp designed by a Norwegian student.

Lies, legends, and myths have survived this horrific event. Almost none are true. What happened that evening was a home invasion by a mentally ill woman intent on murder. The victims were innocent in deed and purpose. In that day, no one knew how to deal with mental illness or even simpler matters like divorce. When Kathleen Drewry burst in upon John Drewry and Miriam Thurmond, she committed one of the most heinous acts imaginable, attempted murder in a private residence. To be sure, John Drewry had been almost clueless in how to handle an erratic ex-wife, although there is no doubt he was trying. No psychologist today would other than advise against attempting to "manage" a situation in the way he did. Of course when it

Margaret Mitchell, ever the center of attention, Georgia Press Institute, 1943. *Hargrett Rare Books and Manuscript Library, University of Georgia*

went to trial, legal theories were advanced, the unsworn testimony of a person afflicted by severe borderline personality disorder and narcissism created fictions that journalists ran with. It was sensational, yet far wide of the mark. An appendix offers an evaluation of how those fictions and legends issued from legal argument and circumstantial evidence.

One other tragedy of 1949 was the death of Margaret Mitchell, famous author of *Gone with the Wind*, known by all in the press association as Peggy and said to be "at her gayest and best at the Press Institute Friday night parties, the wee-hour song fests, the unscheduled story sessions."[62] As a veteran and student, Arthur Darwin had vivid memories of her last Institute and put it this way: "A special occasion was the attendance of Margaret Mitchell, a most gracious and fun-loving lady. The R&B had a hospitality room in a local hotel for meeting selected guests to relax and swap stories. Off the formal slate, Miss Mitchell was plain old Peggy Marsh. Mr. Marsh was confined to a wheelchair but joined right in the fun. We wound up the evening squalling bawdy songs and parodies of headlines from the *Atlanta Constitution*." On the night of August 11, 1949, the diminutive Mitchell, unawares, stepped in front of a speeding car on Peachtree Street and died five days later without regaining consciousness. Gone was a personality that held enthralled Georgia journalists and Grady students equally. She was 48.

# THE FIFTIES AND SIXTIES 3

AS THE FORTIES DREW TO A CLOSE, NEW COURSE SEQUENCES PRESAGED ACADEMIC DEPARTMENTS. The school received accreditation from the newly formed American Council for Education in Journalism that Drewry was instrumental in organizing, and the faculty talked about a curriculum aimed at consumers as well as practitioners. The school also promoted interdisciplinary studies. Already photo- journalism had allied with physics to explore optics and the physical processes of image construction. The eminent Lamar Dodd, whose legacy in art left his name on the school that became a UGA point of pride, also taught art in advertising for Grady and appeared on its faculty roster. Meanwhile students and faculty in art transformed the Grady walls with murals recounting the history of printing and publishing.

Lamar Dodd with Grady students.
*Grady College Archive*

Jean Charlot did the fourth mural. Charlot, a dual citizen of France and the United States, lived for a considerable time in Mexico City where he came under the influence of Diego

Rivera. He spent much of the forties in Georgia, painting some murals for the Works Projects Administration's Federal Arts Project, including one for the post office in McDonough, titled "Cotton Gin." He came to UGA in 1941 under auspices of a Carnegie Corporation grant that enabled him to be an artist-in-residence for three years. He first did the fabulous mural on the face of the Fine Arts Building at Georgia. Then, at the invitation of Drewry, he did a fresco in the Journalism Building that is oddly ironic, even if impressive, for it spans Cortez's invasion of Mexico in the 16th century to paratroopers dropping on Nazis in WWII, and its theme is "the scoop." In addition, he did a book with the UGA Press, *Charlot Murals in Georgia*, with an introduction by Lamar Dodd.[63] Guests for the dedication of the Grady mural on March 24, 1944, were appropriately a group of South American journalists. A master's thesis by Doris Pogue from Birmingham, Alabama, resulted in the sixth and final Grady mural. It celebrated both business and journalism. The murals were a Grady idea and spoke volumes.

The volumes established the school as a collection of storytelling disciplines: literary, visual, auditory, all representing ideas, issues, institutions and individuals—the democratic arts. In the fifties, journalism schools would explain over and again that they were about "communications" and, as such, should be understood as foundational. Drewry and the college were quite defensive about the "new" emphasis, finding it not new at all. Typical was the declaimer in the '54 Annual Report:

> *Communications* is the new word for *journalism.* At least one of the oldest and best schools of journalism is now the Institute of Communications. The University of Chicago, which for years has been almost contemptuous of journalism courses, only this session announced a graduate program in mass communications. The courses leading to the new degree look very much like those which have been offered in other institutions under the label 'journalism' on which the [Robert Maynard] Hutchins-minded classicists have not looked with favor. True the Chicago descriptions suggest the results of an exercise in [Alfred] Adler-semantics, but what these sociologists plan to teach is, in the final analysis, journalism. (Adler founded a school of "clinical" psychology, which pushed professional development for practitioners—a little ironic.)

This defensiveness at Grady about journalism versus communications would continue for the rest of the decade. For Drewry, journalism was the organon. Advertising was the business side of journalism and depended upon

Charlot beneath a conquistador. *Hargrett Rare Books and Manuscript Library, University of Georgia*

The centerpiece connecting the fresco that spans both sides of the open door reads "Time Discloses All Things," a Romanian proverb. Inside a student leafs papers. *Hargrett Rare Books and Manuscript Library, University of Georgia*

examining the "psychology of business" as one course title had it. In fact, the first graduate course at Grady, 1932, was in advertising, its fraternal association with the business of journalism making it a natural. In addition, the first master's degree in Grady, 1938, prominently featured advertising. (It was a master of arts degree in Franklin College with a major in journalism; thus, a nose under the tent of graduate education.) Public Relations was but the beginning of a journalist's story; i.e., promotion begets news and must understand its values and requirements to be successful. Radio, even with entertainment thrown in, was yet another form of journalistic storytelling, offering public service, news, and commentary. "All this emphasis on the word communications," Drewry said, "is a little amusing to some of us who for 30 or more years have been saying that journalism is not restricted to newspapers, but embraces all the agencies of communication."[64] The identity debate continues to this day, if a bit more comfortably.

(A recent syndicated column by David Brooks observed that social issues cannot be resolved without journalists entering "the realm of fiction, biography and journalism," a recombinant DNA as it were. ". . . the best journalism," he declared, "respects the infinite dignity of the individual and the unique blend of thoughts and feelings that go into that real, breathing life."[65] Brooks was asking how to understand teenage pregnancy and its declining rates. Although a bit wistful, his thought is profound: that it takes a lifetime of reading and reflection, or what E. O. Wilson styled as "consilience," the ability of "all ways of knowing," even discordant ones, to "jump together" in new ways of thinking.[66] So as it seemed to Sanford and Drewry, we plunge in to all our devices and frames to tell stories that pass the "truth of reality" test.)

Part of the identity issue had to do with faculty continuity. Until the thirties there had been only Sanford and Drewry, then were added Crouse and Kempton, neither of whom was there for as much as ten years. Of course, journalism had not yet fully defined itself as an academic discipline and doctoral education in journalism was only emerging. The result was that faculty members rotated in and out as what today are called adjuncts. Returning veteran Harold Davis was not wide of the mark when he observed, "Some of the professors he (Drewry) hired were good and some were poor, but Mrs. (Margaret) Margie Neeson, who stayed one year, was superior. She was Canadian and taught a course in book review. We read a book a week for her and wrote a comprehensive review. She invited a few of her students to her home to visit her and her husband Jack, a drama professor."

So the curriculum through the forties and into the fifties remained a function of Drewry's personality and energy. Davis again, "I am sure he (Drewry) ran the school on a shoestring. There really was no permanent faculty except himself (not quite true) and he brought in professors who would stay three or four years and move on. He required that each professor say good morning to him upon entering each day and good evening upon departing. College professors don't like that." Davis went on to a distinguished academic career himself, completing a doctorate in history at Emory and founding the Communication Department at Georgia State University, where eventually he became academic vice president. So he knew of what he spoke. More direct was the following from Louis T. Griffith, a faculty member emeritus, "In those days (forties and fifties), the school afforded a single telephone line—in the dean's office. Faculty members had pigeon-hole boxes in his outer office, and the day's routine included an early visit to bid him good morning and to check our boxes for messages or mail, which he handled personally. We repeated the procedure after lunch."[67] So much for privacy.

Although born on Boston Massacre Day, March 5, Harold Davis retained an affinity for the mother country. Seen here in front of portrait of King George III. *Courtesy Priscilla Arnold Davis*

Interestingly, Drewry himself gave some insight into his feelings about the more transient faculty. Just months before Drewry experienced his own world of pain, he inflicted some in the Annual Report for '48-'49. He complained, "Some faculty members in every department, it can be said with regret, seem to be more interested in what they can get out of doing than in how they may contribute to the objective and good name of the institution which provides them with employment. The 'gimme' attitude is not restricted to students."[68] Whom he references is not clear, and Harold Davis spoke of the uneven quality of short-term faculty; but Drewry's lament, even if only "dean-speak," was mean-spirited at best, especially in an annual report.

In the present academic environment remembering how controlling deans once were is difficult, and Drewry was no exception. One faculty member described him as a martinet.[69] Another said that Drewry never really discussed salaries with faculty members. Instead, he drew up the list, put a salary figure by each name, then carefully scissored the paper so that he could roll up each name and figure into a tight ball. When the summoned faculty member entered his office, Drewry would place the tightly wound strip of paper into the individual's hand. The faculty member would be out the door before unwinding the result.[70] It was peculiar, to say the least, and controlling, but it was the Drewry way and in that day there was no challenge. To be sure, Drewry complained in his annual reports about low pay for journalism faculty compared to comparable units in the university but in the absence of open negotiation with his faculty and consequently the opportunity for push back, it had little urgency and therefore little effect.

Fortunately, by the late forties and lapping over into the fifties, help arrived in the form of some full-time faculty growth. Marion Tyus Butler, a 1934 graduate of the school, joined the faculty in the mid-thirties while pursuing a Ph.D. at LSU. Following a tour of duty in WWII, he returned to fulltime teaching, thereby enriching the news-editorial sequence. By the mid-fifties, Butler would be director of the Alumni Association. Over the years Grady graduates provided more than their share of Alumni Association leaders, but Butler was an original and hugely successful. Joining John Talmadge in the advertising sequence was Hamilton Frazier Moore, who brought an emphasis in public relations that was added to the sequence in 1953. Reflecting his wide-ranging interests in literature, Moore developed a Southern Writers Workshop in 1958 that became a popular feature of the school's offerings. (In 1935, Moore did his master's thesis at UGA on, "Charles Colcock Jones, Jr., Romanticist," whose father figures prominently in the history of the slaveholding South for establishing the Dorchester Mission School near Savannah for the purpose of educating and Christianizing slaves. This family of letters was immortalized in Robert Manson Myers's 1972 book, *The Children of Pride*. More will be made of this later.)

Frazier Moore, a moderating force in volatile times. *UGA Photographic Services, Grady College Archives*

Frazier Moore was the future. (His son of the same name, an AP television critic in New York and Grady grad, recently completed his two terms on the Peabody Board.) Still, changes were evolving. By request and mutual agreement, John Talmadge moved to the English Department in 1953, demonstrating once again the fungible nature of faculty members in journalism with those in arts and sciences. Drewry himself was always more advertising than not; but in the day, most viewed journalism as inseparable from its allied disciplines: advertising, public relations, and broadcasting in its developing forms.

Talmadge was an interesting case in point of the interrelatedness of disciplines. An Athens native, he got his undergraduate degree at UGA before going to Harvard for a master's in English. In Cambridge he studied under the famous and notorious George Lyman Kittredge, one of America's most recognized literary critics of the twentieth century, Shakespeare scholar, and folklorist. Kittredge had a reputation for intimidating his students. Some said brutalizing was more like it. Talmadge was not excepted, but rather than fleeing the course, he went to the great man's house one evening to confront him. When Mrs. Kittredge answered the door and said he was out but would return soon, Talmadge could have fled then. Rather than take flight, Talmadge waited, partially concealed by a telephone pole. As Kittredge passed, Talmadge stepped alongside and startled him. Talmadge explained his purpose, and pausing, Kittredge finally gathered himself and said, "Stay in the course boy, you'll be all right." He did, and he was.[71]

After leaving Harvard, Talmadge went to New York and got employment in an advertising agency, thus his role in Grady. Harold Davis did not think much of him as a teacher (partly because it was about advertising); but as a conversationalist, he had few equals. Talmadge, along with fellow faculty member Louis T. Griffith, provided the college with its first opportunity to tout research with publication of *A History of Georgia Journalism*. Done under auspices of the Georgia Press Association and covering the period from 1763, but mostly 1887 to 1950, it was a truly notable achievement, unusually well-written. Griffith, as common for Gradyites, moved on to play a significant role in university publicity, eventually becoming executive assistant to President O. C. Aderhold.

Talmadge and his wife, like Franklin Butler and his, frequently had Harold Davis and his friends over for evening conversations, occasionally with drinks. They would go well into the night. Davis said, "It seemed to me that Franklin Butler knew everything. Mention anybody, ancient or modern, and he knew. But what made him remarkable, other than his singular use of the English language, was his overview of the world. He had a clear concept of how he thought everything fit together and what it meant. I had never met anybody like that." He thought much the same of Talmadge.[72] (Sounds like Bill Gates's infatuation with "Big History" today.) Of such are great educations made.

1942 graduate, George Octavius Marshall, Jr., recalled doing very little studying in the "J-school" and used that time to compile points toward being a "BMOC " (Big Man on Campus). He achieved his goal in short order before going into service, but he too was getting an "education." After service and a 39-month bout with debilitating tuberculosis, he went on to a Ph.D. in English at the University of Texas and a legendary career on the faculty at UGA.[73] (A variety of sources reported that Grady was "study-lite," but not uniformly, as Harold Davis's course on book reviewing required one book a week with written review. Moreover, as the experiences of so many indicate, Grady was heavy on engagement with things that mattered: writing for the *Red & Black*, doing magazine features, writing ad copy and public relations releases, radio and newspaper commentary, interning across all media. There was plenty to learn by doing.)

Worth McDougald, a force of nature and inimitable. *Grady College Archives, courtesy Melissa McDougald Odum*

Giving definition to the broadcasting curriculum was the arrival of the inimitable Worth McDougald. He was one of three brothers from Statesboro, Georgia, who obtained their degrees at Emory, which he completed in 1947 following a tour of duty with the Navy in the Pacific during WWII. Upon mustering out, he joined the staff of a radio station in Statesboro as news director and began a career path that brought him early to Drewry's attention. Joining the faculty in 1949, he was soon called back into active service during the Korean War. On returning, he resumed teaching and the pursuit of a master's degree that he received in political science at UGA in 1954. He completed a Ph.D. at Ohio State University in 1964, also in political science. McDougald could breathe life into anything, as he did for Radio-Television-Film as sequence head, but his almost thirty year assignment, 1963-1991, as Peabody Director, defined him. McDougald may have been overly sensitive, shredding screening reports on Peabody entries that he himself thought overly critical[74] and leaving meetings with the dean with intentions other than what was agreed upon.[75] Personalities do govern performance.

It is notable that by 1960 there still had been only two full professors of journalism, Sanford and Drewry. Faculty members came and went, and to at least two students who would become faculty members by the end of the

Drewry era, it appeared almost by design.[76] More than a little evidence exists that Drewry delayed re-accreditation in his last two years as dean, 1968-69, to avoid exposure for want of a more evenly balanced faculty and a curriculum grown like Topsy.[77] Be that as it may, Drewry was the public face of Grady and among state and national communication professionals a better profile is difficult to imagine. For all his peculiarities, he was "the Dean."

## EMERGING FROM THE SHADOWS: WOMEN AND CIVIL RIGHTS

The fifties did achieve better definition of the school's main sequences: Radio-Television-Film, Advertising, Public Relations, and Journalism. (Although these four sequences would in 1988 become three departments, they and the ones that follow should be understood as "majors," each requiring common "core courses" before proceeding with an emphasis area.) The academic units remained small, as did their faculties; but each had a better articulated mission despite other narrowly-tailored sequences such as Journalistic-Literary Appreciation, even one in Airlines Stewardess-Reservationists, and another for Pre-Divinity, likely owing to Franklin Butler's presence. This, not to mention curricular collaborations with Agriculture, Law, Home Economics and Education, but one sequence would take the cake. It was designed for women.

The second full academic year of the fifties saw Grady's overall enrollment down from 281 to 208, but that reflected the state of Georgia's adding a 12th grade. The male/female ratio widened in favor of the boys at 127 to 81. Because the Grady School attracted more women than most, it apparently felt the need to do more. Thus, it added an Editorial-Secretarial sequence, "useful to young women who plan to combine editorial and secretarial-clerical duties." How deflating, except it was the attitudes of the day. Yet, one must remember that Lessie Bailey Smithgall started as a "continuity secretary," a critical position in dramatic broadcast productions, and clerk-copyists figure prominently in literature: Henry Miller's *Tropic of Cancer* and Gustav Flaubert's *Bouvard et Pecuchet*. They do so because, á la Diderot and the Encyclopedists and like monks of yore, endlessly copying texts is the surest route to knowledge; but somehow, the new sequence intended less. Secretarial duties were no longer a male but a female domain and not exalted. Just as a teaching certificate was something for women to "fall back on," so would be the secretarial option.

**TOP LEFT:** Margaret Childs, first female editor of the *Red & Black,* 1944. *1945* ***Pandora***; **TOP RIGHT:** Sara Massey, sister of Dyar and Abit, all three were campus leaders. Sara was second female editor. *1945* ***Pandora***; **BOTTOM:** Maurine Nevin and *Red & Black* staff. *1946* ***Pandora***

That said, women continued to step forward. Margaret Childs from Abbeville was the first woman editor of the *Red & Black* in 1944, and two quarters later Sara Massey of Athens, sister of famous UGA alums, Dyar and Abit, took the reins. Mary Lou Nevin followed Massey in the summer term, and Nevin's sister Maurine succeeded in turn. The Nevin women were daughters of the editor of the *Dalton Citizen* and the *Dalton News.* (*Red & Black* editors seldom served more than an academic quarter.) Of course, women dominated the campus in those critical war years, and both Emory and UGA announced special journalism courses "following announcement of a nationwide program to train capable women and draft exempt men for newspaper work to fill wartime emergencies . . . ."[78] Other women students were stepping up, but not until 1953 would another woman serve as editor and she for only one week. It was a time to stand and deliver and Priscilla Arnold did.

The principals in the unfolding drama were Priscilla Arnold (Marietta); Gene Britton (Moultrie), who would later become an Episcopal minister in Athens; Bill Shipp (also Marietta) and Walter "Bucky" Lundy (Cairo). Each would play pivotal roles in the late fall of 1953. The issue, of course, was race. Everyone knew the run-up to the Brown decision was underway, and all knew its implications. Moreover, the university had its own African-American applicant in Horace Ward, a most-likely-to-succeed Atlantan who had applied for law school in 1950. As this story broke, university officials were holding Ward in interminable limbo. Eventually, Ward was drafted into the military in 1953, thereby having to defer both a possible admission to the University of Georgia and a certain acceptance at Northwestern. (There was reasonable suspicion of state complicity in his being drafted.) After graduating from Northwestern Law School, Ward would go on to a highly successful legal career in Atlanta, eventually becoming a federal judge and much honored and acclaimed by the university that spurned him then. He would also play a critical role in a case that embarrassed UGA at the top of its football fame in the early eighties.

Priscilla Arnold at typewriter; standing, Bill Shipp and Walter "Bucky" Lundy, who resigned as editors in 1953 rather than yield editorial independence. *1953* ***Pandora***

In the fall of 1953, Lundy was editor-in-chief of the *Red & Black*, Shipp, managing editor, and Arnold, news editor. On November 5, they published an unsigned editorial, written by Shipp with "Lundy over his shoulder,"[79] captioned CREATED EQUAL:

> "[Georgia Governor] Herman Talmadge (Gene's son) has again shown the Mr. Hyde side of his political personality. He has condemned judicial efforts to give the Negro a chance to get an education equal to the white man's as 'the most foolhardy sociological calamity in our national history.'

> In a speech at the Southern Governor's Conference, Georgia's chief executive said erasing segregation in schools is 'a step toward national suicide.'
>
> We have commended Talmadge in the past for his good work in getting Georgia on the highway of progress. But we cannot commend him for wanting to deny a segment of mankind its right to an equal education.
>
> The governor says we are spending millions to give Negroes equal education in segregated schools. Even a schoolboy economist should realize that it is impossible to support two 'separate but equal' school systems.
>
> With communism knocking at the Negro's back door, we cannot afford to let educational segregation barriers stand. It is as plain as the Red flag in Russia that continued segregation and suppression can and will cause the death of democracy by the hands of its own leaders."[80]

That created a firestorm—lit by Board of Regents member, arch segregationist and Talmadge ally Roy Harris, an Augusta attorney and owner/publisher of the *Augusta Courier*. In vituperative column after column he attacked the editors and demanded that the university cut funding for the student paper unless it submitted to greater editorial supervision by its Board of Control, attacks which in turn brought personal threats to the students and their families.[81] Drewry, like the rest of UGA officialdom, caved and created a "Management Conferences" course, which put the paper under direct faculty supervision. Dan Kitchens, who a year before was student editor, was now on the faculty as a graduate assistant and assumed that responsibility. In case of disagreement between the faculty supervisor and the paper's editors, the issue would go back to the Board of Control for resolution. At that, Lundy and Shipp resigned, whereupon Priscilla Arnold became acting editor and Gene Britton acting managing editor. After putting out the last fall edition, they too resigned at the end of the second meeting of the board, when it refused Arnold's request to re-consider and rescind the new arrangement.[82]

Lundy went on to a distinguished career in the diplomatic service, and today lives in Arlington, Virginia. Shipp became one of Georgia's truly great opinion writers and legendary political editor for the *Constitution*. He lives in Acworth, just outside Marietta, and only recently discontinued a syndicated column. Britton went into the Episcopal ministry and recently passed away in Athens. Priscilla Arnold married Harold Davis after graduating in 1956 and remains an active lay leader in the St. Dunstan Episcopal Church in northwest Atlanta. Harold died in July of 1997 at age 70.

Through all the travail at the *Red & Black*, Drewry kept a low profile, but behind the scenes he supported the increased supervision. He later touted it as creating a "combination lab and student publication." In his 1954 Annual Report, he noted that the Board of Control was "to serve in an advisory and control capacity to insure that editorial and business policies—particularly those which might seem to be prejudicial to the welfare of the University—represent considered decisions, objectively arrived at." It was not even a good sentence for the punctilious Drewry and in its evasions positively offended the principle of student editorial control. Buried in an Annual Report, its purpose was to please his masters.

What surprised Shipp most was the "vehemence" of the response by UGA officials. The student response was nothing to compare, little more than a shrug. Shipp said that although Dean Drewry "failed completely," he was even more disappointed with Dean of Men William "Bill" Tate's reaction, which could often be, and was in this case, "in your face." Still, it was Drewry through his graduate assistant Dan Kitchens who conveyed the message that Shipp should resign. Lundy did not know of that back channel to Shipp but vividly recalls meeting with Drewry and other members of the Board of Control on the afternoon of November 30. He recalls Priscilla and Gene being there also but not Shipp. During that meeting, he said, " Drewry asked (perhaps hypothetically) about accepting my resignation only if at the same time I withdrew from school." When Lundy said he did not "think that should or would be a consideration," Dean Drewry "retorted that I might feel differently when spring came, and I wasn't graduating." That night at the popular Snack Shack on the edge of campus, Lundy and Shipp in the company of several other *R&B* staffers made the decision to resign and either wrote their letters that evening or in the morning and took them to Drewry's office, eventually leaving them with his secretary or slipping them under the door.[83]

By spring cooler heads prevailed and Lundy graduated. Shipp, who had started on a journalism scholarship at Emory in 1951, left that program when Ray Nixon's departure in 1952 spelled its imminent demise, and started at Georgia in the fall of '52 and became news editor of the *R&B* by spring of 1953. Although no longer on the *Red & Black* following his resignation, Shipp remembers staying another term or two before volunteering for the draft in summer 1954. (Unlike with Horace Ward, there was no suspicion of Talmadge involvement. Shipp was clear. He volunteered.) Thus ended his formal education a year before graduation. On returning from

Bill Shipp, reporter, later the state's most influential political columnist. *Hargrett Rare Books and Manuscript Library, University of Georgia*

Europe in the summer of 1956, he signed on at the *Constitution*.[84] A Georgia star was rising but without a Georgia degree.

Arnold and her fellow editors considered Drewry's failure to come to their aid as at best abandonment, at worst betrayal of a trust. Drewry's behavior was consistent with his reaction to all issues affecting race—public silence. Except that behind the scenes he made it clear that the student editors were the problem and that he would fix it. In addition to his communications to Lundy and Shipp, Drewry also managed to give Arnold a "talking to" about her decision; but then so did her father, a Talmadge supporter who worried openly about the resignation's effect on her future employment.[85] Arnold, who worked as a student assistant for Drewry, also thought him "manipulative." Her future husband, Harold Davis, who admired Drewry, agreed, but discounted its importance in his overall personal assessment of the great dean. It had been a classic example of the children, qua young adults, leading.

Only the twisted illogic of race could account for Drewry's actions, sorry as that excuse is now. Lundy put it best, "As I've aged, the irony of having done the most important (maybe only) important thing in my life at age 20 hasn't escaped me. I hope that what you [this author] or anyone writing on the subject can portray is how deep seated the prejudice still was in mid-century. I don't believe my children have ever taken the R&B incident seriously. They just can't relate to that kind of world."[86]

In that same year, 1953, the NAACP held its national convention in St. Louis and pledged to overcome segregation within ten years. Most white people yawned a "whatever" or "no chance." Yet in 1963 the walls came down with the final act coming when Governor George Wallace of Alabama stood in the schoolhouse door at the University of Alabama, only to retreat. Of course the vestiges of segregation and voting denial would be fought out for years, but at least, as of 1963, no southern state could claim not to have yielded on the principle. Walter Lundy lived in San Diego when his father was stationed there during the war. His father, a UGA Agriculture graduate, and his mother were opera buffs and had an impressive vinyl collection of the great performances, which the author as a boy observed with curiosity and ultimately passion. None of this made Walter, "Bucky" to friends, the courageous editor he was, but it proved that not everyone, even down South, was alike, certainly not Bill Shipp, not Priscilla Arnold or Gene Britton. The future would be theirs but not yet, proving that if Henry Grady's heirs silenced talk about race, the bull sessions, as college-talk was known then, turned to these important matters. These forward-thinking students were not the majority on campus, but they were influential.

## FIFTIES-STYLED STUDENTS

The Grady School in the mid-fifties produced many others of consequence in that generation. The aforementioned, but also Billy Morris, Carrol Dadisman, Gene Methvin, and from the earlier fifties, Millard Grimes and

Harold Davis, still later Tom Russell. Then the women: Priscilla Arnold, then Dorothy "Dottie" Lundy, Walter's older sister, and future broadcast and ad agency pioneer Ruth Estes Trager.

William S. Morris, III, followed a father who had already wrapped up ownership of the *Augusta Chronicle*. The father was himself *sui generis*, a true journalist without stint. When Billy's father and Augusta's political stalwart and UGA friend and nemesis, Roy Harris, wound up in court, it ended in a scuffle—well, fisticuffs. Morris was the attacker, and they went to the floor, pummeling. Morris later apologized, but tensions between the two quite different publishers would continue. The dispute was over state Democratic Party leadership. Both had been in the legislature and both named regents. Both were publishers, but Morris was the better newsman, as when he bowed to his paper's editorial leadership on how to run the story about the fight. It appeared page 1, right column, a real statement of what came first for Morris as a journalist.[87]

Billy, the son, was a fighter too. He moved up in the family business quickly, and in what appeared to the rest of the family (brother, sister, even mother) as sub rosa, Billy acquired the company's debt and thereby diluted the stock of the other members of the family. It led to a rupture with his brother Charles who developed his own publishing and media empire. Billy eventually built what became Morris Communications with properties from Alaska to Florida. His premier acquisition was Jacksonville's *Florida Times Union*. He also pioneered in specialty publications, including magazines and travel guides—a remarkable empire. Still, in the great recession of the early 21st century because of overleveraging in the nineties, he wound up having to restructure under Chapter 11. (The Morris Publishing Group, like fourteen other newspaper groups nationwide, among other reasons, had experienced the digital fracturing of audience and therefore lost revenue.) On emerging from that burden, he took something of a victory lap, explaining to employees and staff at various Morris properties how he was able to face adversity and transform it into a motivational lesson about perseverance and seizing the moment so that there would be better days ahead. By early 2014 Morris Communications and its Publishing Group were debt free.

Morris established a chair in the college and an internship program that was inspirational from the standpoint of journalism and its management, also its novelty in focusing on the business side. The longtime holder of the Morris Chair was Conrad Fink. If Grady had a Mister Chips, it was Fink. Billy Morris enabled a giant step forward for Grady in management studies with Conrad taking the lead on the newspaper side. Billy, like his father, believed in the fundamentals of journalism. His eulogy for Conrad Fink was memorable. His accumulations, including plantations and a fabulous art collection, did not change his down-to-earth character. He was a world traveler, recognized by potentates, but none of this went to his head. A remarkable man, Morris made his fortune off journalism without corrupting it. He loved the university, served as a regent and was a Saturday afternoon regular in Sanford Stadium. He never cottoned to the Talmadge wing of Georgia politics. When he finished his first term as a regent, Herman Talmadge refused to reappoint him, such was the enmity, but being anti-Talmadge made Morris no less conservative. He and his wife, Sissie, are partners in all the good things he has accomplished. Today, the door swings freely between Augusta and Athens, and Grady is the better for it.

Dorothy Iva Lundy (ABJ 52), Dottie or Dot as she was known to friends, Walter's older sister, graduated in 1952. She had her dad's flaming red hair and a personality to match. She became a blunt, plain-spoken political advertising force in Georgia politics. Dot Lundy Wood's client list included Georgia's most powerful, including Jimmy Carter in his 1970 gubernatorial campaign against Carl Sanders. Because she was so early in the field, she invented her role. Ruth Estes Trager (ABJ 47) also made her mark in advertising, pioneering the role of women executives in broadcast programming and sales promotion with WAGA TV, eventually winding up as an ad executive with J. Walter Thompson in Atlanta. Because she was on the ground as television started, she was able to build, indeed invent, from the ground floor—a firm foundation indeed. She has also been generous with her college, and a mentor to many young women entering the profession.

**LEFT:** Billy and Sissie Morris at graduation *courtesy William S. Morris III*, **RIGHT:** Ruth Estes Trager. *Grady College Archives, courtesy Ruth Trager*

Carrol Dadisman (ABJ 56), another *Red & Black* editor from nearby Jefferson, Georgia, was a poster boy for fifties-style happiness at UGA. He liked everything about it, the J-school with its engaged dean and faculty, the responsibility of being editor and the camaraderie that came with it, football Saturdays, and most of all Mildred, his campus sweetheart who became a life-mate. He followed campus success with an equally sparkling career in newspapers, first as managing editor of the *Augusta Chronicle*, then as editor of the *Marietta Daily Journal* followed by working his way up the Knight-Ridder chain in Macon and Columbus before serving as long-time publisher of the *Tallahassee Democrat*. He was a consultant for journalists in Russia and Ukraine both as a Knight International Press Fellow and with Grady's Cox Center. Over the last number of years he has compiled and written a history of the *Red & Black* that felicitously locates it in the campus life it and he served.

Gene Methvin (ABJ 55) always wanted to play football for Georgia, but being the "littlest" guy out, he had little chance. Legend has it that he got in on one play. Still, a memorable photograph shows him slashing through the line during a practice in "silver britches," ball tightly tucked in both arms. Most boys growing up in the fifties, pretending in their back yards to be one

Happy Days for Mildred and Carrol Dadisman. *Courtesy Carrol Dadisman*

Gene Methvin, gridiron hero if for only one play. *Grady College Archives*

of their Saturday heroes, could only dream of such a moment. Methvin, whose father was owner and courageous publisher of the *Vienna News*, went on to a stellar career with *Reader's Digest* and gave back generously to his university and college. Aspiring students and young professionals, especially, welcomed time with him.

A fifties reminiscence must include Millard Grimes (ABJ 51), the only person who would serve as president of both the Georgia and Alabama press associations. (He was only president-elect of the Alabama Association, before selling his Opelika paper and giving up his presidency—still, highly regarded on both sides of the border.) Starting at the *Columbus Enquirer*, which would soon become the *Ledger-Enquirer*, Grimes possessed the journalistic diligence to succeed at every step from reporter to publisher to owner. He was in Columbus when the legendary Phenix City story erupted on the Alabama side of the Chattahoochee River. It was a story of gambling, prostitution, intrigue, and finally murder when Alabama Attorney General Albert Patterson was shot dead near the steps leading to his law office. Patterson had become a target by trying to clean up Phenix City, whose principal clientele were soldiers from nearby Fort Benning and the gambling and prostitution that preyed upon them.

Grimes, too, was seen as a comer when he left the *Ledger-Enquirer* at age 38, because the business of publishing had its allure and Grimes would make a reputation for buying clusters of newspapers, even across state borders, and transforming them into successful community newspapers. He also owned *Georgia Trend Magazine* for a time, but his lasting gifts have been innovative ways to secure community journalism through creative business practices. Another debt owed Grimes is *The Last Linotype*, the story of Georgia journalism from 1950 (where Talmadge and Griffith left off) to 1985. It is an outstanding example of historical research and compilation that showcases Grimes's considerable talent as a writer. The Georgia Press Association has never been better served. Among Grimes's colleagues during his Columbus days were other Grady graduates, the aforementioned Harold Davis and Ray Jenkins, who won a Pulitzer for his coverage of the Phenix City story.

The fifties was not "The Placid Decade," as some have charged—far from it. Who suited that decade better than Dwight David Eisenhower? In those years of de-mobilization, he beat back a Republican challenge from its always vocal far right and managed the Korean War to a successful draw (all that could have been done), saved the Federal Reserve, and strengthened

Left to right, Dewy Benefield (ABJ 52) news editor, John Pennington (ABJ 51), Millard Grimes (ABJ 51) editor, Norman Friedman (ABJ 51) business manager *Red & Black. Grady College Archives, courtesy Millard Grimes*

most of the New Deal legacy, even as his conservative wing wanted to dismantle it. Remarkable too was his commitment to infrastructure with the Interstate Highway System. In foreign affairs he avoided the interventionist state of later years (Lebanon being the one exception in 1958), and in the last, he warned of the military-industrial complex. The only possible exception to his exemplary service as president was his cautious approach to civil rights, but even there, most now concede the 1957 Civil Rights Act was about as far as anyone could get, given the South's domination of congressional committees. Only by contrast with the thirty-five years that preceded it was there anything placid about the decade. It roared with new life as rock 'n' roll was here to stay.

Before leaving the fifties, two others punctuate the story. Powell Moore (ABJ 59), son of Milledgeville publisher Jere Moore, soon found himself in the Office of Richard Russell, where he served as press secretary and special assistant. Russell was as forward on foreign relations and military preparedness as he was backward on race. He was a towering figure in the Senate who took Lyndon Johnson under wing. When Truman needed someone to chair the Senate Hearings on the firing of General Douglas McArthur, Russell reluctantly agreed. In the most deft and adroit manner conceivable, he steered the committee toward almost unanimous rebuke of McArthur's insubordination. To serve such a man as Russell opened doors for young Powell Moore.

Moore would enter the Defense Department in the Reagan years and rise to head the Organization for Security and Cooperation in Europe. More recently he has been a high level consultant and security analyst with McKenna Long, one of the most influential law and lobbying firms in D.C. Moore remains active on boards of UGA's Russell Special Collections Library and the Cox Center for Education and Research in International Journalism and Mass Communication. He is generous with the college and a friend to its deans. On induction into the Grady Fellowship, Moore said, "The spirit of Henry Grady that was instilled at the John Drewry school has remained with me for half a century. This spirit led us to lift our sights beyond familiar horizons, to seek challenge, not comfort, and to recognize that words can make a difference."

Powell Moore as Assistant Secretary of Defense Legislative Affairs, 2001. Photo by Sam Davis, U.S. Army. *Grady College Archives, courtesy Powell Moore*

Dick Yarbrough as president of DiGama Kappa presenting Broadcaster of the Year Award to Ed Sullivan, 1959. *Grady College Archives, courtesy C. Richard Yarbrough*

C. Richard "Dick" Yarbrough (ABJ 59) has been a stalwart for his university and its Grady College. He has served as president of the National Alumni Association, Trustee of the UGA Foundation, and been a member of the Grady Advisory Board, each of which required many years of time-consuming service. As head of communications for Bell South, he elevated that role to equal that of legal counsel at the highest levels of executive decision making. When called to serve that same function for the 1996 Atlanta Olympic Committee, he turned in a stellar performance not only in getting the games, but also in handling its major crisis, the bombing at Centennial Olympic Park. In the wake of the tragic bombing and the committee's desperation for a way forward, Yarbrough found himself with but three hours to develop and execute the communication strategy for going forward with the games, and he did.

In these later years, Yarbrough has been a syndicated columnist for the Neighborhood Newspaper chain of metro Atlanta and for newspapers throughout the state—a million readers weekly. Famous for spearing ethics violators in government and especially "lizard-loafered lobbyists," he is equally famous for championing public education. He is a much-sought speaker and turns his fees over to Grady. An artist of extraordinary accomplishments, he and wife Jane split time between Marietta and St. Simon's, where he tends to painting and she to him among her many other charities, because, in the judgment of a recent dean, "He needs it." He has been most generous with Grady, establishing first the Yarbrough Lab, then Yarbrough Fellowships, among the most coveted internships at Grady, and now the Yarbrough Distinguished Professorship, which is estimated by UGA's planned giving office to become a Distinguished Chair at over $2 million; this in honor of his family and especially his first grandson, who died suddenly at age twenty-one, an overwhelming loss.

Left to right, provost, now President Jere Morehead, Mary Beth Wansett, daughter of Jane and Dick Yarbrough, and Dink NeSmith then chair of the Board of Regents, announcing the establishment of a Yarbrough Distinguished Professorship, later to become a Distinguished Chair in Crisis Communication Leadership. *Grady College Archives*

## THE SIXTIES COMETH

Charlayne Hunter's being *first* was an accident. Born in Due West, South Carolina, in 1942, her family moved to Covington, Georgia, soon thereafter. As a five year-old, she tagged along with her six year-old best friend to first grade. The arrangement continued for a month without the teacher putting a stop to it. When the rule had to apply, she begged to stay on and authorities relented. Thus, Charlayne Hunter started first grade a year early, so that she graduated from Henry McNeal Turner High School in Atlanta in 1959, not 1960. The result was that NAACP and Atlanta activists chose Charlayne and fellow classmate Hamilton Holmes as most likely to succeed in mounting the ramparts of Georgia's segregated educational system. They did on January 9, 1961, but not without considerable legal wrangling before and after.

There were ugly days leading up, even in Georgia with Atlanta, its "city too busy to hate." Herman Talmadge, son of Gene, went to the Senate in 1956. He was succeeded as governor by two protégés: Samuel Marvin Griffin in 1955, owner, publisher and editor of the *Bainbridge Post-Searchlight*, the only true newspaperman elected governor in the twentieth century; and Ernest Vandiver in 1959, who looked and sounded different from the typical race-baiting politician, but in the end could not free himself, although in Vandiver's case there would be some later expiation. Among other things, Griffin, in true Talmadge mold, tried to interpose himself between Georgia Tech, then in its football heyday, and its invitation to the Sugar Bowl to play integrated Pittsburgh in 1956. Howls of protest from Tech students and wealthy alumni who wanted to spend time in the French Quarter quashed that sorry initiative, but Griffin's jowls shook with "no-never" declarations. He was a darling of White Citizens Council rallies in neighboring states as he and they called for massive resistance to court-ordered desegregation. Herman himself did not arrive in Washington in time to sign with Senior Senator Richard Russell the "southern manifesto," pledging in 1956 to block integration at all cost and threatening with the discredited nineteenth-century tactics of interposition and nullification—only Lyndon Johnson, Texas, and both Albert Gore, Sr., and Estes Kefauver of Tennessee, refused to sign. Herman would have signed it, of course, as the solid Democratic South never broke ranks except for outliers with national ambitions like the aforementioned.

Then Ernest Vandiver, who looked the part of a new southerner but remained a protégé of the Talmadges, pledged "no not one," when faced with the inevitable. When the "not one" became two, Hunter and Holmes, he threatened again to shut down the university rather than see it integrated, thus setting the stage. Already the dastardly consequences of massive resistance had shown itself during the Montgomery Bus Boycott in December 1955, Little Rock in September 1957, and the bombing of the Jewish Temple in Atlanta, 1958, as hate-filled rhetoric and marauding, strutting Klansmen paraded and prated an undying Confederate nation. Charlayne and Hamilton would show up in Athens at the start of the Civil War's centennial year with white supremacy not done yet. UGA students would protest in their own way.

Frat boys sport the flag of defiance. *1962* ***Pandora***

Charlayne's and Hamilton's first days at UGA were not only ugly but also terrifying. Milling crowds shouting racial epithets, setting fires, and hurling glass-shattering bricks, threatened not only peace but safety. Tear gas to quell crowds only made it more ominous. Still, they persevered and succeeded, abetted at the last by Governor Vandiver's refusal to continue battling in the courts, a sensible but politically costly move for his future in Georgia politics. Charlayne enrolled in Grady, and Hamilton pursued premed in Franklin. Ole Miss would follow in the fall of 1962 with a shoot-out that left two dead and some thirty plus marshals wounded. Finally, the University of Alabama would go in last as Governor George Wallace stood in the schoolhouse door only to surrender to the Kennedy administration on June 11, 1963, just ten days after Charlayne and "Hamp" went through commencement exercises in Sanford Stadium. (In the long wait for their admission, Hunter and Holmes had earned credits at Wayne State University in Detroit and Morehouse respectively.) *De jure* segregation was moribund, but its *de facto* vestiges endured. Of interest was that Drewry's annual report for spring 1961 observed twenty-four significant events and achievements that year. Charlayne's enrollment in Grady was noticed at twenty-three. Silence on racial matters perdured among Henry Grady's acolytes.

A personal moment for Drewry is worth noting. When Charlayne walked into her first journalism class with Dean Drewry, an observant student, Tom Russell, later Dean Russell, witnessed a difference. Rather than calling the roll for the obvious purpose of having a teaching assistant record seat assignments alphabetically, as he had always done, Drewry called it with his usual pomp but no one was assigning seats. The reason was obvious and "ridiculous" to the observant Russell. Drewry did not want to make any student have to sit beside her by virtue of the alphabet. The result for the rest of the quarter was a lot of wasted time during the long roll calls, which were thereby necessitated.[88]

Even with denials and circumlocutions, racial struggles of the fifties transformed journalism. It started with *The New York Times*, the most southern newspaper on earth. Its ownership, the Adolph Ochs family from Chattanooga, encouraged its southern bureau in its decision to begin step-by-step coverage of the real story, the movement itself. First was John N. Popham, IV, also of the *Chattanooga Times*, who travelled the South 50,000 miles a year in his green Buick, filing stories for *The New York Times*, including hot spots like Little Rock. (The Georgia Press Institute featured Popham at its 1959 gathering in Athens, along with Joseph Alsop,

Washington correspondent and columnist, and Grady's own Robert Lee Sherrod of *The Saturday Evening Post.)*

Claude Sitton from Oxford, Georgia, a 1949 Emory journalism graduate, succeeded Popham on what Gene Roberts and Hank Klibanoff called *The Race Beat*, title of their Pulitzer Prize-winning book on coverage of the civil rights movement. Sitton eventually became national editor of the *Times*. Then Jack Nelson in the late fifties and early sixties at *The Atlanta Constitution* won a Pulitzer for his coverage of abuses at the state mental hospital in Milledgeville, including appalling conditions on the segregated wards for blacks. In 1965 he became Washington Bureau Chief for *The Los Angeles Times*. Using his Alabama roots and connections, his coverage of events in Selma, Alabama, especially the Viola Liuzzo case, exposed murderous Klansmen. And when national television showed up in places like Birmingham, the world could see for itself, and *de jure* segregation was over. The "race beat" taught journalists how not to compromise.

Nowhere would this be more true than on Ralph McGill's and Gene Patterson's *Atlanta Constitution*. The *Journal* was always softer on race and hot button issues than was the *Constitution*. Ralph McGill, or "Rastus" McGill as he was known in South Georgia, was the most cussed and discussed editor in Georgia. Slowly at first, then steadily, he put the pressure on Georgia, particularly Atlantans, to take the necessary steps. A graduate of Vanderbilt, he started as a sports reporter in Nashville but evolved into a towering giant of commentary at the *Constitution*. No editor since Grady was more celebrated nationally and today the McGill Lecture in Journalistic Courage is a featured annual event of the Grady College. His successor, Gene Patterson (ABJ 43), equally towered above the rest, winning a Pulitzer in 1967 for his commentary

**LEFT:** Ralph McGill. *Hargrett Rare Books and Manuscript Library, University of Georgia;* **RIGHT:** Gene Patterson delivering first McGill Lecture. *UGA Photographic Services*

on efforts of the Georgia Legislature to unseat Julian Bond for his anti-Vietnam War views, this despite Patterson's editorial support for the war. The corpus of Patterson's eight years at *The Atlanta Constitution* is legendary, but singular must stand his column on the bombing of the 16th Street Baptist Church in Birmingham, written on the same day, Sunday, September 15. The lives of four little girls were snuffed out. Titled "A Flower for the Graves," one cannot read his column and not weep.

Stepping up was also happening on the radio side in the fifties by dint of the remarkable Elmo Ellis (né Israel). He grew up in tiny West Blocton, Alabama, where ironically there had been enough heads of household to form a synagogue. Elmo's cousin, Mel Allen, Voice of the Yankees, preceded him at the University of Alabama, while Elmo, following a brilliant stint as an undergraduate, wound up in Atlanta by 1940 as a producer for WSB-Radio. After service in WWII and trying his hand as a producer in New York, he came back in 1948 to manage WSB-Television, but radio was his métier. Following the political leads of William B. Hartsfield and Ivan Allen, Jr, he built community radio around the theme of a "city too busy to hate." WSB vans showed up at community celebrations from picnics to parades with reporters wading into the crowds so all Atlanta could celebrate with them. It was brilliant listener strategy. The station even expanded its call letters of **W**elcome **S**outh **B**rother to include all people, if ironically today, accompanied by "Tara's Theme."

Ellis was also known as a demanding boss but one who got results. After 1964 he cemented his reputation as general manager of WSB Radio & Television. He earned a master's in broadcasting from Emory before that program shut down in 1953 and continued to teach an occasional course in what remained of the Emory program. Ellis was very active with the Grady School in advisory and professional-in-residence roles and a regular at the Georgia Association of Broadcasters Institute, also hosted by Grady. A dedicated liberal in terms of race relations, his alma mater gave him its highest honor, the Hugo Black Award, who Ellis first investigated because of Black's political association with the Klan in the twenties. Satisfied that the true Black shown through as a New Deal Senator and a staunch supporter of the Brown decision in 1954 as a Justice of the Supreme Court, Ellis accepted. He retired as Vice President of Cox Broadcasting in 1982 and continued as an author and editorialist. Born on the 11th hour of the 11th day of the 11th month in 1918, he died June 24, 2005, still known as the man who "removed rust from radio" and "broadcasting's Ralph McGill." As a fearless radio editorialist, he received a Peabody in 1965.

Elmo Ellis, right, with Ivan Allen, Jr., mayor of Atlanta, center, recognizing Margaret Mitchell in the Atlanta Shining Light campaign, the brainchild of Jim Tate (ABJ 42) who led Atlanta Gas Light into the forefront of progressive corporate communication. *Courtesy* ***Atlanta Journal-Constitution***

All these happenings and Hunter's and Holmes's courage changed everything. UGA would no longer be for whites only, and over the years it would come to represent all citizens of Georgia. Vestiges of segregation remained. One does not end 350 years of slavery and segregation overnight—but end it did—at least legally. While the vagaries of racial attitudes still have play, the university is far closer to its ideal of serving all Georgia citizens equally, not to mention a burgeoning global presence. Of all colleges, given its First Amendment standing, Grady has benefitted most. Thus began the sixties.

## TURBULENT DECADE

The social ferment of the fifties leading into the sixties was not spent. 1963 was pivotal. As noted, it was the year of Charlayne's and Hamp's graduation. In January of that year, Martin Luther King, Jr, was holed up on a former slave plantation near Savannah, the earlier mentioned Dorchester Mission School, which Grady faculty member Frazier Moore had written about. King and lieutenants were plotting their assault on the Big Apple of segregation, Birmingham, Alabama, which commenced on April 3. Soon there issued "Letter from Birmingham Jail," rhetorical touchstone of the movement. (Addressed to eight white clergymen, the lead minister being Episcopal Bishop Charles Colcock Jones Carpenter, whose great grandfather of the same given name had established the Dorchester Mission School.)

By early May, demonstrators, including children, were spilling out of the Sixteenth Street Baptist Church into Kelly Ingram Park, where the aptly named "Bull" Connor and his minions awaited them with police dogs, water cannons, and paddy wagons. As the jails filled and the Kennedy administration pressured, the Birmingham business community caved and the "whites only" signs came down. On June 11 Governor Wallace made his infamous "stand in the schoolhouse door" at the University of Alabama, and Kennedy went on television the same night and declared segregation "no longer a legal but a moral issue." (That same night Mississippi NAACP Secretary Medgar Evers was shot dead from ambush.) Then on August 28, King led a march on Washington that ended in his ringing declaration of "I have a dream." Three weeks later "Dynamite Bob" Chambliss and accomplices bombed the Birmingham 16th Street Baptist Church and crushed out the lives of four little girls. Then on November 22, an assassin's bullet killed President Kennedy and left the nation and the world aghast. These triumphs and tragedies yielded a moral capital sufficient to pass the Civil Rights Act of 1964 and a year later with events at Selma the Voting Rights Act of 1965.

When President Lyndon Johnson signed the Voting Rights Act on August 6, 1965, only three days remained until the Watts suburb of Los Angeles erupted in fire and violence that made the rest of the nation aware of its own racial passions. For another three years it would rage in Chicago, Detroit, Boston, and the nation's capital itself. In the meantime, a movement

Dan Rather on left, eventual Grady faculty member Dan Keever on right, both covering 1968 Democratic National Convention. Rather and Keever are looking in the same direction because Keever's colleague had called out "Dan" to get his attention and both "Dan's" reacted. *Courtesy Dan Keever*

mobilized against the war in Vietnam. Then 1968 came to resemble 1848, the year of the Great Deluge in Europe, as uprisings worked their way through the eastern bloc, and the Prague Spring was brutally suppressed by 200,000 Soviet troops. In the United States assassinations rang out again, King on April 4 and Robert F. Kennedy on June 6. Lyndon Johnson had already renounced a second run at the presidency in late March, but still the Democratic National Convention ended in shambles as Chicago Mayor Daley's bullies beat anti-war demonstrators outside and punched CBS's Dan Rather on the convention floor. It was all too much and students were no longer the students of their parent's generation. They were in tie-dye and in the streets.

What a time for journalism! On February 27, 1968, Walter Cronkite, the most trusted anchor in news, said it was time to end the war by negotiation, a sobering truth to power. Still, the war would drag on for another five years, punctuated on May 4, 1970, when Ohio National Guardsmen opened fire on anti-war demonstrators, killing four Kent State University students

Charlayne Hunter and Tom Johnson both bound for the history books. *Grady College Archives, courtesy Tom Johnson*

and wounding eleven more. These events and times produced an amazing group of students at Grady who would go on to amazing careers and accomplishments. One might start with Tommy Johnson (Wyatt Thomas Johnson) of Macon, Georgia. Johnson was a proud protégé of one of Georgia's all-time great publishers and owners, Peyton Anderson, Jr., of the *Macon Telegraph and News*. Tall and ruggedly handsome, Johnson was a reporter on the *Red & Black* when Hunter and Holmes showed up in 1961. He immediately gained Charlayne's trust as she and he both were destined to become Grady grads, and the student paper played an especially constructive role in that transition.

Hunter and Johnson also went on to spectacular careers. Having won the confidence of the legendary Calvin Trillin (Trillin did a book on Charlayne's and Hamilton's experience at UGA), Hunter started at *The New Yorker,* and following a stint as investigative reporter and news anchor with WRC-TV in Washington D.C., she joined *The New York Times* in 1968 as a metropolitan reporter, covering especially the African-American community. She joined the "McNeil-Lehrer Report" in 1978 and became the PBS NewsHour's national correspondent in 1983. She moved to Johannesburg in 1997 where she became South African correspondent for National Public Radio and later bureau chief for CNN. She and husband Ronald T. Gault lived in Johannesburg for fifteen years. They now divide time between Martha's

Vineyard and the Tampa Bay area and maintain a winery in South Africa. She remains close to the college and serves on the Peabody Board.

On becoming a Grady Fellow, Charlayne said, "I am often reminded of my own desire to become a journalist, back in the time when young black girls growing up in the segregated South were not supposed to have such dreams. When I told my mother of my dreams, inspired by the comic strip character Brenda Starr, she didn't tell me to 'can' the pipe dreams and do something real. She simply said, 'If that's what you want to do, fine,' for instinctively my mother knew that dreams propel ambition. As a result, my life as a journalist has exceeded even my wildest dreams." Charlayne kept her eyes on the prize.

In 1965, Tom Johnson joined the first class of White House Fellows and mightily impressed Lyndon Johnson himself. When President Johnson returned to Texas in 1969, Johnson (no relation to the president) became his executive assistant, and at age thirty, head of Johnson's Texas Broadcasting Company as its executive vice president. He was named a director of City National Bank in Austin and head of Johnson's exclusive franchise in the state capital, KTBC. After Lyndon Johnson's death, Tom remained close to the family, especially Lady Bird, but moved back into newspapers as publisher of the *Dallas Times Herald*. He followed that with a thirteen-year stint as president and later publisher of *The Los Angeles Times*. In 1990, Ted Turner asked him to become president of CNN, just in time for the outbreak of the Gulf War, which helped define that cable channel. He remained president until 2001 at which time he retired, but he remains active on foundation boards and as a faithful confidant to Grady deans. He, along with his friend J. B. Fuqua, went public about their experiences dealing with severe depression, a real service to mental health.

As Charlayne and Tom graduated, change was coming to Georgia and none too soon. In 1962, on a suit brought by UGA alumnus (38) Morris Abrams of Savannah, the Supreme Court overturned Georgia's County Unit system. That system had put a stranglehold on Georgia's larger counties. On statewide ballots, say for governor, it allowed Echols County in Southeast Georgia, the state's least populated county, to give two "units" to its winning candidate, whereas Fulton County (Atlanta) with at least 150 times the population, gave only six "units" to the candidate it voted for. Thus, one voter in Echols could cancel fifty in Fulton. The Talmadge machine relied on this rural formula. With the "unit system's" demise, Georgia would elect its first truly "New South" governor, Carl Sanders, a UGA alum, undergraduate and law, and Augusta native. Among Georgians, especially in metropolitan Atlanta, he cut a figure like John F. Kennedy nationally. For a brief time in the South, progressives like Sanders, Terry Sanford in North Carolina, and LeRoy Collins in Florida had a chance.

Higher education would be a principal beneficiary. In his first two years in office, '63 and '64, Sanders keynoted both Press Institutes at Grady, but then neither Sanders' accomplishments nor JFK's assassination could stem the Goldwater tide in Georgia. As George Wallace predicted, when the Kennedy administration confronted him at the schoolhouse door in Tuscaloosa, the Democratic Party would lose its presidential base in the Solid South, and so it did. At the state level, voters remained loyal to the party of their fathers, the Democratic Party; but it tacked steadily in a more conservative direction until at last it too became solidly Republican. Still, the New South optimism that Sanders brought signaled a real growth spurt for Atlanta. By the end of the decade, its population would top a million and skyscrapers dwarfed its tallest building at the start of the decade, the Fulton County Bank Building. "The city too busy to hate," as Mayor William Hartsfield styled it, gave the state a metropolitan feel that belied its rural heritage. It was Henry Grady all over again, boosterism at its best.

As the Grady School ran up to its 50th anniversary in 1965, and with Sanders's fresh face to inspire, the times did feel like Henry Grady redux. Drewry declared '62-'63 to be a "true New South year" on the occasion of Grady's birthday, May 24. He noted that Sanders had been present for both the Radio and Television Institute, which Sander Vanocur of NBC News headlined, and the Press Institute. At the Peabody Awards that year, Jackie Kennedy's "Tour of the White House" with CBS's Charles Collingwood, received a Peabody and JFK sent a special note commending the board for its decision, saying with humorous modesty, "As an occasional amateur performer on radio and television, I extend my warmest greetings to all of the professionals you honor today."[89] Kennedy wit at its best, and the professionals included in addition to Collingwood, Cronkite for news and Carol Burnett for entertainment. Soon, in May, Kennedy would be saluting

Left to right, Cronkite, Drewry, Collingwood, Burnett, and Cerf. *Associated Press Photograph File*

Alan Shephard's orbits of the earth and preparing for the confrontation with Wallace at the schoolhouse door. Charlayne and Hamp were preparing to graduate. Things were getting on, a New South indeed. The next year the Peabody went for news coverage of the Kennedy assassination. Present to receive the award were Thomas Moore, president of ABC-TV, NAB president LeRoy Collins (himself a former New South governor of Florida), CBS president Frank Stanton, and NBC president Robert Kintner—the world upside down in a flash.

With such an array of New York news executives confirming its importance, Grady pushed forward. Drewry had been lobbying for a new building from the beginning of the decade and signs were encouraging. Interestingly, the school celebrated its 50th in the spring of 1965, rather than its actual start date of the fall. They also celebrated the twenty-fifth anniversary of the Peabody Awards, which was chronologically true to its founding year 1940 but not its first presentations 1941. Perhaps they were simply "truing up," getting both, 50th (school) and 25th (Peabodys), done in the same year. Governor Sanders was back to keynote the Press Institute, and all other institutes and workshops joined in the "shout-out" to Grady and the Peabodys.

Of interest, there was some dissension on the Peabody Board. Drewry said that despite criticism of television as a "Vast Wasteland," Newton Minnow's complaint in 1961 as FCC chairman, the jurors had found much to praise. Former FCC chairman and Peabody Board member, Paul Porter, begged to differ, saying the board almost decided to make no awards for 1964 and for that reason decided to abolish traditional "categories" in favor of "distinguished achievement" irrespective of categories. The exchange foreshadowed the future; i.e., awards based on one criterion, "excellence" regardless of categories. Although the board may have wanted to move in that direction, it was not yet prepared to turn away from categories, as future awards would show. That year awards went to "CBS Reports;" to William H. "Bill" Lawrence of ABC for news commentary; to Julia Child's "The French Chef," WGBH, Boston; and to NBC's "Hallmark Hall of Fame." All great programs, but consensus in American culture as well as politics was showing strain, a sign of times to come.

As most agree now, the assassination of Kennedy was not the end of American innocence or consensus. Indeed, a consensus formed around his death about the way forward on race and on war, with the most recent readings of the Kennedy legacy convinced that he, against all advice within, had determined to get out of Vietnam. Whatever, accumulating events from

1965-on clearly destroyed any consensus that might have emerged from Camelot. The manufactured Gulf of Tonkin Incident triggered a wholesale invasion of South Vietnam by American forces and bombing of the North. America's college generation was put on alert, both ways, stay or go. The burgeoning anti-war movement, first at Berkeley then Stanford and Columbia, overshadowed the more timid movement on southern campuses, but come there it would. By 1968, with the January Tet Offensive in South Vietnam, the abnegation by President Johnson in March, and the gut-punching Chicago Democratic Convention in August, not to mention the April and June assassinations of King and Robert Kennedy, all hell was breaking loose.

Still, everything is local and adults have a different way of framing things, especially if they come out of the tumult of world wars and a Great Depression, not to mention the Korean War coming close on heel. So, what happened to Grady in the run-up from 1965 through 1968 was both profound, indeed inspirational. In that time occurred the 50th anniversary of the school, already noted, the announcement and construction of a new Journalism Building, and the retirement of John Drewry in 1969, all occasions of justifiable celebration and self-congratulations.

A journalism building of its own was a big deal. Drewry had been urging it since the early sixties. His wide knowledge of journalism schools and travels on accrediting visits convinced him that one did not merit "elite" status without a separately dedicated facility. The Commerce-Journalism Building of 1928 was for its time state-of-the-art, and its subsequent expansion in the late forties seemed at first blush more than adequate. Besides, it had a privileged location, adjacent to the Main Library on North Campus, but time is the enemy of adequacy, especially with the advent of television and film with its space needs. As early as 1940, Grady had formed a partnership with WGAU-Athens and WSB-Atlanta to provide UGA radio programming. WSB paid for the conversion of a classroom into a studio. Then in 1953, Emory closed its journalism program after Raymond B. Nixon, its longtime director and Henry Grady biographer (1943), left for Minnesota. Grady got their remaindered equipment and still more pressure on space.

Finally, in 1955, WSB-TV expanded the 1940 idea for a radio partnership to television. The banner read "'CAMPUS GEORGIA'—WSB-TV—JOURNALISM WORKSHOP," and proclaimed: "The nation's oldest chartered state university and the South's first television station joined forces January 22, 1955, to provide laboratory facilities for carefully selected young people interested in TV careers and productions of a series of television programs called 'Campus: Georgia.'" The Sunday *Journal-Constitution* said, "WSB-TV Saturday will become the first commercial television station in the South, and possibly in the nation, to provide its facilities to journalism students for program production." Although these Saturday shows were produced in WSB facilities, students did much preliminary work at Grady, a public/private partnership for the benefit of all but still more pressure on Grady's facilities. (The University of Missouri acquired KOMU-TV, an NBC affiliate, and began airing December 21, 1953, under Journalism School management. WNDU, Notre Dame, was also an NBC affiliate operating from 1955 to 2006 when Georgia-based Gray Television bought it for $85 million. The only other currently university-owned commercial TV station is the University of Alabama's WVUA-TV, unaffiliated, which is housed in Bryant-Denny Stadium as anchor to a $19 million Digital Media Center, adjacent to its College of Communication and Information Sciences.)

By 1965 the Regents approved an architectural proposal for a new Journalism-Psychology Classroom Complex, just south of Baldwin and north of Memorial Hall at the corner of Baldwin and Sanford, an ideal location since it also overlooks Sanford Stadium. It was formerly the location of Woodruff Hall, the physical education facility where the Bulldogs played basketball. If it rained during a game, they said, you had better have an umbrella—or was it, the only place where basketball could experience a rain delay. All hopes were set for a 1967 completion, but it would not open for

Ground-breaking for Journalism Building, Governor Sanders with shovel, Drewry at right. *Grady College Archives*

another two years, at which time it provided the most fitting possible setting for the send-off of legendary Dean Drewry. Dedicated May 24, 1969, Henry Grady's 119th birthday, the principal speaker was Eugene Black, Grady's grandson and recently appointed Chair of the Peabody Board. The good thing was that Journalism would finally have its own building as Psychology (one of the most popular majors in Franklin) and Journalism would be two buildings forming a complex linked by covered walkways on the ground level and a street-level plaza that joined each facility to two lecture halls. It was perfect.

When it opened, it even looked good in a 1960's way. It was modern, if stolid, with far more brick than glass. The insides constituted something of a maze and had no access for the disabled, with the result that combination "outside" stairways and elevators had to be retrofitted in 1980. Cold days can be numbing on the walk or ride up. (Always irreverent students called it "the Cutlip shaft," so named for the college's then dean.)[90] Still, like a 50s or 60s new car, the new 1969-model building felt like all chrome and steel with leather interior, and the new owners were proud to give it a spin. Studio space on the first floor was cavernous as befitted early television production and only as the faculty grew would office space seem cramped. The dean's suite had a conference room and across the hall an expansive reading room that would be named for Drewry. Of course, later, less enthralled and more sardonic students and faculty would call it the "Dreary Room."

The college occupied the first three floors: First or ground was mostly for Radio-Television-Film; Second or street level contained the dean's suite, faculty and departmental offices, seminar rooms, and combination lab-classrooms; and Third was mostly laboratory and classroom space. The university reserved the Fourth and Fifth floors for general classrooms that Grady shared with foreign languages for the most part. Today the college occupies the Fourth as well, with designs on the Fifth. As for the outside elevators, some said it was done by an architect after losing a son or was it his wife, no one knew for sure, to a freak elevator crash—some also say it was a fact.[91] Buildings have their stories too.

Change had come for the Peabody Awards also. For its first twenty-eight years, it had known only Ted Weeks and Bennett Cerf as board chairs. The new guy in 1968 would be none other than a grandson of Henry W. Grady, Eugene Black, Sr. (His father of the same name, although never adopting the Sr. designation, married Grady's daughter Augusta.) Black was a UGA alumnus, graduating Phi Beta Kappa, and president of the World Bank from 1949-62, thirteen of its first sixteen-year existence. He was also recipient of numerous honorary degrees, some twenty in all, including from Yale, Princeton, Columbia, and Oxford. Staffers at the bank, who admired him greatly, called it Black's Bank. In 1962 he became chairman of the Brookings Institution, the position he held when asked to serve as chair of the Peabody Board. Black was an adviser to presidents and world leaders, especially on Southeast Asia economic and social development. He was a director and board member of venerable institutions such as the Chase Manhattan Bank, Ford Foundation, and *The New York Times*. (Bennett Cerf stepped down because he had become a director of RCA, which he thought might present a conflict of interest.)

**ABOVE:** Eugene Black talking with ardent Grady supporters Don Carter, left, and Jasper Dorsey, right. *Grady College Archives;* **BELOW:** John and the wonderful Miriam Drewry applauding the first recipients of the Drewry Early Career Award, 1977. *Grady College Archives*

Black was back on campus a short year later, not only to dedicate the new building but to say farewell to Drewry. The formal adieus went on for four days that surrounded the dedication of the building and Grady's birthday, banquets and plaques galore. Memorable was a bench with Drewry's name and placed on the Sanford Street side of the new Grady Building. At a banquet, sponsored by the alumni, eloquence abounded and gifts included a trip around the world and a commitment to fund a chair in his honor. But most memorable, the city of Hahira, the enunciation of which he was so fond of exaggerating for each class of incoming students, made him an honorary citizen. And so it went, a forty-seven year career of significant accomplishments for a college and university. For the next fourteen years, he maintained an office in the building and his wife Miriam would drive him over most days where he worked on his book column, visited with faculty and students for a long and, for him, a gratifying goodbye. As with so many pledged funds, the chair in his name never materialized but the resource room named for him was fitted out suitably and his books made for a handsome wall, a truly significant memorial to the legendary dean.

## WERE THEY WEIRD OR JUST WIRED?

Oh those students of the sixties! Times were a-changing, but not completely and not yet. Still, things were blowing in the wind. As the decade started, they were in Bass Weejun loafers, button-down collared madras shirts, Villager dresses, and twisting and shouting all night long. Vince Dooley arrived in '64 to rescue Georgia football and by the fall of '65 would open the season with the "flea flicker" play that beat Alabama and Bear Bryant by a point. Although Bama would go on to another national championship that year with Joe Namath as quarterback, Dooley had thrown down the gauntlet. The "Flea Flicker" is still thought by many Bulldog faithful to be the school's most famous play and is subject of a lithograph that hangs in the college today courtesy of a gift to Dean Clark by John Furman (ABJ 63).

Bryant sweats. Dooley wins with the famous "flea flicker" play. Georgia 18-Bama 17. *1966* ***Pandora***

Things did not begin to sober up until that year, 1965, then only gradually. By 1968, marijuana smoke hung in the air, hair got longer and stragglier, dresses shortened up, and tie-dye shirts spun eyes like pinwheels, but not for everybody. Most students, even those with more radical thoughts, clung to southern manners if not mores and took a "my-country-right-or-wrong" position on Vietnam. They would form the phalanx of a rising conservative Republican majority in Georgia. The decade began with about as many Grady students as in 1950, approximately 280, which still made it sixth largest in the nation. By the end of the sixties, almost 1,000 students occupied its new building, making it 3rd among the nation's largest journalism programs.

Perhaps the most optimistic sign of the times was the emergence of the *Athens Daily News* in 1963. The instigator was Claude Williams, Jr., (BA 44) (ABJ 48), a highly enterprising and successful advertising salesman, who succeeded in a variety of venues from radio to outdoor advertising and from newspapers to banking. Co-conspirators were initially Millard Grimes (ABJ 51) and then more directly Glenn Vaughn (M 53). Both had been highly successful in Columbus, Georgia. The idea was to compete as a morning paper with the staid, old *Athens Banner-Herald*. It was a spark that led to

Claude Williams, Lewis Grizzard, Glenn Vaughn, and Mark Smith and the "new" journalism, Gradyites all. *Grady College Archives, courtesy Claude L. Williams, Jr.*

fifteen years of remarkable vitality for newspapering in the Classic City and a laboratory for university students, especially for Grady and the *Red & Black*. During that time an alternative weekly also formed as the *Athens Observer*, and as the word alternative suggests, an alternative in politics as well. The *Observer* even experimented with cable news.

Billy Morris (ABJ 56) would enter the picture in 1965 along with his brother, Charles, buying the *Banner-Herald* and within another two years the *Daily News*, but the competitive spark had been lit and would last well into the eighties as the two papers continued to compete under common ownership. The *Daily News* got the jump on offset printing featuring the best, most comprehensive photography; the best sports coverage from UGA to little league; and local news. It energized everything. Grady students were principal beneficiaries. Mark Smith (ABJ 66) was one of those. Himself scion of a leading newspaper family in Georgia and Alabama, dating back to the nineteenth century, his father and mother owned and operated the *Eatonton Messenger*. Thus, he grew up in the business, but the *Daily News* would start his personal journey. Famous is the picture of Mark with Claude Williams,

Jr., Glenn Vaughn, and Lewis Grizzard, a true Grady foursome in their *Daily News* days.

When Billy Morris snapped up the Athens papers in 1965 and 67, Mark Smith, after serving a stint as publisher of the *Banner-Herald*, moved to Augusta and over a period of forty years climbed the Morris Communications ladder, eventually becoming corporate vice president for sales and marketing. He was also at point on a number of acquisitions, such was his business savvy. He left Morris in 2003 to form Smith Communications, Inc., which owns the family's *Eatonton Messenger*, along with two other newspapers covering five counties and another five regional magazines. More recently, Smith formed a highly innovative Middle Georgia Printing Co-op when he purchased the former presses of the *Macon Telegraph* and now does the print runs for over thirty newspapers in middle Georgia. Smith holds the distinction of serving on the Grady Advisory Board, now known as the Board of Trust, longer than any other and is its longest serving chair. All deans from Drewry to the present have benefitted from his manifest commitment to the college. Mark Smith and Claude Williams are both Dean's Medalists. Interestingly, when Mark headed for Georgia in the fall of 1960, it was to study archeology, because he had tired of the newspaper business, having grown up in it. Fortunately that aim did not last. Fortunate also, that a serious automobile accident only delayed his Grady degree to 1966.

Also in the sixties was UGA's second most famous student from Wrightsville, Loran Smith (ABJ 62). No fan of Georgia football in the glory years of the seventies and eighties will ever forget the combination of Larry Munson in the booth and Smith on the sidelines. It sounded like domination. But Smith was more than a sideline reporter. It would be hard to imagine anyone who has written more about the university. He remains to this day a syndicated columnist, sharing reminiscences about Georgia's people and commentary on its culture. A million Georgians read him each week. So who makes Loran second-most-famous from tiny Wrightsville in south central Georgia—Herschel Walker. Life is not always fair, but it is to the swiftest—although come to think of it, Smith was a track star in his college days, but nah.

Loran Smith (ABJ 62) with Don Rountree (ABJ 63) Grady Fellows. *Grady College Archives*

Lewis Grizzard (ABJ 84)[92] became a legendary authority on UGA football, humorist, columnist,

Lewis Grizzard, only one like him. *courtesy* ***Atlanta Journal-Constitution***

and author. Until recently, the college still had his typewriter, off which flew some of the funniest regional humor ever generated. (It mysteriously disappeared.) Jim Minter called him the best journalist he ever hired at the *Constitution*. A much sought after speaker, he lived hard, drank even harder, and as a result departed far too early. He was an eighteen year-old sports writer for the *Red & Black* when he started with the *Daily News*. Such was the energy being generated in Athens as media lab. All who knew Grizzard have a story to tell. No one who ever heard it will ever forget his most memorable punch line, and apologies to those who did not: "That dog will bite you!" Of course, it was what went before. Thousands will know it, apologies again to the rest, but shoulders are still shaking in Dawgland. (Google it.)

Grizzard did have a roommate who is now a Grady Fellow, Randall Abney, from LaFayette, Georgia, about as far northwest as one can get in the state. Abney showed the entrepreneurial spirit by getting into cable early and pulling programming from Ted Turner's start-up TBS, especially Braves Baseball and spreading it over North Georgia. Among his and wife Carolyn's, also a Grady Fellow, later ventures would be a lens-crafting operation in Italy that won an Academy Award for innovation in the technology of film-

**LEFT:** Carolyn and Randall Abney front row right, other Fellows include front row, left, Edwin Pope, and to his left, Phil Gailey, Steve Koonin, Bo Spalding, and Jim Tate, 2010 Fellowship Gala—a power lineup. **RIGHT:** Tom and Wendy Dowden with Ann Hollifield, center, first holder of Dowden Professorship for Media Research *Grady College Archives*

Brian Johnstone. *1968* ***Pandora***

making. Thus Grady's second Oscar. Carolyn and Randall are also a driving force in UGA's Osher Lifelong Learning Institute (OLLI). World travelers, collectors of art and books, connoisseurs of good wine, their thirst for knowledge is unquenchable, their zest for life infectious.

Tom Dowden (ABJ 62) also made his mark in cable before diversifying. He used his good fortune to endow first a media lab in Grady and later a professorship in media research. He took his inspiration from Drewry's oft-repeated aphorism, "Remember, in deciding your future career choices, that work is work only if you had rather be doing something else." Similarly, Brian Johnstone (ABJ 68), a Scot who became Executive Director of Public Affairs at Lockheed Martin Aeronautics, drew his inspiration from the persona of Dean Drewry, which he described as looming large. "Who could forget," Johnstone said, "Drewry's assurances that he routinely communicated with the long-deceased Henry Grady, whom he declared was in 'journalistic Valhalla.'"

To capture the true spirit of the sixties, one has to look no further than the Grady women who were moving to the fore. Just as women's suffrage took a back seat to emancipation, so too did the women's movement of the last half of the twentieth century await a completion of the African-American part of freedom's agenda, but arrive it did. Industrialization, corporatization, mechanization, technology, education, health and medicine—all required new roles for women, and they stepped forward. Rebecca Leet (ABJ 71),

**LEFT:** Rebecca Leet. *Grady College Archives, courtesy Rebecca Leet;* **RIGHT:** Gloria Ricks Taylor with Margaret Thatcher. *Grady College Archives, courtesy Gloria Taylor*

former Executive Director of D.C.-based Public Leadership Education Network (PLEN), put it most succinctly, "UGA began—and almost ended—for me with the *Red & Black*. I joined my first week as a freshman and, as editor in 1970, barely survived a vote of the Board of Regents to expel me for publishing the first ads for contraceptives and abortion counseling." Like Priscilla Arnold before her, it did not take much for a woman to be "out of place," but students like Rebecca were willing to take risks in order to move things forward.

So too was Gloria Ricks Taylor (ABJ 66) from Soperton, Georgia, who being told in one of her last Grady classes that women needed to start from the bottom; e.g. clerical, copywriting, or whatever and then hope for the best. Her first job as an advertising assistant for a textile company was through university placement, not Grady. The ad read, "A man is preferred although a woman will be considered." At that she took her show on the road with the Hearst Corporation, first to London, then back to New York as head of corporate communications at Hearst. In that role she has connected the college to the likes of Frank Bennack, Jr., one of the most powerful figures in media and publishing and also in philanthropy, and to David Barrett, former CEO and Chairman of Hearst Television as well as DiGamma Kappa Award recipient and speaker for the occasion. Taylor continues as a leadership consultant for Hearst and is an on-site confidant to Grady deans, having served on the Board of Trust's executive committee from its creation. She is also recipient of the Grady Dean's Medal. Her service to Grady is reminiscent of the pre-Regents era when UGA was governed by Trustees, one of whom was always Athens-based, as is she.

**LEFT:** Pat Mitchell welcoming a gathering of Peabody Award recipients at Paley Center. *Grady College Archives*; **RIGHT:** Betty Hudson with friend and colleague Tom Brokaw and Peabody Director Horace Newcomb. *Grady College Archives*

Pat Mitchell (ABJ 65, MA in English 67) first taught at UGA before going on to head National Public Radio and now serves as President and CEO of the Paley Center for Media in New York. A Grady Fellow, she is a native of Swainsboro, Georgia, and never is without Georgia on her mind. Then Betty Hudson (ABJ 71), daughter of Grady great, Willis Johnson (ABJ 43), is the funniest woman on this or any planet, with an unrivaled sense of humor. Beginning at NBC News in New York, she is now Executive Vice President for Communications at the National Geographic Society. She has served in full measure numerous boards at both Grady and UGA, and received the university's 2003 Distinguished Alumni Award. She now dates herself from having been among the first students in what was then the "new" Journalism Building, making her as old as, well, a venerable building.

Maxine Clark (ABJ 71) did not let the transformation pass her by either. Growing up in Miami, Florida, she made her way to Athens majoring in Marketing and Advertising, where Ron Lane was one of her most admired professors. Retailing was her future, starting with Payless Shoes and moving to May Department Stores, a giant holding company of among others, Neiman Marcus. Still, she wanted more. Taking inspiration from conversations with a friend's daughter, she launched Build-a-Bear Workshop in the late nineties, which became a phenomenal success. Headquartered in St. Louis, these workshops can be found all over the United States and abroad. She recently sold the company, and Maxine and her husband Bob Fox, an entrepreneur in his own right, devote themselves to philanthropy. Together they received St. Louis's highest honor for service, the Harris Community Service Award. She is a trustee of Washington University in St. Louis and

Maxine Clark advising Grady students to "do what you love and love what you do." *Grady College Archives*

**LEFT:** Carolyn Tieger announcing establishment of a Distinguished Professorship with Cully Clark on left, Parker Middleton on right. *Grady College Archives*; **RIGHT:** Tieger, sixties-style. *Grady College Archives, courtesy Carolyn Tieger*

generous to many causes, including hospitals and public education. A loyal friend of Grady, she also is a recipient of its Dean's Medal.

Carolyn Caudell Tieger (ABJ 69) from just up the road in Homer, Georgia, made her way down the road to Athens and on to a remarkable career in public affairs public relations. Fellow Homerian, Phil Gailey (ABJ 66) preceded her at Grady and went on to fame at the *St. Petersburg Times,* both keenly interested in politics and the world beyond. Carolyn's journey, after a stint with the Reagan administration, took her to the Washington, D.C., Office of Porter Novelli, which she served as Partner and Managing Director. She now lives in Naples, Florida, and continues a highly successful private consulting practice. In the spring of 2013, she announced the immediate establishment of a professorship. By an additional planned gift it will become the Carolyn Caudell Tieger Chair in Public Relations for Public Affairs Communication. Her goal is to build a stronger interdisciplinary relationship between Grady and UGA's School of International and Public Affairs, and it will. "It seems like just yesterday," she said, "when I stood in the parking lot near Grady College with my parents as we prepared to say our goodbyes. . . . I still remember what I wore—a yellow pleated skirt, a madras shirt and brown Weejuns." She credits the Grady Fellowship for bringing her back into the fold and providing her an opportunity to give back and "help build the future of Grady's next 100 years."

So, where did all the hippies go? Most found happiness and warm memories of their Grady days. Of course most were never hippies, but all were daring in spirit and got the beat.

# THE SEVENTIES AND EIGHTIES 4

"AS A MATTER OF FACT, STUDENT RIOTS OF ONE SORT OR ANOTHER, PROTESTS AGAINST THE ORDER THAT IS, KICKS AGAINST COLLEGE AND UNIVERSITY MANAGEMENT, INDICATE A HEALTHY GROWTH AND NORMAL FUNCTIONING OF THE ACADEMIC MIND." "If our colleges do not breed men who riot, who rebel, who attack life with all their youthful vim and vigor, then there is something wrong with our colleges. The more riots that come on college campuses, the better world for tomorrow." William Allen White, *The Emporia Gazette*, April 8, 1932

Students protest Vietnam War, November 1969, across from Memorial Hall. Grady Building in background. *Hargrett Rare Books and Manuscript Library, University of Georgia*

John Drewry's successor was Warren Kendall Agee, Dean of the William Allen White School of Journalism at the University of Kansas. Near the end of Agee's first full year as dean, on May 4, 1970, at 12:24 p.m., shots emptied from M1 Garand rifles of the Ohio National Guard into protesting Kent State students, leaving four dead and eleven wounded. It was America at yet another crossroads. Debates flared across campuses over whether to continue or suspend classes for the remainder of the semester. "Moratorium" they called it. Students marched, faculties met, administrators sweated decisions. Students at the University of Alabama burned the ROTC Building. At Chapel Hill, they marched by the thousands and surrounded the building where faculty debated moratorium at microphones that fed loudspeakers for the crowd outside. There, classes became optional for the remainder of the spring term. At Georgia, the immediate protest drew perhaps 500, most may have been onlookers, to the Academic Building in hopes of getting an administrative response. Later, more joined the march to the president's house on Prince Avenue. Despite three arrests (later released) and a minimalist response to close classes on May 7 and 8, not much else happened. As university historian Tom Dyer observed, ". . . an essential conservatism among Georgia students militated against any sustained tradition of liberal activism or student radicalism."[93]

Still, things were changing. At the close of the sixties, the Women's Student Government Association demanded an end to more restrictive rules of conduct for female students. The university soon obliged, ending as most universities already had, the era of *in loco parentis*, where universities acted as local parents. Quite simply, universities did not want the liability that came with the authority it assumed. What was less apparent but would become more troublesome for deans especially was a change in what faculty expected in terms of governance. It would have great consequence for Agee.

Agee in every respect had the right credentials as a credible successor to Drewry. Born in Sherman, Texas, in 1916, he received his bachelor's degree cum laude from Texas Christian University in Fort Worth in 1937. For the next ten years he worked on the editorial staff of the *Fort Worth Star-Telegram*, at which time he assumed an instructor position at his alma mater while pursuing a master's at the University of Minnesota in 1949. It was a route followed by many in that day as we have seen at Grady. Obtaining a doctorate at Minnesota in 1955, he moved quickly through the ranks, becoming professor in 1957. He was already serving as department chair, starting in 1950 and ending in 1958, when he became dean at West Virginia University. He left Morgantown two years later to become the first national executive officer for the Society of Professional Journalists/Sigma Delta Chi, traveling some 60,000 miles to restore its reputation among practicing journalists and educators. He returned to Texas Christian in 1962 as Dean of the Evening College. By 1965 he was named dean of the William Allen White School of Journalism at Kansas, the position he held before accepting appointment at Grady. In 1956 he served as president of the American Society of Journalism School Administrators (ASJMC today) and in 1958 led the Association for Education in Journalism (AEJMC today). He co-authored a highly regarded textbook on mass communications and served on a number of editorial boards. He was the ticket, or so everyone had a right to think.

Dean Warren Kendall Agee.
*Hargrett Rare Books and Manuscript Library, University of Georgia*

William Allen White was to the Midwest what Grady was to the South, a regional champion who was highly regarded nationally. White, 1868-1944, was a great friend of Teddy Roosevelt and detested William Jennings Bryan's version of Democratic populism, which gained some traction in Kansas. As Doris Kearns Goodwin said of those times, "Voices had been raised to protest the concentration of corporate wealth and the gap between rich and poor, yet the doctrine of laissez-faire precluded collective action to ameliorate social conditions. Under Roosevelt's Square Deal (also called New Nationalism) the country had awakened to the need for government action for problems caused by industrialization—an awakening spurred in part by the dramatic exposés of a talented group of investigative journalists he famously labeled 'muckrakers.'"[94]

Although White was not a "muckraker," per se, Emporia, Kansas, was a wholesome place, but corruption shouted "here I come" in Kansas City, and he cheered the reformers on. White supported Roosevelt's third party "Bull Moose" campaign against incumbent Republican President William Howard Taft and Democratic candidate Woodrow Wilson in 1912. Later he supported Wilson's League of Nations proposal, wildly unpopular with Republicans. A through and through Republican, White never voted for Franklin Roosevelt, even though he liked him personally and supported a number of New Deal programs. He wrote beautifully and brilliantly, both fiction and nonfiction, and received numerous awards, including two Pulitzers. Greatly admired for his reformist pleadings, he nonetheless remained a small-town Midwestern progressive, which was not the future that awaited the nation soon after his passing. Had he lived long enough, Dwight Eisenhower, with his small-town Kansas background and own brand of progressivism, would have been his beau ideal. The School at Kansas and the library at Emporia State in his hometown were named for him.

On arriving, Agee made the comparison between Grady and White and made friends accordingly. He commended the strength of its faculty and the new building as Drewry legacies and claimed Drewry as a personal friend. He also arrived to much congratulations, as from Walter Cronkite who applauded his "appointment to the prestigious Georgia job."[95] Agee had big plans and his first annual report laid out a detailed agenda. A handsome, pipe-smoking, amiable man, he looked the part, but it was to be a more difficult six years than anyone imagined. Still, the plan he articulated at the end of year one was the future and the energy with which he prosecuted it was amazing, at least until he was derailed in 1973. The faculty called him "iron pants" for the long hours he put in and seven days a week at that. Yet soon students would be calling him "jelly fish" for a less admirable quality, an anxiety about confrontation that made him appear weak and indecisive, even nervous in meetings.[96]

On arrival there were pressing issues that included reining in an out-of-control curriculum and gaining re-accreditation which given the last review was no sure thing. As early as 1963, a re-accreditation report had been a warning shot across the bow—a curriculum weighted more toward the professional than liberal arts, the presence of only one full professor raised questions about its promotions policy, and low salaries were flash points. To be sure, Drewry had an answer for each, but although the accrediting body granted re-accreditation, it requested by March 15, 1965, "a progress report in these areas."[97] Drewry really had let things get out of hand and the chaotic nature of the curriculum was one of them. An undated and unsigned document in the same file, revealed Drewry as taking evasive actions with his own faculty to maintain the status quo. Ernie Hynds, a recent permanent addition to the faculty, said that Drewry really did rule with an "iron hand" and that no progress could be made on curriculum until he stepped down.[98] Students wound up taking far more hours in journalism than standards called for and the accrediting body had signaled its displeasure.

"The faculty and students cooperated wonderfully," Agee recalled, "arriving on campus almost a week before normal time in order to undergo almost a complete change in students' programs. We created a highly compact but flexible program of communications study supported by greater breadth and depth in traditional liberal arts areas."[99] He got approval for reducing the core curriculum of required basic journalism courses from forty to fifteen quarter hours, increased emphasis on writing, and separated the advertising and public relations program. (For those unfamiliar with the quarter system, students took three courses, five hours each, per week; thus 15 hours credit per quarter or 45 hours total over a normal academic year—fall, winter, spring.) Agee succeeded in eliminating sequences in Journalistic-Literary Appreciation, Journalistic-Secretarial, and Journalistic-Home Economics. The overall effect was to reduce required communications hours from 38 to 29.5 percent of a student's total for graduation, more nearly the 25 percent called for in accreditation standards. Ernie Hynds, longtime professor of journalism and department head in the nineties, recalled the faculty having already made the curriculum adjustments prior to Agee's arrival. The speedy resolution (one week) would seem to support Hynds' recall.[100] In spring 1970, the college received re-accreditation in Advertising, News-Editorial, Public Relations, and Radio-TV-Film. It was a herculean undertaking, but more was to come.

The 1970 report of the accrediting body was revealing and deserves consideration as a demarcation point in the history of the school. It is clear that the time for new direction was due. Drewry's long tenure resulted in truly impressive accomplishments, but the faculty he assembled was too inbred and idiosyncratic for the times. The curriculum that freighted as many as seven sequences and additional cooperative programs with other UGA units was unwieldy and consumed too many credit hours. Agee wisely took a year to straighten things out. The following findings and conclusions in the 1970 report are of interest. The total budget had risen to $643,489 for an impressive increase of $395,034 over three years. Agee's twelve-month salary was $27,000. Five professors made between $15,400 and $17,300 (four of those on nine-month contracts); four associate professors made between $12,000 and $13,500; fourteen assistant professors ranged between $8,500 and $12,000; with thirteen instructors, all on nine-month arrangements, making $7,500-$11,200; for a total of thirty-six faculty and two administrators who also taught. The number of majors included 510 men, 423 women, and 42 graduate students for a total of 975. (Recall that Grady had less than 300 students just ten years before.) Juniors and seniors in the sequences reviewed included 332 in Advertising-Public Relations, 45 in News-Editorial, and 107 in Broadcasting.

The review team noted an increased emphasis on research by the new administration, found faculty salaries adequate with heavy teaching loads, promotion policies in the process of being clarified across the university, and faculty participation in policy development non-existent until the current year. The team found student placement "haphazard at best" under the previous administration but now moving in the right direction. Of interest to the current generation of faculty, the team found the new building commendable, but "some classrooms are cramped and uninviting and the school is already short of faculty office space." It also found funding limited for faculty travel and for student scholarships. It rated library holdings for journalism education as excellent but periodicals in the reading room were "provincial." Clearly the accrediting team found Drewry's oversight wanting and the new directions promising. Proof, perhaps, that Drewry's tenure was overly long, and as will be seen, his continued presence over the next thirteen years seemed at best superfluous, at worst unwelcomed.

Agee saw it that way also. In a letter to Provost S. W. Pellitier he complained of being stymied in the use of a six-office suite for a communications research center because Drewry "demanded this space and occupied it" without regard to its potential use or even his own plans when it was built. Agee went on to say that Drewry resisted new changes and made himself available to at least two faculty members "whose views coincide with the old ways of doing things. . . . There [in his office suite] they can find reinforcement in looking backward."[101] The old and the new, as it often is. Little could Agee know it would play out in similar ways in his own demise as dean. (The space identified is the suite of offices, middle of the back hall, second floor, and is now occupied by Advertising and Public Relations faculty members.)

The accreditation report found the "new curriculum" a positive step forward but worried about "grade inflation" despite assurances to the contrary, especially when compared to grades outside journalism. Faculty morale was high, with a few exceptions, and "all faculty seem enthusiastic about the new direction of the school." It found professional experience among faculty ranging from "somewhat below average to good," with research productivity "only average" but with new "impetus." A telling finding was "evidence of excessive inbreeding of faculty, and noted that attempts should be made to hire other than Georgia graduates." It declared the ratio of journalism to liberal arts courses "dreadful" as noted in the previous report, and in need of "immediate remedy," which it found in progress. Bottom line, the visitors noted "that, while commendable improvements have been made in the quality of the curriculum, teaching and grading in recent months, additional efforts are essential to raise the standard of instruction, to make the content of courses more challenging and especially to stiffen grading practices in a few courses." That said, the visitors voted unanimously to re-accredit.[102]

Had the visiting accrediting team been able to pull back the covers, they might not have been as pleased. A new arrival on the faculty after the team's departure, Al Hester, believed Agee to have inherited a faculty also characterized by its "slackness," which included fraternization with students, parties fueled by booze, and drunken faculty members in bed with students.[103] Coming from Wisconsin, more noted for its graduate program, the contrast was striking, at least so it seemed to Hester. It read like John Updike's *Memories of the Ford Administration* (Knopf 1992), a novel that centered on seventies-style campus life, or perhaps Richard Russo's hilariously funny *Straight Man* (Random House, 1997). Only what Hester saw going on at Grady may have been more ridiculous than funny, although as we shall see later, it was another sign of the times.

That said, Agee had a long range plan that he also laid out in his first year with the following goals: 1) To become one of the nation's top-ranked schools of journalism and mass communication; 2) To develop a well-balanced and fully promotable faculty worthy of annual merit pay based on superlative teaching, theoretical research, and/or public service; 3) To equip the school with laboratories and equipment essential to instruction, research and service; 4) To attract more superior students, including minorities; 5) To employ and retain minority faculty; 6) To bring the faculty into full partnership in the school's administration and development; 7) To strengthen the school's relationship with outside clientele through the establishment of a School of Journalism Advisory Board, Journalism Alumni Society and other organizations as needed; 8) To gain full academic respectability of the school with the university community; 9) To seek a Ph.D. program and communications research center for the school and a change in name to the School of Communications or the School of Journalism and Mass Communication; 10) To strengthen the school's administration through employment of a business manager, appointment of an associate dean, development of an office for undergraduate affairs and employment of a supervising broadcast engineer; 11) To raise admission standards and to study the possibility of converting the school to a two-year and graduate program; 12) To improve student internships and employment services; 13) To increase financial support through grants and scholarships; 14) To develop the reading room into a Learning Resource Center through addition of auto-tutorial services; and 15) To move the George Foster Peabody Broadcasting Awards collection to the main library and to obtain funding with which to process the items for scholarly research.[104]

With a few modifications and adjustments for new technology and terminology, Agee had laid out the second half of Grady's first 100 years. He set about furnishing the new building with laboratory and instructional equipment, a radio station for students (WUOG), a $65,000 gift from Gannett, matched by the university, for a photo lab that quadrupled photographic facilities, and cameras from WSB. Step by step his goals were falling into play. So much to do, but far more serious issues loomed. The university was re-considering its tenure and promotion guidelines. In his second annual report, Agee worried over its consequences for a professional school, specifically what to do about faculty whose professional experience made them invaluable in certain courses. "Under the current guidelines," he feared, "such teachers are unlikely to be promoted beyond the rank of assistant professor regardless of their merit and application."[105]

Still, Grady took steps. A 20 percent enrollment increase in '71-'72 caused Agee to eliminate his associate dean's position and reassign that person to fulltime faculty responsibilities. That action added further to the strain on his time and to the "iron pants" legend. Large lecture sections admitted more students in order to accommodate demand without enlarging lab enrollments for accreditation purposes. (One cannot overestimate the effects of explosive enrollment growth from 1960 into the early Agee years.) Still, Agee kept his eyes on his goals with respect to a communications research center and a partnership with Morehouse and Clark University in Atlanta to develop a Black Studies program. He could boast that "a Syracuse University study this spring revealed, in the opinion of 109 journalism school administrators throughout the country, the Grady School has made the greatest improvements of any school in the nation in the past five years." No doubt that assessment came in large measure owing to Agee's continuing work in national organizations and considerable correspondence with leadership, witnessed by the quick turn-around of the accrediting council. The impressive new building also factored in as enviable. Agee said that the goal of current efforts is to be considered among "the half-dozen top-ranking communications units in the country."

## 1973, YEAR OF TURMOIL

Then 1973 arrived and things fell apart. As he later recalled, "I came to the University at the wrong time." It started at the top when President Fred Davison decided he could no longer run the university like a dean, as the university was too large for that, and he simply could not sign off on all faculty recommendations and decisions. He needed a provost. In 1968 he turned to the department head in Chemistry, S. William Pelletier, to assume that responsibility. This action led to a lengthy dispute over institutional direction and accordingly promotion policies. The direction for most flagship universities was now research; therefore, it came to the foreground in promotion and compensation decisions. Agee had warned in his 1971 annual report that it threatened professional schools, and indeed the impending crisis would break first in Journalism.

Moreover, Agee had promised his faculty a more open administration and greater faculty participation in decision making about policies and directions, and he meant it. However, Pelletier had other ideas about promotion and merit pay. He insisted that departments be originating units, with schools and colleges serving as forwarding units. Final decisions would be made by university committees organized around the social sciences, arts and humanities, and physical sciences, then on to a general committee of the university that would make the final determination as to whether an individual would be recommended for promotion by the president to the Board of Regents—whew! Things came to a head in the spring of 1973.

As prelude, Agee had to dodge incoming fire from respected journalists who complained about the quality of Grady graduates. In a "Dear Fred" letter to President Davison, dated February 14, 1973, Jim Minter, managing editor of *The Atlanta Constitution*, said that he had surveyed his top editors, each a Grady alum, and other newspaper people and found Grady's preparation of future graduates woefully lacking and less qualified than graduates of Auburn (ouch), Emory, and Florida (double ouch). Minter went on to enumerate that instructors at Grady were "only vaguely acquainted with the business [of journalism]," "the curriculum was outdated," and "the Red and Black is not properly used to train graduates." Minter enclosed a lengthy undated memorandum to him from Bill Shipp with full condemnatory findings and conclusions. He even included an observation of a student intern, Rex Granum, saying that he had learned little or nothing in his journalism classes. These were the kinds of complaints all journalism schools heard. Did a journalist even need a journalism degree, people asked? By

Jim Minter as managing editor of *The Atlanta Constitution*. Courtesy ***Atlanta Journal-Constitution***

citing Emory, Minter included a university with no journalism program and only an occasional course, taught usually by someone working at various Cox properties; for example, Marcus Bartlett, general manager at WSB, who would soon join the Grady faculty.[106]

Agee responded with his own "Dear Fred" on February 27. It was an expansive letter in which he recounted conversations with an equally impressive array of journalists at the Georgia Press Institute. Reg Murphy, editorial page editor of the *Constitution* said he was impressed with the curriculum turn-around since 1969 and added, ". . . the Atlanta newspapers had had two good Auburn University graduates but he did not view Auburn as a consistent source of good newspapermen as is the University of Georgia." Agee cited Durwood McAlister, managing editor of the *Journal*, as saying he had "almost quit looking at Florida graduates" and that a recent Missouri graduate "was completely unacceptable." Agee conceded he had not talked with Minter but cited a 1972 letter from him in which he found that "your 1972 crop has some impressive young men and women who are definitely good prospects."[107] Agee cited other examples of success and speculated that the problem faced by those who hire and fire journalists is that the current

Advisory Board leadership meets with President Davison. Left to right, Don Carter, Carolyn Harris, Davison, and Jasper Dorsey. *Grady College Archives*

crop of students, whatever the professional school, law for example, or liberal arts degrees like history, are more interested in "social issues" than "objective reporting"—a clear generational knock. Finally, Agee added a further thought that presaged what was to come. "We are now completing a year's study," he wrote, "of the proper theoretical and professional mix required in our school and should be able soon to report fully on our needs."[108] Part of this discussion would include the freshly minted advisory board, which reported its own critical review of the curriculum and faculty, delivering it in November, 1974. Faculty leaders like Wally Eberhard and Al Hester in turn were critical of Agee for allowing the board to overstep its bounds, especially with an "extremely flawed methodology" for arriving at its conclusions.[109]

Back and forth it went even as more recent faculty members like Eberhard and Hester brought with their Ph.D.'s extensive professional experience. They knew the requirements of the newsroom. Truth is, J-school faculties have always worried over student preparation, often complaining themselves about poor writing skills among students. Part of the complaint is that English Composition classes in Arts and Sciences do not get desired results to begin with. They come to journalism and mass communication unprepared. The larger truth is that four years of college does not a writer make, at least for most. For she who would be a writer, it is a life's journey. Accomplished professionals wince at their early efforts. Of course some students, or at least a few, depart Grady "camera-ready," thus Jim Minter's brag about the "1972 crop." What can be said is that the students who aspire to be writers most often get it through magazine classes, feature writing, investigative reporting and of course the *Red & Black*—and that's only print journalism. All communications disciplines are writing-intensive. Minter's and the board's complaints about students or faculty not knowing the business side led to major investments over the ensuing years with the result that Grady's reputation as a leader in "management and economics" is strong. Still in all, a recent meeting of the Board of Trust, April 2012, went into a "thought summit" about what members might contribute to encourage even better results on the business side in all Grady degree programs. It is ongoing, but back in 1973 events were about to overtake talk.

1973 was another of those sea-change years. The Watergate hearings led to President Nixon's infamous declaration that he was "not a crook." Henry Kissinger signed the Paris Peace Accords, and the last soldiers left Vietnam although Saigon would not fall for another two years with helicopters taking desperate people from atop the CIA Compound and American Embassy. Then, in May, fury broke loose in Journalism. It started when Agee, who identified with the administration's desire for higher standards, failed to recommend merit pay increases for 10 of the 36 faculty members in Journalism. It was almost bound to happen because only twelve members of the faculty held a Ph.D. and not all of them were productive researchers. Moreover, among junior faculty and instructors there were "givers and takers" by Drewry's own lights from an earlier annual report or "slackness" to hear Hester describe it. Clearly Agee wanted a system that recognized professional contributions along with research, but the faculty read his salary recommendations as toting water for Davison and Pelletier—that he was not his own man.

In fact, Agee and sequence heads had engaged in an elaborate review of each faculty member to make recommendations, although it is true that Agee could have done a better job of communicating his final recommendations to sequence heads in the run-up to May 23. A memorandum from VP for Instruction William L. Hays to Chancellor George L. Simpson, June 1, 1973, details the elaborate steps Agee and sequence heads took in evaluating faculty, including one nine-hour session with dean and sequence heads. (The author has read each rather detailed evaluation and found them among the best he has ever seen.) Still, Agee did not communicate his final recommendations to sequence heads until after the president and provost approved them on April 18, which in fact did zero-out the ten faculty members who Agee had recommended for less than two percent raises. Agee shared the final recommendations with sequence heads on April 24, accompanied by evaluations, at which time Emery "Pete" Sasser, sequence head in journalism, began sharing salary recommendations and evaluations on a selective basis with his faculty.[110] As Al Hester said, "Agee didn't telegraph his moves sufficiently," even with thorough planning and preparation such as occurred in this instance.[111] So the storm was brewing a month before the fateful meeting on May 23.

Some faculty contended that it was more an issue of process, saying that the absence of guidelines and of faculty participation in evaluations, promotions, salary decisions, and employment were troubling. Of course, process is always the default when rewards are denied; but in this instance, they were right. At a special faculty meeting on May 23, called ironically to complete administrative faculty forms, Daniel W. Kitchens, an instructor and *Red & Black* advisor, called for a vote of "no confidence" in Agee. (Kitchens was *R&B* editor the year before the gang of four editors resigned in 1953 over Roy Harris's interference. At that time, as a graduate assistant, he became the paper's adviser. He still was.) Kitchens also believed he had the support of powerful alumnus Billy Morris in this action and perhaps others.[112] Associate Professor "Pete" Sasser seconded the motion, and it carried by written vote of 25 to 8.[113] Clearly Agee had a problem on his hands. Tom Russell, who would be appointed assistant dean in the quarter following the vote, said everyone knew it was going to happen. Still, Agee was blindsided.[114]

Someone alerted the media. Already with close ties to the college, they spared nothing in getting the word out about the revolt among Grady's faculty. In part it was an echo of the "green eyeshades" preference of newspaper journalists for practical training versus the research/communication direction of a research university—Minter's complaint about lack of "preparation." President Davison quickly voiced his confidence in Agee and in the goals and procedures he had instituted at Grady. "In the four years Dean Agee has headed the journalism school," he said, "he has moved rapidly to upgrade the quality of his faculty and to implement high standards." Davison was hot now and complained that there had been little or no concern expressed previously to the administration about Agee's leadership. He added, "I personally consider it beyond the bounds of professional conduct that such a meeting was held and that the press was notified in advance."[115]

At Davison's request, Agee called a meeting of the faculty the following day. Davison, Pelletier, and two university vice presidents, William L. Hays and S. Eugene Younts, attended. The meeting took place in the conference room just off the dean's office. It was cramped. Davison castigated the faculty for its action and said the vote had no standing with the administration because no formal complaint had been filed prior to the vote. He said that he and the administration set the standards for excellence. He called it a "gross display," "disgusting and uncivilized behavior," and a "miserable performance." Pelletier likened the faculty's handling of the matter to "gutter people."[116] Pelletier even taped a piece of foam over an air vent at the bottom of a door to prevent anyone from listening in, presumably journalists. He was that way.[117]

In its defense, the faculty finally complained about no forewarning of poor evaluations or zero pay increases, and Davison agreed to set up a committee including the two vice presidents, Dean Agee, and several faculty members to come back with recommendations about procedure, which they did on September 20, recommending "extensive and detailed guidelines for faculty employment, evaluation, promotions and salaries."[118] The faculty adopted these new procedures and guidelines in an October meeting. Despite some progress, later Dean Tom Russell remembers the establishment of a separate committee under Gene Younts to offer direction for Agee, but it devolved into interminable meetings with no real results.[119] Agee's tendency to such meetings without decision complicated things. "Indecisive" was the most common complaint about Agee.

In their letter of delivery to President Davison, vice presidents Hays and Younts expressed their personal confidence that matters in Journalism had been addressed. They also recommended that the university "recruit as soon as possible at least three outstanding senior faculty members, one for each sequence, to shore up apparent weaknesses. Each of these persons should have a national reputation as a productive person and be a pacesetter with instinctive leadership abilities that inspire colleagues." The end of faculty unrest was not in sight for Davison and company as fire broke out in Commerce & Business Administration and also in Arts and Sciences. Not until October could Davison put matters generally to rest in a comprehensive report to the faculty about new goals, guidelines, and procedures that would enable the university to join the ranks of modern research universities. To improve communication, he established an Academic Affairs Advisory Council that included all deans and directors of significant academic programs.[120] It was a smart document but could not by stroke of pen make turmoil go away or what Pelletier artlessly described in his files as the "faculty fracas."[121]

## AN UNSETTLED PEACE

Wally Eberhard always engaged. *Grady College Archives*

Over Agee's remaining two years, the school continued to grow. Enrollments rose to 1,300. New faculty members were recruited, quality improved and research took off. Among the new faculty were Wallace B. "Wally" Eberhard, who combined nine years of professional experience with depth interest in journalism history. John W. English, who had considerable experience in the Far East and six years of newspaper work, was a prolific writer for magazines. English paired well with Albert L. "Al" Hester, former city editor of the *Dallas Times-Herald* with eleven years of newspaper experience. Al would lead the charge in the mid-eighties for a focused interest in international studies and research. Then came Joseph R. "Joe" Dominick, head of Radio-TV-Film, an excellent researcher and top performer in Broadcast Education Association circles. His textbooks in various editions were and are among the most popular. Finally, James E. Fletcher arrived from the University of Kentucky with extensive military and educational experience and proved to be another top researcher. Each held or would hold Ph.D.'s. Part of the success owed to the maturing of doctoral education in journalism and mass communication. Part owed to moving toward genuine academic departments, as opposed to sequences, thereby creating scholarly critical mass.

Agee made progress on almost all his goals, including: a placement program, a research center, planning for doctoral education, moving to slow enrollment by adopting a grade point average of 2.5 for admission, and a faculty recommendation to admit students only as juniors and seniors. All these things happened in various ways. Grady was approaching the time it would become a college but that awaited a doctoral program. (In those days Grady was always referred to as the J-school, a tendency that lingered into this century to the chagrin of many mass communications faculty members.)

Fletcher addressing a class. *Grady College Archives*

In the meantime, Agee had grown tired of administration and become increasingly pessimistic. In a report to the Alumni Association in May 1975, he said, "So now, a bit weary, I muster out of the paper war." He also cited growing health problems "induced by a taxing work load, including the pressures of building the school on many fronts simultaneously and rapidly amid campus and school-wide controversies." It led him "to initiate talks with the president and provost aimed at ending my twenty-five years of school administration and beginning a third career as a full-time professor."[122]

For all his accomplishments, and they were considerable, Agee, the sterling candidate, seemed uncomfortable in his own skin. The person the faculty called "iron pants" for his long hours, was ill at ease in meetings. Although the faculty handled its vote of "no confidence" poorly (Davison was right, no process was followed and Agee was blindsided),[123] the vote was still 25-8. Agee's social skills did not live up to his resume. It was a sad performance for a man who put in the hours, had good ideas, and had such distinguished credentials and connections. He was a man out of season. In a personal letter to the journalism advisory board dated May 22, 1975, he put it oddly if poetically as he intended, "... I am anxious," he wrote, "to become reacquainted with the real me lurking somewhere within the mantle of the deanship that I wear seven days a week and 24 hours a day."[124] Letters of support for Agee poured in from the school's external constituencies and at the conclusion of his final meeting with the Journalism Advisory Board he had created, he received a standing ovation. After stepping down in 1975, he remained on the faculty for another ten years with creditable accomplishments, especially in the international arena.

## THE SEVENTIES: UNCOMFORTABLE SHOES

The seventies marked a real transition in faculty governance and made for some grim scenes on campuses across the country, not just in Athens. Faculty Senates formed and challenged presidents. The University of Alabama's young (thirty-one when he assumed office in 1970) and fair-haired president, David Mathews, left for Washington to become Gerald Ford's Secretary of Health, Education and Welfare. When he returned a short time later, a newly formed Faculty Senate went after him in a most confrontational manner, resulting in his eventual departure for the Charles Kettering Foundation, where he remains today. Virginia Trotter, who joined him at HEW, returned to UGA and became provost, later down-graded to Vice President for Academic Affairs, following all of the aforementioned controversy over Pelletier as provost. Neither presidents nor deans ruled in the old way.

Davison's presidency itself was at best premature. He assumed the office at age thirty-seven, except for Harmon Caldwell, the youngest president. Born in Atlanta and growing up in Marietta, he went to Emory at Oxford, a two year program, then earned a doctorate in veterinary medicine from Georgia in 1952. After private practice, he went to Iowa State University in 1958, where he earned a Ph.D. in pathology and biochemistry and became a

President Fred Davison. *Hargrett Rare Books and Manuscript Library, University of Georgia*

research associate there. He developed a research interest in the comparative toxicity of stable rare earth compounds for the Atomic Energy Commission. It all sounded so impressive that he was made Dean of the UGA College of Veterinary Medicine for two years before becoming Vice Chancellor of the System. In another year, 1967, he would be president of the University of Georgia. What did he know, impressive as he was, except how to impress people? He had little academic acculturation. Perhaps it was the Kennedy years that valued youth. Whatever, he made up for lack of maturation with what the faculty at Grady, and truly all over campus, believed to be a brash, sometimes overbearing style, more a politician some said, but at the same time not very "politic" in his dealings. Leon "Buddy" Hargreaves, Dean of Forestry, called him "baby Fred." Other deans picked up on it.[125] Still, he would have a nineteen-year run of considerable accomplishment.

Interestingly, the enterprising *Athens Daily News* under Glenn Vaughn's leadership scooped the appointment. Having access to the list of candidates, they checked the travel plans for each and realized none of the external candidates were on their way to Georgia, which left Davison the obvious, if inexperienced, choice. So, when publisher Vaughn checked with president Claude Williams, Jr., to ask if it were alright to run with the story before the announcement, the result was that Vaughn showed up in Atlanta for the announcement carrying copies of the *Daily News* with banner headlines, already hot off the morning press.[126] The further result was that Davison seemed the accidental president.

The seventies were generally a hard grind. Watergate; the ouster of Vice President Spiro Agnew and the resignation of President Nixon; the inglorious ending in Vietnam; unease over feminism and confrontations over the vestiges of segregation; stacked heels, bell-bottom pants, and polyester leisure suits for men; short skirts, big hair or straight hair and heavy eye makeup for women; angry rhetoric on all sides; the election of James Earl Carter, only five short years after he ran a racist campaign to defeat Carl Sanders for governor of Georgia; the Iran hostage crisis; stagflation and long lines for gasoline: it is all a wonder now. It got so bad that Americans were even asked to turn out the Christmas lights in 1973. The wind that blew out of the sixties was an ill wind of dashed hopes on the left and outraged anger from the right. Only the Saturday night line-up on TV ("M.A.S.H.," "Bob Newhart," "Mary Tyler Moore," and "All in the Family") offered anything like genuine laughter.

What the seventies needed was a good horse, and it got three, including the greatest of all in 1973, Secretariat, but then Seattle Slew and Affirmed had cases of their own to make. And down the stretch they came!

## TRANSITION

Agee's last major act was one prayed for, but the old saying was never truer. The college, for all its travail through the Davison/Pelletier decision to ratchet up research and stand by Agee, was offered the opportunity of recruiting three senior positions of high national repute. Agee landed three, on the face of it, "stars." The first was Vernon A. Stone of the School of Journalism at Wisconsin, an elite program in research and graduate education. Second was Scott Munson Cutlip, also of Wisconsin. Overtures had been made to him previously without success. This time he accepted. Stone and Cutlip got on well enough at Wisconsin, but more was to come. The third was Marcus Bartlett, who had just retired as executive vice president of Cox Broadcasting, Inc., after forty-two years in the business. He had taught part-time in Emory's journalism program that had been terminated twenty-five years earlier and limped along with a course or two from time to time. He was clearly "the professional." Bartlett liked to say he had taught two department heads at Georgia, Worth McDougald and Ernie Hynds,

**LEFT:** Vernon Stone soon to be a problem for Agee. **RIGHT:** Scott Cutlip, huge reputation, controversial yet successful dean. *Grady College Archives*

when they were undergraduates at Emory. Hynds also said Bartlett played the organ at his and Mary Ann's wedding.[127] None of the three would work out, at least as "stars," despite the promise.

Stone soon became Grady's surrogate dean for Provost Pelletier. By the provost's own judgment, Stone was the man with the firmness to get the job done. Agee was not. Clearly the administration had lost confidence in him.[128] In any event, when Agee stepped down, President Davison liked Cutlip and asked him to serve as acting dean for a year. Cutlip initially resisted because he wanted his summers to complete a history of public relations. Davison and Pelletier, assured him he could have his summers, and so he signed on. The acting year would lead to a total of eight years as dean, as no suitable alternative was found from outside, and in fact, Cutlip liked it. He kept his summers too, which rankled other deans and put an undue burden on his assistant dean, Tom Russell.[129]

Interestingly, the regents confirmed Cutlip for full appointment on a vote of 11- 2, the two coming from regents influenced by Grady alums who were suspicious of a "public relations" man taking the helm of a J-school. It was typical journalistic hubris, ignoring the basic democratic principle that all ideas, issues, individuals and institutions need their best representation. In that sense, PR professionals are no different than attorneys. Put the best case forward within ethical bounds, and Cutlip was the godfather of the educational profession of that principle. He and Allen H. Center wrote the bible of public relations textbooks. In fact, Cutlip and Center have no first names on Google, such remains their legacy as co-authors.

Cutlip was born July 15, 1915, in Buckhannon, West Virginia. He was at some point orphaned and taken in by an uncle, George, who reared him on a farm just out from town.[130] He no doubt grew up going to Stalnaker's Hardware Store, an emporium where one could get more than tools, and fished for mountain chub in French Creek with a bent pin hook and wadded piece of bread for bait, as boys are wont to do. He attended West Virginia Wesleyan in Buckhannon but eventually graduated from Syracuse. From 1933, he wrote for the *Buckhannon Record*, then later for the West Virginia Publishing Company in Morgantown. He got his bachelor's at Syracuse in journalism and political science before winding up in Australia with the Army Air Force. He eventually landed at the University of Wisconsin in 1946, teaching journalism and pioneering in public relations. There he had a special program for army officers and joined with Allen Center to do their famous textbook.

Among faculty members of the Cutlip period, admirers are few, certainly among the print journalism faculty. Among students, Swann Seiler, famous Grady alum, says Cutlip was in the halls greeting students and putting an arm around them. She admired his student-centeredness. While Agee wearied, Cutlip never gave that appearance. His florid face, considerable paunch, and bright smile, inspired confidence at the Athens Country Club, if not altogether in the halls of Grady where he was viewed as excessively confrontational and capricious, even mean, some thought.[131] President Davison, a man of personal rectitude, liked him, no doubt in part for the kind of advice only a skilled PR practitioner can deliver a chief executive, although what he thought about Cutlip's notorious fondness for drink is not known. When Pelletier informed Cutlip of Agee's decision to step down, he assured him, no doubt acting for Davison, that he was the best person to bring calm and unity to the school as acting dean, despite Pelletier's continued use of Stone to counsel him on college matters, at least for a time.

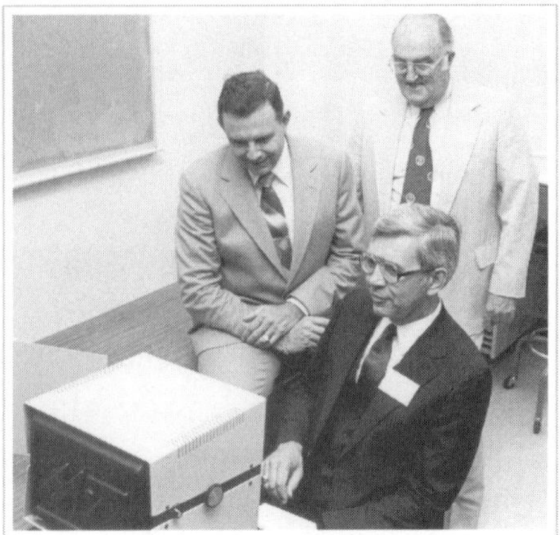

Davison and Cutlip overlooking Carrol Dadisman at computer. *Grady College Archives*

In fact, Davison's admiration for Cutlip's savvy ways and two-fisted approach, plus Cutlip's staunch support for Davison's plan for building a modern research university, brought Cutlip into Davison's "kitchen cabinet."[132] Also in Davison's inner circle were Ralph Beaird, Dean of the Law School, and Barry Wood, Vice President for External Relations and Assistant to the President. The camaraderie spilled over to the Athens Country Club where town and gown leadership intersected. Beaird and Cutlip were frequently on the golf course where every time Cutlip drove the ball, he would sing out, "Love to hit that ball!"[133] During Cutlip's deanship he traveled the state, using his connections with Georgia journalists to promote Davison's administration and its agenda, always with an eye to the General Assembly and its support for UGA measures.[134] This special connection to the administration had value for the college, but at the same time engendered suspicion about whom Cutlip served.

Tinkam, Reid, and Krugman, the future now. *Grady College Archives*

Cutlip's administration as dean achieved much, proof that a school or college's mission and the ability to get things done is always greater than the particularities and peculiarities of its leadership. The college finally became a "high demand major," meaning enrollment in the junior year. The doctoral program was implemented in 1983 with its first two students, meaning Grady would become a college (a designation that typically accompanies offering the full complement of degrees). He continued Agee's success in hiring highly qualified faculty. Among those recruited during Cutlip's tenure were names that would have great influence well into the next century, people like Leonard N. Reid, William E. Lee, Conrad Fink, Dean M. Krugman, Barry L. Sherman, Kent R. Middleton, Ruthann Weaver-Lariscy, Robert Willett, and Spencer F. Tinkham. They were among the twenty-two hires Cutlip made in eight years, bringing total faculty strength to forty-one over the thirty-six he inherited. The number of new hires also meant a lot of people left. More importantly, most of his hires held Ph.D.'s with concomitant improvement in research output. It was a real turning point for scholarship. That said, some faculty believed that Cutlip "imposed" certain candidates, which included Conrad Fink who held only a bachelor's degree.[135]

But as with all deanships not all was sweetness and light and particularly frustrating for Cutlip was Vernon Stone. Although the two had gotten along well enough at Wisconsin, good relations did not transfer to Athens. Cutlip believed that Stone thought he should have been named dean on Agee's stepping down.[136] Indeed Stone enjoyed a special relationship with Provost Pelletier during Agee's term. Be that as it may, when Cutlip had been dean for only seven months, Stone filed suit against him over what he considered an insulting salary raise of $800. When Cutlip explained that all three faculty members at similar rank and time of service received only a 2.5 percent raise, Stone was not mollified and especially when Cutlip noted that Stone's research productivity had fallen off. When the case was thrown out of Superior Court because the dean had the necessary discretionary authority, Stone appealed to the United States Court for the Middle District of Georgia claiming $100,000 in damages and naming President Davison and the Board of Regents as well. That too was denied, so Stone went to the Fifth Circuit, which affirmed the decision of the District Court. (Although a bit much, it is not unusual for a dean's life to be complicated by such as this. Adverse findings or conclusions about faculty promotion and reward are often tendentious and occasionally badgered by legal action.)

That was just Cutlip's first year. When a search failed to turn up a suitable successor, Cutlip chose, with strong internal support, to stay on. Originally he and President Davison discussed a "two-year" fixed term, concluding that he could fix what ailed the college in that time. However, the letter of appointment was silent on the term matter and what started as an expectation of two ran an additional seven years. In his letter recommending the appointment to Chancellor Simpson, June 8, 1976, Davison said, "There is a cohesiveness in the school which has not been apparent for a number of years and morale has never been better." He also pointed to "an overwhelming consensus" among faculty and leadership "that Dr. Cutlip continue his effective leadership."[137] Cutlip was Davison's man.

The internal appointment of Cutlip was controversial from a process standpoint, along with that of Ralph Beaird in the Law School. One of five candidates in the Grady search protested, and the chair of the search committee for Grady's dean, Hardy Edwards, Dean of the Graduate School, even recommended in a letter to Davison, May13, 1976, that the Equal Employment Opportunity Office review the search. Nothing came of it. Edwards and Cutlip were known antagonists. Edwards had turned down Cutlip's application for graduate faculty status on the grounds that his principal accomplishment was the textbook, not original research.[138] Cutlip did get strong endorsements from Worth McDougald, Tom Russell, Frazier

Moore, and from Marcus Bartlett, the other "star." Clearly a consensus had developed in the college.[139]

However, in the seven remaining years Cutlip's abrasive style continued, even to alienating much of his support in the college and among external constituencies as well, but not Davison. A disagreement with the Georgia Association of Broadcasters erupted in 1978 and got so acrimonious by 1982 that GAB pulled the Georgia Radio and Television Institute out of Athens and to Macon, where Mercer, Wesleyan, and Macon Technical School took over. When in 1982, Cutlip wrote the GAB's executive director, Bill Sanders, threatening to go forward with the Institute in Athens in any event,[140] it was idle, because GAB had taken legal action to acquire the Institute's name as registered trademark. Clearly the college had issues with GAB also. Still it all seemed so unnecessary. As early as December 1978, Sanders had written President Davison, "These confrontations continue to occur, and my office keeps trying to put out Scott's fires. There is growing sentiment . . . to move the Radio-TV Institute out of Athens."[141] It did not abate. By January of 1983 Grady sponsored its own University of Georgia Radio-Television-Cable Institute that featured John Chancellor of NBC News. GAB was not listed as a sponsor but apparently made no protest, despite the registered name, the addition of "cable" being the only exception.[142]

One other issue dangled, although on the surface it appeared not so problematic, but that was before Cutlip weighed in. What to do about *Red &*

From left, Bill Sanders of Georgia Association of Broadcasters, Dean Tom Russell, and Mike McDougald, 1988, during better days for Grady and GAB. *Grady College Archives*

*Black* independence? Although it maintained an editorial office in the Journalism Building until 1980 (more and more was being done off campus), the college's input was largely entrusted to its faculty advisor, Dan Kitchens, who was well liked by staffers for the thoroughness of his critiques and concomitant improvement in their writing skills. The over-reach of 1953 was in the past, but not so for President Davison. By his legal counsel's interpretation, the president was the paper's publisher, and he did not want to be held responsible for editors' oft too-liberal views. *Red & Black* staffers did not want him or anyone else in that role either. Typical of the complained-of "liberal" drift was an editorial series in 1977 by news editor Patricia "Tricia" Templeton (ABJ 78), titled "Racial discrimination still a reality at the University."[143] It was just this type of *Red & Black* meddling that put the administration's teeth on edge. What could not be gainsaid were the numbers Templeton revealed. At the time African-American enrollment stood at 3.5 percent or 753 of 21,238, and African-American faculty members constituted only 19 of 1,650. Davison had Cutlip's ear on such matters.

When as editor-in-chief a year later, Templeton learned that Davison and Virginia Trotter, Vice President for Academic Affairs, would join a journalism Advisory Board meeting to report on the state of the university, she and a reporter showed up. By her lights, it was an "open meeting," and Davison did have a reputation for being inaccessible, certainly to the *Red & Black* but also to the *Athens Banner-Herald* and *Daily News*. Tom Landrum who was in the university's PR office at the time, remembered Templeton as "giving Fred [Davison] fits."[144] Moments before the meeting was to start, Cutlip spotted the two and said they would have to leave. When Templeton protested on open meetings grounds, Cutlip said it was closed because personnel matters would be discussed, all the while moving toward them in what appeared to be a menacing, angry manner. He later claimed in a private letter that he was calm.[145] Whatever, Templeton and the reporter departed, and later editorialized that the Dean of Journalism was no journalist and needed a course in ethics.[146] In response, Cutlip claimed somewhat defensively in the same private letter that he was author of the Wisconsin "Open Records Act." That said, it was confrontational, and the adult in the room behaved poorly. One faculty member from that era characterized Cutlip as a "bully." When asked for an example, he cited the Templeton case.[147] Being a dean requires an area of emotional intelligence called equanimity. Cutlip was not overly endowed with it.

**ABOVE:** Grady Advisory Board, Cutlip presiding. *Grady College Archives;* **BELOW LEFT:** Patrica Templeton as *Red & Black* editor. *Hargrett Rare Books and Manuscript Library, University of Georgia;* **MIDDLE:** priest and Rector of St. Dunstan's, Patricia Templeton. *Courtesy of Patricia Templeton;* **RIGHT:** Priscilla Arnold Davis, congregant at St. Dunstan's. Twenty-five years prior to Templeton's ordeal, Davis also exhibited courage as *Red & Black* editor. *Courtesy Priscilla Davis*

There was a final act. When Templeton learned that later in the same meeting of the advisory board, Cutlip insinuated that she was "sleeping with sources to get information for stories that put the administration in a bad light," she confronted him. He called her "an impudent little bitch," a comment that was "shouted down the hall in full hearing of many."[148] Today, Templeton is a priest and Rector of St. Dunstan's Episcopal Church in Atlanta. One of her faithful parishioners is Priscilla Arnold Davis, who as a *Red & Black* editor in 1953, twenty-five years before, resigned rather than knuckle under to intimidation by Regent and rabid segregationist Roy

Gene Patterson, Sam Griffin, Tom Wood, James Newman, and Tom Lloyd, chiefs on Grady's Advisory Board. *Grady College Archives*

Harris. She, too, went unsupported by her dean but not in such a farcical and outrageous way.

Suffice to say the journalists in the room were outraged, when they learned about it, some only after the incident. Don Carter, Vice President of News for Knight Ridder; Carrol Dadisman, Executive Editor of the *Columbus Ledger-Enquirer*; Gene Patterson, Editor and President of the *St. Petersburg Times*, all remonstrated with Cutlip, but the most outraged was Tom Wood, President of Atlanta Newspapers, Inc., not only over the "open meetings" matter but especially the insinuation that Templeton was sleeping with a source or sources to get damaging information about the administration and its handling of the Library issue. Wood had his managing editor investigate and found that as a "stringer" for the *Constitution* her "spot coverage" was entirely consistent with that of their "experienced reporter" assigned to the story. Moreover, Wood said Templeton did meet with "one (member) of the Library staff, but it was to do research. . . . Ms. Templeton has never dated, been engaged to, nor socialized with (him), or anyone else connected to the library." He then demanded proof of such wanton allegation as Cutlip made at the meeting.[149] Of course, Cutlip had none.

Also called on the carpet by Cutlip was Jim Galloway, an *R&B* editor the year before and, at the time, *Pandora* editor. Apparently Cutlip had learned that Galloway and fellow editor Sandi Martin planned to include photographs that would have intimated "sex in the dorms." Imagine that! In any

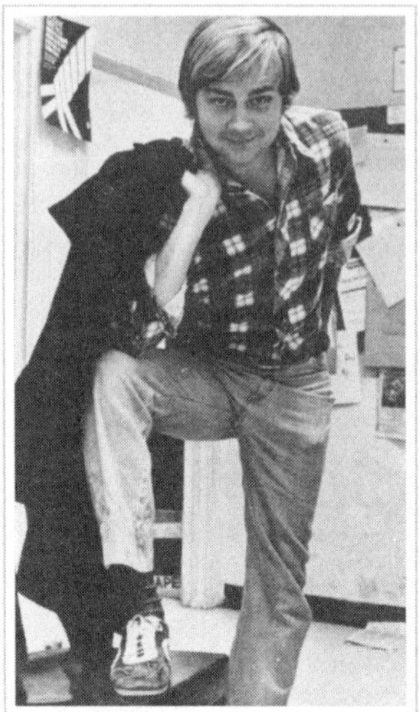

Jim Galloway, 1977, now the *AJC's* political correspondent. *1977* ***Pandora***

event they were scolded for the thought and in the end decided on their own not to include them. Currently, Galloway is Georgia's most highly regarded state capitol journalist with his "Political Insider" column for the *AJC.* Again, Cutlip was running interference for Davison, otherwise known as bad PR counsel. Tom Wood, then President of Atlanta Newspapers, Inc., said a consensus emerged among journalists that while Cutlip may have written the bible on PR, "he hadn't read it."[150]

(Of interest is that Davison knew about all these confrontations because Cutlip and principals regularly copied Davison and his files are replete with it. Still, Davison remained close to Cutlip and valued his counsel up to and including the Jan Kemp case. A contemporary observed that Davison was aggressively defensive toward opposition, perceived or real, although he could be positively "gregarious" with people he considered as friendly or admiring, a volatile mix. Longtime and highly regarded member of the Grady faculty, William "Bill" Lee, said the same of Cutlip. "You wouldn't want to be perceived by Cutlip as an enemy." Lee was relieved to count himself among the dean's friends.[151])

With all this going on in 1978 and in order to free himself of *R&B* nuisance, Davison appointed a committee to study the feasibility of independence. The committee said it was doable but without recommendation, pushing the decision to Davison and the Regents. Davison recommended in favor, but the decision was almost inevitable as the *Red & Black* already had moved its editorial offices in 1980 from the Journalism Building into an old bank building on North Jackson Street. The Regents approved independence on an 8-7 vote (one regent switched to create the majority) and formed a non-profit corporation to oversee the independent operation.[152] Elliott Brack of the *Gwinnett Daily News* was elected president of the newly formed directors and continued in that position until 2012 when events re-formed the board. Journalism faculty and students remained active in developing stories and bylines for the *R&B.*

## REMEMBERING CUTLIP

Despite a couple of rough budget years, the overall trend during Cutlip's administration was considerably up. In fact, during his eight years compensation rose sixty percent, although there was not a corresponding improvement in the operating budget. Still, he partially offset this deficiency through grants and gifts. A proposal written by Al Hester resulted in a gift from the James M. Cox Foundation establishing the Cox Electronic News Laboratory. Anne Cox Chambers and heir apparent Jim Cox Kennedy attended the dedication. Cutlip also worked on scholarships. The school had only two $250 awards that Tom Johnson had arranged through the Peyton Anderson Foundation. By 1983 the school had $200,000 in endowment that yielded $25,000 a year for that purpose. (Normally an endowment of that amount would yield approximately $10,000 annually at a five percent spending rate. Thus other sources, such as annual giving, must have augmented the yield.) In all, the school accumulated $975,000 over Cutlip's eight years—$125,000 from the alumni association that Agee had formed; another $150,000 from the Cox Foundation and Atlanta newspapers that alums William I. Ray and Jim Minter helped arrange; and $67,000 from the Knight Foundation to support graduate students. It was a good start to fundraising in an era that previously had not paid much attention to that opportunity. Perhaps it owed to Cutlip's having written a book on that subject—and read it.

There were other grace notes in the Cutlip years, among them the founding of the McGill Lecture Series and the establishment of the Atrium Award. With $25,000 raised from alumni and friends to establish the lecture series, Gene Patterson (ABJ 43) fittingly gave the inaugural lecture in honor of his mentor and friend, calling McGill a "Rock in a Weary Land." (Isaiah 32:2) It was an auspicious launch for a series that has attracted top-flight journalists to the campus in the years since. Among the first to follow Patterson were Tom Wicker of *The New York Times*, Anthony Lewis also of the *Times*, then John Siegenthaler, an aide to Attorney General Robert F. Kennedy during perilous times in the civil rights movement and president, publisher and editor of the *Nashville Tennessean*, followed by Katharine Graham of *The Washington Post*. There was also the Atrium Award, established jointly by Grady and the Atlanta Apparel Mart, to recognize top fashion journalism in six categories in an $87 billion fashion industry nationwide. With alumna Susan Harte (MA 75), a business staff writer for the *AJC*, and magazine professor John English's fingerprints all over this

Grady faculty, September 1980. First Row: Warren K. Agee, Roland Kraps, Worth McDougald, Frazier Moore, James Frost, William Martin, George Abney, Bruce Swain, George Hough, Alfred Wise; Second Row: Charles Kopp, Frank Kalupa, Donald Wright, Wallace Eberhard, Mark Bartlett, Ernest Hynds, Scott Cutlip, Beverly Bethune; Third Row: Dan Kitchens, J. Thomas Russell, Roger Wimmer, Kent Middleton, James Womack (part-time), James Fletcher, Ed Lynch, William E. Lee, Paula Poindexter; Fourth Row: David Clavier, Margaret Johnston, Barbara McKenzie, Leonard Reid, Lee Wenthe, Joseph Dominick, Graeme Bond, Jeff Clark, Al Hester, Ronald Lane, Richard O'Brien, James Foey, Robert P. Crow. *Grady College Archives*

award, it brought national attention to Grady for the next twenty years, 1980-2000—more evidence that Grady not only set standards but juried them. George Hough, head of Journalism, also played a key role in launching the Atrium Awards.

But it was for the faculty assembled on Cutlip's watch that most credit is due him. That legacy endures.

## CRAZY IN THEIR OWN RIGHT

No history of the Agee and Cutlip years, the seventies as they became the eighties, is complete without a look back at its students. The seventies may have been something of a grind, historically and politically speaking, but weird clothing styles and morphing social roles could not dampen youthful exuberance and expectation. Take for example, the "rat pack," as a gang of four guys who purloined Sinatra and pals' moniker and made their way. Tom Landrum, who reminds everyone his undergraduate degree was in history (72), got his master's in public relations (87) from Grady. Even before, he was palling with the likes of Rex Grannum, Joe Belew, and Charlie Hayslett, an irrepressible group that would go on to careers of impressive achievement.

Landrum retired at the end of the 2013-14 academic year as UGA's Senior Vice President for External Relations and had previously served Presidents Davison and Knapp as a communications specialist. Landrum's appreciation for his graduate mentor, Spencer Tinkham, resulted in generous gifts to support the work of Dr. Tinkham and his students. He also does advanced seminars for Grady's best and brightest.

Rex Grannum went to Washington with the Carter administration and soon got on with ABC News where he landed in its London Bureau for much of the eighties before taking charge of its Atlanta bureau and later moving into private consulting with Prism Public Relations in D.C. Joe Belew also went to Washington where he became head of the Consumer Bankers Association. His sudden and untimely death in 2009 at age fifty-nine filled a D.C. church with mourners; such was his infectious personality and genius. He was like so many who leave Athens—it never left him. The week before his passing, this writer was in a local haberdashery where they were packing a rack of suits to be sent to his D.C. address. A clerk exclaimed, "What a great guy!" Finally, Charlie Hayslett, who as a student was married with children, working and struggling to get through, found company in this band of brothers. Hayslett has his own agency in Atlanta specializing in a broad range of communications services to over a hundred clients, many of them Atlanta's top brands. He has generously connected the college's master's program in health journalism with the Healthcare Georgia Foundation, a mutually profitable relationship that continues.

Swann Seiler (ABJ 78) must be included here too. Of the Seiler family that furnishes the Uga Mascot for UGA, Swann has served as President of

**ABOVE:** Tom Landrum, so cool. *Grady College Archives, courtesy Tom Landrum*; **MIDDLE:** Rex Grannum, a little more serious than customary. *Grady College Archives*; **BELOW:** Joe Belew, "great guy." *1972* ***Pandora***

**ABOVE LEFT:** Charlie Hayslett rounds out the "Rat Pack." **ABOVE RIGHT:** Swann Seiler with Dean's Medal, flanked by Tony Barnhart and her dad, Georgia legend Sonny Seiler. **BELOW:** Pulitzer Prize-winning Deborah Blum talks with students under a flowering dogwood. *Grady College Archives*

the National Alumni Association and Chair of the Grady Board of Trust. She is also a Trustee of the UGA Foundation (formerly Arch) and a Dean's Medalist of the college. During Cutlip's tenure, she greatly admired his attentiveness to students and his connections to university leadership and has encouraged all subsequent deans in that respect. In a 2001 interview, she was asked who, outside family, influenced her professional career most. Without a blink, it was Scott Cutlip. "He actually spent a great deal of time with me," she said, "and actually encouraged me to major in public relations rather than broadcasting." Calling him "one of the true giants in the field," she continued, "He passed away last year and I miss him."[153]

Then there are the Deborah's: Blum (ABJ 76), Norville (ABJ 79), and Roberts (ABJ 82). Blum is a renowned science writer, having won a Pulitzer in 1992 for a series she did on primate research while at the *Sacramento Bee*. That series became *The Monkey Wars*, published by Oxford University Press in 1994. Her interest in literary journalism has led to three other books, among them *The Poisoner's Handbook: Murder and the Birth of Forensic Medicine in the Jazz Age* (Penguin, 2010). That book made her a contributor to the Nieman Story Board and distinguished journals such as *Lapham's Quarterly*. A past president of the National Science Writers Association, Blum holds a distinguished professorship at the University of Wisconsin, where she also received a master's degree in science writing in 1982. In March 2010 she was back at Grady talking about *The Poisoner's Handbook* before a totally engrossed audience.

Norville and Roberts are both famous in the world of television. Norville, a Dalton native, made her way to NBC where she hosted *Today* and substitute-anchored the *NBC Nightly News* and the weekend *CBS Evening News*. Since 1995 she has been host of the syndicated *Inside Edition*. Norville has received two Emmy Awards, the first for covering the democratic uprising in Romania for NBC News and the second with CBS's *48 Hours*, for coverage of flooding on the Mississippi River. Roberts, from Perry, Georgia, started as a local television reporter in Columbus, Georgia, then Knoxville, Tennessee, and in Orlando, where she covered NASA. By 1990 she was in New York at NBC serving as a correspondent for *Dateline NBC*. She went to ABC in 1995 as a correspondent for *20/20* and as substitute anchor for *World News Tonight* and *Good Morning America*. She also has won two Emmy Awards and a Clarion award for coverage of abuse in the Amish community. Roberts is married to Al Roker and lives in Manhattan. She and Norville remain close to Grady and among numerous other contributions, co-hosted the inaugural Fellowship Gala Tribute Evening in 2008.

Donald A. Perry (ABJ 74) was the kind of person about whom it could truly be said, if you had him as a friend, you did not need but one. He grew up south of Valdosta on the Georgia side of that great dividing line that separates the Empire State from the Evil Empire. Fortunately for Grady, Don was always on the right side. At the time of his untimely death in 2012, he was head of communications for Chick-fil-A, a trustee of the UGA Foundation, a tireless board member for Grady, and a marvelous counselor to its deans.

**ABOVE:** Deborah Roberts and Deborah Norville with Mr. Grady at 2008 Inaugural Fellowship Gala. **BELOW:** Deborah Roberts gives University's 2006 Hunter-Homes Lecture before joining students at Grady. Professor Dwight Brooks, back row, right *Grady College Archives*

His services filled a 1000-seat church and annex and another 1000 gathered around screens in the atrium of the Chick-fil-A Headquarters. Don's take-away as a student was the writing course he took from Professor Margaret Johnston. "I believe," he said, "that Grady will be at its best in the next 100 years preparing all categories of graduates as effective writers." No truer words from an everlasting friend.

The seventies also gave the college Bruce Finland (ABJ 74) and Glen Wilson Finland (ABJ 74). Sitting across from her in a broadcasting class, Bruce was smitten and still is, for good reason. They, too, went to Washington, he as an entrepreneur in e-business before anyone knew to talk about electronic networking as a discrete enterprise zone. His first application was in e-learning. He later sold it, and remains at home in the private entrepreneurial sector. He even drew up a forward-looking business plan for the college to get into the arena of online learning long before MOOCS became talk of the town. Glen has followed her passion—writing. She received an M.F.A. in Creative Writing from American University, where she also teaches. It was in a Broadcast News Writing class that Bruce's "extraordinary teacher," Bill Martin, would launch him on a "lifelong career," and "the sweet, smart, beautiful, captivating girl sitting next to me in class would become my partner for the next 35 years"—and still counting.

**ABOVE:** Don Perry works with a student.
**BELOW:** Bruce and Glen Finland with Coach Dooley at 2012 Fellowship Gala *Grady College Archives*

Glen Finland's recent highly acclaimed book, *Next Stop*, about her family and autism, was so compelling that she received a Dean's Medal during the 2012-13 academic year, in what the college styled The Year of the Story. Also honored and recognized that year were other writers and graduates of the seventies and early eighties, Chris Dixon's *Ghost Wave*, Steve Sears's *The Indomitable Investor*, Sam Starnes latest novel *Fall Line* and others. Grady has always been about writing, something that J. Thomas Russell foregrounded on becoming dean in 1983. Grady even got a National Champion writer out of the class of '82. Justin Gillis from Vidalia was so named by the William Randolph Hearst competition. Justin went on to a brilliant career at the *New York Times*, where, as environmental reporter, he won special acclaim for his coverage of the 2010 BP Gulf oil spill.

**ABOVE LEFT:** Steve Sears with mentor Conrad Fink. **ABOVE RIGHT:** Justin Gillis, Hearst Champion Writer, 1982. **BELOW:** Brenda Hampton with Grady Ambassador Christina Jones. *Grady College Archives*

Brenda Hampton (ABJ 72) was born to be the maven of television storytelling. After all, her father was a television repairman who took her on Atlanta house calls. Well, he was also an electrical engineer for AT&T, but which job impressed her more? Today she is the most successful producer in the history of Warner Brothers Television. If her only contribution had been creator, writer, and producer for "7th Heaven," eleven seasons with seven million viewers per episode would have justified her seat on the front row, but add to that "Fat Actress," and "The Secret Life of the American Teenager," among others and you begin to get the picture. A Fellow of the Grady College, her accessibility and creative input has been lavished on Grady deans. With her three adopted children, she selects a state each year and off they go in the SUV, on the road again, a blithe spirit indeed.

## FINAL SCENE

This chapter closes both with a remarkably unattractive exchange between Cutlip and Agee but with a coda for perspective. Agee had gotten a pretty good parachute on stepping down: current salary; reduced teaching load compared with other faculty in rank; a half year's leave to the University of Texas; and above all, a secretary. When Cutlip sought to terminate the secretarial part of the arrangement five years later, Agee resisted, even reminding Cutlip of a letter from Pelletier outlining the original agreement.[154] Cutlip rightly retorted that no such agreement is forever, but it was the tone.

When anyone asserts the need for frankness and candor, they are about to unload, and Cutlip did. The most cutting of all, "When you were compelled to resign the deanship," he wrote, "you were more than amply rewarded for your six years in this office, particularly in view of all the difficulties you had." Then, "Quite frankly, Warren, I think you would greatly lessen faculty resentment of your rather cushy situation if you pulled your full share of the teaching load and did not expect perks other faculty members don't have."[155] So sad, but think what the college accomplished in both tenures. Agee and Cutlip knew what needed to be done. Their plans were good. Their personalities complicated things. Yet faculty, staff, students, alumni and friends, The College, saved them, as did the larger university cushion them from folly.

There is always a coda, and in this instance it begins with the deaths a day apart in June 2005 of Agee and Vernon Stone, two of the "four stars" brought to Grady in the seventies. Stone, whose lawsuit over compensation clouded his tenure at Georgia, went on to direct the School of Journalism at Southern Illinois University for eight years and retired as professor emeritus from Missouri in 1992. He is remembered fondly and well in the world of broadcast journalism. He served as director of research for the Radio-TV News Directors Association for twenty-two years and is credited especially for his contributions to the advancement of women and minorities in that arena. In a beautiful tribute by Jill Geisler of the Poynter Institute, titled "What we measure, what we value," she credited his research for changing the demographic landscape of broadcast news, and Grady's own Lee Becker, who has done so much to advance that type of research through the Cox Center's annual surveys, joined a program at AEJMC in 1998 that presented Stone the Distinguished Broadcast Journalism Educator Award, a real punctuation mark for his career.

Warren Agee, who passed away on June 14, 2005, the day before Stone's passing, was remembered by Ernie Hynds as a real "gentleman and scholar." Tom Russell described him as a "very kind hearted, nice person" and incredibly devoted to his job, "often seven days a week—always in coat and tie."[156] It may be that as Agee said, "I came at the wrong time." It remained for a student in those days to sum it up best. Steve Oney (ABJ 79) who wrote the book on Leo Frank cited in the foreword, appreciated Agee for bringing writers-in-residence to the faculty—Paul Hemphill in 1973, Bill Hedgepeth, the year after. Oney's take on Agee was that "he didn't want to make waves, and the early 70's—a more restive time on the Georgia campus than the late 60's—was all about making waves. Agee would have been a good dean in the late 50's," Oney believed, then continued, "In fairness to Agee, some of the faculty members—and a lot of the students—were generally insubordinate."[157] Be that as it may, Agee brought with him outstanding credentials and an extraordinarily well thought out plan for the future.

Scott Cutlip, who died of cancer in Madison, Wisconsin, on August 18, 2000 at age 85, received high acclaim and great respect from public relations educational and professional associations. It is almost impossible to think of a significant award that was not bestowed on him. He is remembered affectionately and well by many, even those who concede his abrasive side. Jim Minter, editor of *The Atlanta Journal-Constitution*, liked him because he likes "characters." Friends at the Athens Country Club liked him for much the same reason, and for sure, President Davison embraced him. Ruthann Lariscy and Spencer Tinkham said he could be "gracious and kind" in finding support for faculty research. Tinkham remembers first hearing the phrase "a widow's mite" when Cutlip apologized for not obtaining as much funding as he had hoped. Karen Miller Russell, recalls her days as a graduate assistant of Cutlip's at Wisconsin in the early nineties. Cutlip went out of his way to get

**LEFT:** Ruthann Lariscy and Spencer Tinkham. **RIGHT:** Karen Russell with one of her books, *The Voice of Business*, 1994. *Grady College Archives*

Scott Cutlip and Bill Lee with symposium co-director Albert Pearson, Dean Rusk, and law dean Ralph Bearid. *Courtesy of William E. Lee*

funding for her research from PR legend Harold Burson, and succeeded. Russell was grateful for the helping hand.[158]

Although Dr. Russell may have been the last faculty member Cutlip influenced to come to Grady, it remained for Bill Lee, who was among the first in 1977, to sum it up. Lee is a highly acclaimed scholar in the law of mass communications and a much-respected teacher. No student ever forgets his high expectations of them or his way of standing and delivering in the classroom. He, along with Kent Middleton, also recruited to UGA by Cutlip in 1980, publish a highly influential textbook, *The Law of Public Communication*, now in its ninth edition. Lee remembers especially his first day on campus. Cutlip took him to lunch with former Secretary of State Dean Rusk, then on the faculty of the UGA Law School. On one wall of Rusk's office was a signed Norman Rockwell portrait of JFK, on the other, one of Lyndon Johnson, the two presidents he served. At lunch they hatched a proposal for a First Amendment Symposium, a relationship between law and journalism that radiates out to this day. Lee who described Cutlip as most knew him, "blustery, larger-than-life, who bellowed," is still grateful for this nudge toward the career direction, law, he ultimately took. This too should be remembered.[159]

# 5 J. THOMAS RUSSELL COMPLETES THE CENTURY

BORN IN FLORENCE, ALABAMA, IN 1941, TOM RUSSELL GREW UP IN ATLANTA. After attending Florida Southern, a Methodist school in Lakeland, Florida, for one year, he reversed course and made his way to Athens and the Grady School. Receiving his ABJ in 1963, he completed a master's in Advertising at the University of Illinois, and his Ph.D. there in 1969, thus punching his ticket on what in the college is now called the Illinois Railroad. After acquiring some experience in Atlanta on the business side of advertising, he joined the Grady faculty in 1966 and by 1979 obtained the rank of full professor. He served stints as assistant dean for both Agee and Cutlip, but stepped away from that role in 1979 to become sequence head in Advertising. When Cutlip announced his decision to step down from the deanship, and following a comprehensive search, the college found its best option was at hand, and so Tom Russell became Dean Russell. He held that position for the next seventeen years, closing out the century as the second longest serving dean in Grady's history. (Sanford also led the school for seventeen years, 1915-32, but as director, never dean, and with supra appointments as president and chancellor.)

Russell was among the faculty's most accomplished researchers and edited the *Journal of Advertising* from the college. Grady was also home to the *Journal of Broadcasting* and another journal in critical studies. Clearly its research reputation was burgeoning. When Agee became dean, only twelve of thirty-six faculty members held a Ph.D. In Russell's first year that number had swelled to twenty-six of forty-one, with one other Ed.D. Also, Russell's first year was the college's first for offering a doctoral degree with the original two students increasing to seven in the second year. This academic maturation accounts for some of the low faculty tolerance for imperious administration.

Dean Tom Russell. *Grady College Archives*

In Russell's first year, the surest sign that the seventies were in the rearview was the final episode of M.A.S.H. To be sure there were earlier signs, for one, The Reagan Revolution. When Reagan launched his 1980 campaign on August 3 at the Neshoba County Fair near Philadelphia, Mississippi, he made it both symbolically and abundantly clear that he intended to make good on the "southern strategy" that Nixon embarked on in 1968 and that Reagan had nearly perfected in his primary run against Gerald Ford in 1976. Despite Reagan's occasional nods to FDR, he intended no New Deal in his revolution. The era of "welfare queens," to which he alluded and supporters in his camp trumpeted, was over. Compared to Jimmy Carter's national "malaise," Reagan was upbeat about America as a "city upon a hill," a reference to the beacon the Puritans intended of their Bay Colony. American exceptionalism was back. Unlike Carter, Reagan was easy to like and in that respect truly like FDR. In Georgia, Democrats George Busbee and Joe Frank Harris were governors during the eighties, and their Lieutenant Governor was Zell Miller, who as governor in the nineties, would play a big role in higher education by establishing the HOPE Scholarship program. Still, the tide was running "red" in Georgia politics and would soon enough extend beyond presidential elections to the Republican Party's current super majorities.

Interestingly, the last significant Democratic vote-getter in Georgia was a Grady graduate. From Bainbridge, Georgia, Lera Catherine "Cathy" Cox (ABJ 80), started in newspapers, *Gainesville Times* and hometown *Bainbridge Post-Search Light*, but soon turned to law and politics, receiving her law degree from Mercer. First a state representative from her home district, then two terms as

Secretary of State (first woman to hold the position) where she pursued reforms that in her second run for office in 2002 gave her the largest Democratic vote-majority at 61 percent. Her run for governor in 2006 resulted in a primary loss, but by then no Democrat was going to win. The last Democratic governor would be Roy Barnes, a one-term governor, 1999-2003, who, among other reasons for losing his last election, incurred intense opposition for supporting removal of the Confederate battle emblem from the state flag. Still, Cox was the last credible candidate to become not only the last Democrat but also the first woman governor of Georgia. She is now President of Young Harris College, and was last seen by this writer at a Chick-fil-A Foundation board meeting, where Jay Smith, past president of Atlanta Newspapers, Inc. and Vince Dooley were also present.

Cathy Cox, President Young Harris College. *Courtesy Cathy Cox*

Moreover, the religious right was asserting itself. The social liberalism of the sixties and seventies (some would say hedonism) was coming under increasing attack. The political right began using the term "political correctness" to denote (a) people who, among other things, felt that African Americans should be called whatever they wanted to be called; for example, African Americans not blacks, and (b) more generally, anyone who asserted a liberal point of view, for example, support for affirmative action and quotas loosely defined. All of which started to have consequences for higher education, which was viewed as a bastion of liberal thought, and to some extent it was. Agee was the first dean to call for increased minority enrollment and hiring, and Cutlip was the first to hire an African American on the faculty, Paula M. Poindexter, although she stayed only one year before leaving to take an industry position in public opinion research for the *Los Angeles Times*. Still, educators wondered how they could achieve progress on diversity without counting heads; i.e. quotas, not as rigid formulas but as a way of measuring progress and developing goals. Because Republicans had held the White House for all but four years from 1969-1993, the courts began a rightward turn against affirmative action, thereby making policy assertions, if not action, on that front more difficult if not impossible.

One thing UGA really had going for it in the eighties was football, the Herschel Walker era, a national title (1980) and three consecutive SEC championships to boot, but even that soured a year later with the infamous Jan Kemp (ABJ 70) case. In 1986 a jury finally determined she had indeed been fired for protesting academic fraud for nine football players in 1981. Of course, the case was more complicated, but it was hard to get beyond the headlines. President Davison seemed forced to step down after a 19-year run. The Regents did not actually fire him, just delayed his annual appointment, upon which he resigned in pique.[160] Complicating matters for the college was the general knowledge that Scott Cutlip was among a small inner circle of advisors for Davison, his "kitchen cabinet," who had advised the president to "stonewall" Kemp,[161] and indeed Cutlip held the title of Special Consultant to the President. If so, it was truly unfortunate.[162]

Cutlip could not let it go. Two months after the verdict he lit into old friend Karl Meyer, editorial page editor for the *New York Times*, blistering a front page story by Dudley Clendinen that Cutlip considered "biased to one side" and unfair to Davison. Cutlip had known Meyer at Wisconsin and said things in Wisconsin athletics had been every bit as bad as at Georgia, even worse. Cutlip conceded college athletics generally were out of control but said Davison was a victim of his subordinates.[163] In another year Clendinen would be in Atlanta, joining Bill Kovach in a shakeup at the *Atlanta Journal-Constitution*.

While Cutlip fenced for Davison, the UGA and Grady faculties engaged the more serious implications of the case. George Octavius Marshall (ABJ 42), highly regarded member of the English Department and local leader of the American Association of University Professors, spearheaded a University Council effort to weigh in on next steps to find ways forward.[164] In a memorandum to the Journalism faculty, Kent Middleton, then in his sixth year and already president of the University Council, urged participation in meaningful debate and support for Council's "efforts to investigate issues stemming from the trial." He said that Davison's resignation made it more, not less imperative for that kind of engagement and that the *Red & Black* planned to run a series as did the *Banner-Herald.* [165] One other positive outcome was that two Grady graduates, Randall Savage (ABJ 72) and Jackie Crosby (ABJ 83) won a Pulitzer Prize for their stories in the *Macon Telegraph and News* that dealt with the problems surrounding college athletes and their academic work or want thereof.

Ironically, over ten years later, Cutlip would be quoted as saying, "Fred [Davison] had an intense dislike for media . . . and he was supported by people supporting that dislike." Cutlip enumerated among them "the president's wife and secretary," and, in particular, one of his [Cutlip's] own golfing buddies, Ralph Beaird, then dean of the law school, among those who harbored "an intense hatred of the media." Left out by Cutlip was his own subordination to Davison that involved bullying *Red & Black* and *Pandora* editors and his intercessions with media on behalf of the inaccessible president, proof that Cutlip knew better but, co-opted, failed to do better. Today one recoils at how artless and awful the messaging was by attorneys for the state and between and among principals for the university (to read it is to become sickened). As Grady Fellow Tom Landrum put it, a sour relationship with media invariably pre-dates a "crisis." If one has no "proactive [system] with the press in good times," it will not happen in bad. Thus Davison and those who were responsible to him were left twisting in the breeze of recriminations, each against the others. It was as bad as it gets, and a Grady dean could not wash his hands.[166]

Another irony for Grady was that only six months before the university fudged for nine football players in 1981, nine Grady students had confessed to cheating. The difference was Grady took steps. The students were in a journalism course and assigned to survey Athenians on inflation, crime, taxes and "other issues of the day," then to report on it. It was an upper division class. The "Grady nine" filled in the questionnaire without actually conducting the interviews, their only excuse being "it was only a class assignment." The *Red & Black* editor-in-chief, Brian O'Shea, enlarged the "nine" to a more general problem of degradation in education.[167] It was yet another example of *R&B* journalism discomfiting the administration, only now it was Dean Cutlip's watch. The further irony was that the teacher-of-record for the survey was Paula Poindexter, Grady's first African-American faculty member. She would leave by the end of the academic year, but for an opportunity in industry research, not for fingering shame. After ten years at *The Los Angeles Times*, she returned to academe at the University of Texas and recently served a term as President of the Association for Education in Journalism and Mass Communication Education.

The 1984-85 academic year saw a strengthening of longstanding ties to the University of Illinois in the field of advertising with the announcements that Drs. Karen King and Peggy Kreshel would join the faculty in fall and spring of the coming year. Already Drs. Frazier Moore, Tom Russell, Len Reid, Dean Krugman and Spencer Tinkham earned their credentials there. Moreover, Professor James W. Carey, Dean of the College of Communications at Illinois, was on campus during the Winter Quarter as a Distinguished Visiting Bicentennial Lecturer, honoring the 200th year of the university's chartering. Long one of the nation's leading thinkers about communication theory and practice, his lecture, "The Struggle of the Written (and the Spoken) Word," keynoted the 1985 meeting of the Georgia Press Association Institute. The Illinois Railroad indeed. 1985 also gave evidence of a continuing struggle for the written word in its News-Editorial Sequence. The quest for enrollments in that area was not new but certainly intensified that year as faculty sought to understand why and to develop a recruitment effort to overcome low demand, a pattern that continues to the present day. A preliminary finding was "that many students see print media as unexciting places to work, and with limited long-term economic outlook."[168] Although little was new in that finding, it did prompt more effort to counter what some perceived as a trend. Underwritten by a $10,000 grant from the *AJC*, faculty spread out over the state, visiting newsrooms, doing high school workshops, and developing young alumni groups to promote interest. Although the digital revolution has added more fuel to that fire, writing across all media and especially in the new applications of social media remains a core Grady commitment.

Also in 1985, the contours of Grady's contributions to international studies began to take definite shape. Warren Agee received a second Fulbright for work concerning the press in Portugal. Al Hester extended his work with the U.S. Information Agency in Tunisia, directing a workshop to improve writing and editing among Third World journalists. Hester wrote and published a *Handbook for Third World Journalists* that with USIA support received wide distribution. Additionally, John English directed three workshops on writing and editing in Kuala Lumpur, Malaysia. By 1986 Hester's work in Nigeria, Zambia, Lesotho and Malta was done under the official heading of the college's Center for International Communications Training and Research. (The center had been approved in 1985.) Roland Page in AdPR was a contributor, as was Kent Middleton in Journalism. The advent of what would become in 1990 the Cox Center was well underway.

July 1, 1988, was a date to remember as the school became a college, with a full complement of degree programs and academic departments (no longer sequences) in Journalism, Broadcasting, and Advertising-Public Relations. Also the college had just received a re-accreditation report that highly complimented all its academic and professional programs. The site team reported favorably on all twelve standards. By the end of the eighties the departments and programs of the college had attained the essential configuration that would carry it for the last quartile of its first 100 years. Institutes

Left to right, David E. Easterly, president of Atlanta Newspapers, Inc., Al Hester, journalism sequence head, Dean Russell, and Jim Minter, editor *AJC*, 1985. *Grady College Archives*

and centers would be added but core programming and indeed much of its faculty, in place in 1988, would resemble that of 2015. All deans before and after Russell joined in his view that the disciplines of communication had more in common than not; thus communications being more than catch-all.

## ATLANTA AS LABORATORY

As the college made its turn to current form in the years 1986-88, there was a back story burning in Atlanta that added spice. His name was Bill Kovach. Like Ralph McGill he was an East Tennessee boy-made-good. He headed *The New York Times* Washington Bureau when the Cox family (some said the two-sister owners, some say its publisher Jay Smith) decided a change needed to be made in Atlanta. In fact, it was Garner Anthony, husband of Barbara Cox, successor to Jim Cox, Jr., as family czar. Some believed the *AJC* was a relic of Henry Grady's time, when boosterism, especially about the business community, caused the newspaper to turn a blind eye to social ills emerging from segregation and corporatism. Those who thought that way decided Atlanta needed not a paper of record but one of consequence. So out went Jim Minter (ABJ 51) and with him a tolerance for Lewis Grizzard-style, humorous southern cover-up, or so some thinking went. "If you don't like the South, Delta is ready when you are," chuckled Grizzard. In came Kovach to change things.

Ownership did have concerns about the paper's direction and reputation and brought in Thomas "Tom" Winship, a highly respected journalist who had done wonders with the *Boston Globe.* It was Winship who said they should go after Kovach and needed to strike quickly because Kovach was already looking to make a change. (Winship had talked with Phil Gailey [ABJ 66], then with the Washington Bureau, and Mary McGrory of the *Post*, over drinks, who advised that having been passed over for the executive editor position at the *NYT*, Kovach indeed was looking to move.)[169] His arrival in December 1986, saw the departure not only of Minter but also eventually Bill Shipp, intrepid 1953 *Red & Black* editor and much admired political columnist, albeit too liberal for many readers. Yet what made the *Atlanta Constitution* singular was liberal commentary combined with more conservative reporting, a progressive combination that was just right for ambitious Atlanta.

Kovach was charismatic and determined to turn the *AJC* into a version of *The New York Times*—long-form investigative reporting and no *USA Today* flash and dash. He brought with him Wendell "Sonny" Rawls, Jr. and James Dudley Clendinen, two east Tennesseans, each *New York Times* prodigies and each *New York Times* credentialed; but the threesome were also and truly John Siegenthaler protégés. Rawls and Kovach were native east Tennesseans, and Clendinen, although from a *Tampa Tribune* family, was Vanderbilt educated. Kovach got what he, and perhaps ownership, wanted—two Pulitzers, one for investigative reporting on discriminatory lending practices by Atlanta Banks with respect to minorities, "red-lining," and another by recent arrival from Charlotte and political cartoonist Doug Marlette. There would be another four nominations. It was breath-taking and job-ending, but not for the reasons most often ascribed.

Bill Kovach. *Courtesy* ***Atlanta Journal-Constitution***

The story-line went this way. When Jay Smith, said, "You're fired," after only weeks before praising Kovach for coverage of the Democratic Party Convention held in Atlanta, cognoscenti cried foul. (This convention is remembered for the longest, most boring nominating speech ever by none other than Bill Clinton. It was also the convention that nominated the lack-luster Michael Dukakis.) Those crying loudest said, "Pressure from the Atlanta business community." Novelist Pat Conroy and his friends at Atlanta's Old New York Book Shop on Piedmont Road were in full throat. Conroy, along with Sonny Rawls, assistant managing editor for news under Kovach, even wrote a screenplay idealizing Kovach and castigating his detractors as refugees from a New South parade, or worse still, Midwestern Babbits. Conroy imagined Robert Redford playing Kovach (Kovach was and is very good-looking), a reprise as it were of "Absence of Malice," only Redford in for Newman. Warner Brothers acquired the rights to "Above the Fold" but never produced it.[170]

Of course ownership and publisher denied it. Jay Smith, president of Atlanta Newspapers, Inc. (effectively publisher), said repeatedly that he simply no longer trusted him, and interestingly Kovach never said it was pressure from the business community, although he left sufficient room for his admirers to continue the fiction, if such it were. Jay Smith, in fact and on request of the Kovach team, played an active role in the prize-winning story on "red-lining," even to keeping it on point. Moreover, he and ownership enabled the Kovach newsroom to grow from approximately 350 staffers to 450. So clearly other issues existed; for example, questions about management; details such as circulation that an editor, Kovach, should have understood and did not; and to management style, some finding Sonny Rawls more an enforcer than an enabler. So, when twenty-three months into the job, Smith told Kovach that Rawls would have to go, Kovach resigned rather than accept the mandate, a principled reaction, and Smith accepted. In the end, Kovach departed for the Nieman Fellowship program at Harvard, where he eventually became its curator. Ron Martin who followed him at the *AJC* was indeed out of the Gannett *USA Today* School, but he got good marks from seasoned *AJC* reporters. Even an examination in the *American Journalism Review* determined there was more sound than fury in all the hullabaloo, and more than a few said that Kovach simply tendered his resignation one too many times.[171]

Rawls actually stayed on another nine months, raising at least some question about his failure to embrace the principle his friend Kovach had stood on; and Jay Smith made an interesting side-trip to California, his purpose to visit Robert Redford. At some point the screenplay wound up in Redford's hands, whether put there by WB or Conroy is not known. Fellow Atlantan Jane Fonda arranged Smith's introduction. Smith reported Redford as "courteous but his questions very direct." Smith's mission was to explain that the villain in the screenplay was the son of a Cincinnati car salesman,

Jay Smith. *Grady College Archives, UGA Photographic Services*

himself, and not family heir Jim Cox Kennedy, who in 1988 had just succeeded his stepfather, Garner Anthony, as Chairman and CEO of Cox Enterprises.[172] No evidence suggests that the visit influenced Warner Brothers not to produce, but it is more evidence that the Cox family let journalists run journalism. Conroy would soon move to San Francisco to escape the "banality" of Atlanta newspapers. By then Reg Murphy, former editor of the *Constitution,* and while such a kidnap victim (but that is another story), was at the *Examiner*. Proof, perhaps, that "you can run but you can't hide."

The Kovach episode was reprise of another sort also. Since 1950, when Cox acquired the *Constitution* and thereby both Atlanta's major papers, they were always whipsawed from right and left. For most Georgians, at least those of a conservative bent and that was most whites and certainly those outside the I-285 beltway and in rural Georgia, they were the "lying Atlanta newspapers." For people of a more liberal or progressive bent, like Conroy, the string of liberal editors, McGill, Patterson, et al., were undercut by ownership that reflected its Dayton, Ohio roots. They offer Gene Patterson's resignation in 1968 as case in point; the precipitating issue being coverage of a Georgia Power rate increase, which Patterson, it is said, believed publisher Jack Tarver muzzled in the interest of business. Tarver had a different account of course, and Patterson's own message to staff about stepping down ruled out Tarver as having influenced the "rate" story or being other than supportive in his role as editor. Patterson's reasons may have been more personal.[173] In any event, the Kovach case echoed a familiar theme for those Atlantans who wanted more progressivism and thought they got less. And while it is true that the managerial direction of people like Tarver and later Jim Minter was more conservatively inclined, each took pride in the editorial leadership from the likes of McGill and Patterson and believed themselves to be its defenders, critics notwithstanding.[174] In fact they were.[175]

The story has a footnote, not an endnote. The column that precipitated the rupture between Patterson and Tarver was written by B. J. Phillips, a UGA and Grady student from 1963 to 1967. Although she never graduated, she did write a letter to Gene Patterson that so impressed him that he decided the paper needed a "youth columnist," which it did in part because of Patterson's support for the Vietnam War and the alienating effect it was having on students. Like so many others who figured prominently in Grady's history, Drewry foremost, she was a graduate of Griffin High School. Following the rupture she, like Patterson, went to *The Washington Post* and on to a high-profile career which included stops at *Time* magazine and the *Philadelphia Inquirer*. Patterson had reached for youth before. Soon after becoming executive editor at the *Constitution*, he hired a fresh-faced reporter from Biloxi, Mississippi, Jack Nelson, who instantly took the lead in the newsroom and before leaving Atlanta to become longtime Washington Bureau Chief for *The Los Angeles Times*, won a Pulitzer for investigative reporting. B. J. would be family spokesperson at Patterson's memorial service, and Patterson was at his eloquent best in eulogizing Nelson in 2009.[176]

Gene Patterson addresses Atlanta History Society program on Ralph McGill, 1988. *Courtesy* ***Atlanta Journal-Constitution***

The *Atlanta Constitution* has played a huge role in the life of Atlanta, the state, the region, and nation. It is not and should never be the *New York Times*, the ultimate newspaper of consequence [if there is one] in journalism. The *Constitution* has challenged and aggravated its readers with its liberal/progressive lean from the time of Henry Grady. Ralph McGill, the ultimate mid-century liberal columnist, had no greater supporters than James Middleton Cox, 1920 presidential candidate, a true liberal Democrat, and publisher Jack Tarver, who "steadied the soapbox" for McGill's insistent, persistent, persuasive efforts to move both himself and his region forward. Tarver ran the show from the mid-fifties to the mid-seventies. His caustic, barbed attempts to combine humor with administrative directives rankled and irritated unnecessarily, but as Bill Shipp said, had he not been trying to make "margins" (profits) and been thrown into the newsroom, "he would have been the most liberal of all." Tarver was devoted to McGill and in truth McGill to him, even when Gene Patterson, who had a son-to-father relationship with McGill, resigned. When liberals wanted to blame Patterson's departure on ideological differences with Tarver, McGill and indeed Patterson himself did not accept that interpretation, but that legend lived on in the minds of Atlanta's more progressive, yes liberal, partisans.

(In the end, the crucial breakup occurred when Cox's Dayton operations came South, moving headquarters in the late seventies to Atlanta. Garner Anthony, who succeeded Jim Cox, Jr., wanted to move away from the

Ralph McGill and Jack Tarver at a Georgia Press Institute gathering ca. 1950. *Hargrett Rare Books and Manuscript Library*

*Constitution's* southern identity and in the effort made it what it never was, a pale reflection of the *New York Times.* If one takes that mix and compounds it with personalities, pain is the result; but few who have served the *Constitution* and left have failed to prosper in other ways and in other vineyards. From Grady's time to the present, it has been one of the South's most important papers of record and consequence.)

In the wake of the Kovach episode, the regional division of the *New York Times* did try to make inroads into Atlanta by acquiring first the *Gwinnett Daily News* and then later an attempt on the *Marietta Daily Journal*, all in an effort to take burgeoning North Atlanta away from Cox.[177] The venture failed, ultimately costing the *Times* a bunch, but it did provide one enterprising Grady faculty member a case study. Conrad Fink, he of the signature bushy eyebrows and iconic member of the journalism faculty, a former Vice President of AP News and senior executive at Park Communications, Fink was inimitable and indefatigable. In this instance, he proved, as he did with some dozen books, that research is not reserved for Ph.D.'s alone but can be the provenance of leading professionals as well.

The case study he undertook for the Poynter Institute also underscored what has always been true for the Grady College, that being seventy miles from a major media market while enjoying an idyllic setting in Athens is a huge plus for journalism and mass communication education—the best of both worlds. The *New York Times* attempt on North Atlanta also foreshadowed the *AJC's* move from Marietta Street in downtown Atlanta to Dunwoody, just north of the perimeter, in 2010. Although justified in part by the forced economies of the digital revolution, many speculated that Atlanta's suburban and white middle class was now well north of downtown. (This writer spent the 1986-87 academic year at Georgia State University, visited with Kovach and other players, and knew that Atlanta's population center was indeed well north of downtown. Even in that day, Jim Minter openly expressed the view that a move was necessary. Perhaps the most interesting fact is that it did not come until 2010, again with liberals bemoaning the racial divide it underscored. Of course, pragmatists would say a newspaper must follow its readers.)

## COX AND GRADY

The relationship between Cox and the Grady College has been most interesting and beneficial. Gradyites have played important roles in Cox Enterprises: Harold H. Martin, Gene Patterson, Aubrey Morris, Jim Minter, Bill Ray, Dennis Berry and current *AJC* publisher Amy Glennon come readily to mind. With its Cox Center for International Training and Research in Journalism and Mass Communication and the Cox Institute for Newspaper Management Studies (now Journalism, Innovation, Management and Leadership), the relationship is signature. This major development came about in 1990, when the James M. Cox Jr. Foundation, through his widow (he died in 1974) found great value in Grady's international work and its long suit in newspaper and media management. The widow, Betty Gage Holland, directed significant resources to the college. Holland was more than a benefactor, she was a participant in the programs she supported and a loving friend of all involved. The college redesigned the garden in front of the Journalism Building and named it for her in 1998. The college also presents annually the Betty Gage Holland Award, a $1,000 prize for a student journalist with an additional $1,000 to the publication in which that student's work appears. At her passing, Conrad Fink said, ". . . she never claimed credit, never pushed into the public acclaim that could have been hers. That, I always thought, was a very real manifestation of principle, a selfless service to a higher ideal. The wider world never will know of her goodness in this, but we will."[178]

The gift did not come in the form of endowment but through a donor-advised relationship that Ms. Holland established between the college and the foundation; to wit, $300,000 would be set aside annually to support what became the Cox Center and the Cox Institute. Ms. Holland had come to admire very much the work of Al Hester (international) and Conrad Fink (management studies) and accordingly directed that annual gifts of $150,000 each support their work. The proviso was that it be continued annually at the satisfaction of the principals in the foundation, Ms. Holland and the two daughters of James M. Cox, Jr. by a previous marriage, daughters who very much mirrored

Betty Gage Holland. *Grady College Archives*

their step-mother in manner and spirit of service. There was a stipulation that if the foundation wished to move in other directions, the Cox Center and Cox Institute would be given a three-year grace period before termination. Al Hester remembers vividly a call from Dean Russell during Christmas break, reporting that Larry B. Hooks, an attorney representing Holland's philanthropic interests, wanted a proposal "and quickly." Hester, an experienced grant writer, said yes, and over the holidays proposals for the Center and from Fink for the Institute reached Hooks' desk and won quick approval.[179]

That beneficence was huge in 1990, the equivalent of $540,000 today, and annually. Tom Russell declared it a "game changer" for his administration, giving the college never-before-imagined flexibility in program support—a true discretionary fund especially through the Cox Institute to support research, service and teaching. Although the annual amount has not increased in the years since, it has been continuous. The annual amount is equivalent to the yield from a $6 million endowment, given university spending rates on endowment that range from 4 to 5 percent, and remains foundational for Grady's considerable reputation in international research and training and in management studies. In its centennial year the total amount of funding will have reached $7.5 million. Also, the Cox family and its enterprises have been generous with the university generally. Recently, James Cox Kennedy, Jr., gave a million dollars each to the Terry Business College and to Grady. At Grady it enabled four Jim Kennedy Professorships in New Media, a true windfall for the college, its faculty and students. Grady has been privileged to be included in the family's extraordinary benefactions to many educational institutions and a host of other worthy causes.

But of course the Cox relationship was not only recent. At the 25th Anniversary of the Grady Chapter of Sigma Delta Chi in 1954, George C. Biggers, then president of Atlanta Newspapers, Inc., took the occasion to praise Drewry's stewardship. He noted especially the pipeline from Grady to Cox. All total, there were thirty-nine Grady-trained graduates working in Cox media. "To me," he said, "this illustrates better than any other way I could express how we of the *Atlanta Journal* and *Constitution* feel about John Eldridge Drewry." Imbedded in the 1954 Annual Report, it was like so many other encomiums to the nexus between Cox and Grady.

One other factor that contributes to the Cox-Grady relationship is the sheer number of Cox leaders Grady has engaged, only partly owing to Cox's reputation for churn in management. One person who left early in the eighties was Thomas H. "Tom" Wood, president of Atlanta Newspapers, Inc., from 1977 to 1982 and a member of the Grady Advisory Board in that time. (He was on the board when the infamous ouster of *R&B* reporters from an advisory board meeting brought down the wrath of journalists, especially Wood, on Dean Cutlip.) On May 8, 1982, Wood announced the "unthinkable," a merger of the *Journal* and *Constitution* newsrooms. It came off better than anyone thought—no lay-offs. He resigned three weeks later.[180] Jim Minter, who was editor at the time, said had Wood stayed, the Atlanta papers would have become great.[181] A person of considerable business acumen, Wood's departure led ultimately to a partnership with William H. "Dink" NeSmith (ABJ 70), a true Grady legend. Although Wood himself was not a Grady graduate, the partnership he formed with NeSmith became Community Newspapers Inc., CNI, a blessing to community journalism in four states and to Grady. Wood and Nesmith met on the Grady Advisory Board. So, the happy relationships the college has enjoyed with various members of the Cox family of enterprises may only indicate that the college is not a wholly-owned subsidiary of Cox, as some outsiders have surmised, but better than that, willing partners where and when beneficial.

## THE KNAPP DECADE

While all this was going on, Charles Boynton "Chuck" Knapp was becoming president of the University of Georgia It was to be a good presidency for Grady. Born in Ames, Iowa, in 1946, he received his undergraduate degree from Iowa State University and graduate degrees in economics from the University of Wisconsin, Madison. Following a teaching stint at the University of Texas, Austin, and service as an undersecretary of labor in Washington, D.C., he eventually made his way to Tulane, where he was soon made executive vice president. From that position the regents named him President of the University of Georgia, following an interim year for Henry King Stanford. Knapp was accessible, energetic, and forward thinking. He was instrumental in establishing the Georgia Research Alliance to channel resources to the state's Research I Institutions and in developing Governor Zell Miller's signature HOPE Scholarship program, a lottery funded program that promised a free ride on tuition for Georgia's top performing high school students—mostly from Georgia's more advantaged schools. Knapp's was a ten-year era, 1987-97, of good feelings about UGA and its ascendancy among the nation's flagship universities. His presidency also rode a rising tide of state funding for higher education that separated UGA from the south-

**ABOVE:** President Charles B. Knapp. *Office of Public Information, University of Georgia*; **BELOW:** John Holliman, CNN front man for Desert Storm. *UGA Photographic Services*

eastern pack and made it aspirational to Virginia and North Carolina.

In 1990 Knapp was a visible presence as the college celebrated the Golden Anniversary of the Peabody Awards at a black tie event at Atlanta's World Congress Center, the first time the awards had not been presented in New York. He and his wife even hosted dinner events for the board as it gathered in Athens. It would be Horace Newcomb's first time as a board member. In 2001, Newcomb would become its director. The celebration was a true gala but the awards that year for media productions completed in 1989 served as a reminder of what a bang the eighties ended with. Coverage of Hurricane Hugo and the San Francisco Earthquake won awards. In just over another year the awards recognized the barrage that erupted over Baghdad in January 1991, the First Gulf War, and the legends it would make of Atlanta's CNN News team, including Grady's own John Holliman (ABJ 70). Thus did the eighties become the nineties, natural disasters soon handing off to a man-made one.

Holliman was back on campus February 22, 1991 to speak with hundreds of students about Desert Storm. The whole broadcast area was abuzz with industry relationships that were equipping our students with the latest technologies. At vortex was David Hazinski, a former NBC reporter and co-host of "World Business Review" with Caspar "Cap" Weinberger, Reagan's Secretary of Defense, and an international consultant. Hazinski orchestrated a build-out of real-world studio opportunities for students. Negotiations were underway with WXIA-TV/Gannett Broadcasting in Atlanta to move its Athens bureau on campus. The walls between industry and academe had never been more porous, with huge benefits for students. The operations Hazinski was developing would eventuate in NewsSource 15, a live broadcast aired over cable in Athens in cooperation with CNN. Hazinki's zeal for news was palpable and his relationship to students robust. (No student ever forgets his irrepressible personality or the debt they owe him—or for that matter his salty language.)

**LEFT:** Hazinski demonstrating how it's done. *UGA Photographic Services*; **RIGHT:** Barry Sherman. *Grady College Archives*

It would lead to his becoming a university Meigs Professor, the highest honor for teaching, and Jim Cox Kennedy Professor of New Media. It was also more evidence of the benefits of the Athens-Atlanta communications axis.

Another inimitable Grady personality, Worth McDougald, announced his retirement, effective June 30, 1991. He and John Drewry had been the face of the Peabody Awards for its first fifty years. The college promoted Barry Sherman to professor and on the dean's and president's recommendations the regents confirmed him as McDougald's successor. He would put his own stamp on the program and take the awards into the twenty-first century. The graduate program was hitting its stride with a record 181 applying for the master's program and sixty-one for the Ph.D. Only five would be admitted for doctoral study. A decision made in its inaugural year, 1983, was to grow it slowly. Of special note was the first admission of a student from the Peoples' Republic of China. The Asian presence in the college has grown significantly in recent years with huge benefits for global discourse about communications.

The Cox Center gained additional leverage with a decision made at the beginning of the nineties to concentrate on eastern and central Europe where democracies were emerging from Soviet domination, most with some history of journalism and therefore might provide more fertile soil. However, the shift away from the third world was not total and work continued in Latin and Central America, the Pacific Islands, and to a lesser extent in Africa. The Center's Director, Al Hester, was and is a remarkable person. Born in West Texas and educated at Southern Methodist, he was working city hall for the *Dallas Times Herald* the day Kennedy was shot. So for all who knew where they were that day, he was there. He went on to a master's and Ph.D. in jour-

**ABOVE:** Al Hester with Ibrahim Muhammed Ibrahim who talks about his country, Qatar. *Grady College Archives;* **BELOW:** John English. *Grady College Archives*

nalism from Wisconsin, and then on to Grady, where he became sequence and department head of Journalism and the founding director of the Center for International Research and Training in Journalism and Mass Communication (after 1990 the Cox Center). His global reach was truly phenomenal, his connections through USIA and the Soros Foundation, among other outreach entities, even more so. For the Center's first twelve years, he gave it and Grady the most prominent position in international outreach of any university in the nation, a position it maintains. He retired to Athens in 1997, where he and his wife Conoly have continued to read and write extensively with an emphasis on Civil War and Reconstruction in Athens/Clarke County, Georgia. From West Texas to Dallas on that fateful day to Madison to UGA to all over the world and back to local history, what a life!

Central to the Center's success was Hester's determination to involve as many faculty members as possible. In the early going, names that figured prominently were John English, Wally Eberhard, and Jim Fletcher. English was an original member of the Peace Corps with assignment, 1962-64, in Malaysia to teach English in Borneo. With Hester, he continued to emphasize that part of the world but also the complete mission of the Center. English also founded a cultural studies approach to communication in the college, although "founded" may be qualified when one recalls early faculty members like Crouse whose emphasis was drama and criticism. English's doctoral studies in critical approaches to popular culture informed and enriched his teaching of journalism as genre, an emphasis that is still echoed today by close examination of storytelling in other genres like telenovela in Venezuelan television, a subject of Meigs Professor Carolina Acosta-Alzura's research and teaching. It is also interesting to note that Grady alumnus Larry

Dendy (ABJ 65), recent author of an illustrated history of the campus, was also an early Peace Corps volunteer, as was Kent Middleton, long time department head of Journalism, who took his assignment to Tunisia in 1966. Middleton would do follow-up programs under auspices of the Soros Foundation in Eastern Europe, Bucharest especially.

In 1993 English was instrumental in partnering the college with journalism programs at Columbia, Northwestern, and Southern California on a $3.2 million Pew grant to underwrite a national program for critics, reporters, and editors of the performing arts. It was a three-year program in which the participating schools would bring in three critics annually as fellows both to be mentored by Grady faculty and to serve as mentors. Dr. English also was asked to serve as a judge/panelist for the National Magazine Awards sponsored by American Society of Magazine Editors and Columbia University. The Pew grant represented a significant coup not only for English but for the college's own privileged position among the nation's elite programs. At the end of the three year program, Michael Charles Janeway, famous at *Atlantic Monthly*, but not so well regarded at the *Boston Globe*, would leave Medill at Northwestern and go to Columbia, where he would collapse the arts program into that university. Among the residuals would be *The Journal: National Arts Journalism Program*. The NAJP is now Seattle-based but continues as emphases at Columbia and the University of Southern California-Annenberg.

English also took the whip hand on the magazine program, taking students to New York for their introduction. He was instrumental in Grady's Studies Abroad program, first in Cortona, Italy, but when that location in Tuscany did not lend itself to contemporary art, the program moved to Parma. Beyond Al Hester's program, English was moving the college forward on the international front, proof once more that real creativity and synergy emerges from the faculty in an academic enterprise. Deans and department heads can provide the forum, facilitate creative discussions, and find resources, but as much as their names are associated through external constituencies with leadership, it comes from the faculty with each member generating a universe of possibilities from where they "cast down their buckets." A true academic enterprise that involves teaching, service, and inquiry into the nature of things cannot fail when faculty members follow their passions. No dean embraced that principle more fully than Tom Russell.

As the late eighties moved into the nineties, the language of computer assisted reporting, compugraphics, and desktop publishing made its way into the lexicon. The transition was expensive but in combination with state funding, private gifts, and industry partnerships, the college made progress. One such partnership was with WXIA-TV in Atlanta, where Steve Smith, an executive there, was instrumental in moving their Athens bureau to the college.[182] By the next decade, Smith would be a valued member of the faculty. Dean Russell summed it up, "In a relatively short period of time, the college has moved from manual typewriters to computers, from black and white television studio to satellites, and from simple typesetting to desktop publishing." It seems almost quaint now but then it was the future.

No peer institution in the region could equal Grady's accomplishments in technological conversion and sophistication. (No faculty member ever believes that, but a college like Grady is usually better off than it thinks.) The ultimate beneficiaries were savvy students entering the job market technologically proficient. Faculty research anticipated change coming as revealed in the title of one publication, "Young Readers Respond to Actual Use of a Full-Featured Electronic Newspaper." Kent Middleton played an important role in the conversion. It was one among many probes. Still Grady, and indeed the world, had not seen anything yet. Education was on the cusp of the digital revolution, and it had prognosticators aplenty, but the dot.com bubble had yet to rise and burst. Newspapers especially felt threatened but still confident enough to continue whistling in the dark. Would we be changed, or more of the same, just differently displayed?

Barry Hollander addressing a group of international journalists. Hollander is accomplished in digital applications and also undertook interdisciplinary study in religion to advance his understanding of its role and influence in journalism. *Grady College Archives, courtesy Grady Breadth*

Portentous was work done by recently arrived Dean Krugman, via once again the Illinois Railroad. In the *Journal of American Advertising* (1985), Krugman argued that television would become a central processing unit capable of delivering services well beyond traditional program viewing. The model argued that when interactive computer services entered the scene "viewing" takes on a completely different meaning and requires new explanations. And so it did. The model Krugman developed worked well in predicting the direction of television and newer viewing environments. In more recent times he has scored research successes in the uses and effects of Kindles and other tablets. Grady curiosity and industry have always led the way. (When the revolution manifested itself in the *fin de siècle*, it changed everything. The golden age for "newspaper" journalism was the last four decades of the twentieth century, as it fueled the fortunes of its patrons, the great families of journalism: Pulitzers, Sulzbergers, Grahams, Chandlers, Knights, Gannetts, Newhouses, and Coxes. Even in the middle ranks, Morris, Reynolds, Belo, Gaylord, significant wealth accumulated. It was to these families and the foundations they created that journalism education turned for major backing. Even smaller community newspaper chains were returning significant margins, as much as 40 percent, and they too figured in the equation. With the collapse of newsrooms in the digital revolution that loomed, only horizontally integrated corporations, like Cox Enterprises Inc., [CEI] handled the buffeting well. CEI's legacy media holdings generate less than 10 percent of its corporate revenues.

(Those in fundraising for journalism and mass communication education have had some success with personal wealth accumulated in other sectors, electronic media, advertising and public relations agencies, for example, and through partnerships that yield significant in-kind investment. Still entities that are publicly held answer to investors and most profits are directed accordingly. Thus, fundraising would change significantly in the twenty-first century.)

* * * * *

The 1993-94 academic year brought renewed accreditation preceded by departmental efforts to improve outcomes assessments of student performance, a direction the accrediting council urged. Once again the site committee recommended approval on all standards and the council approved renewal in spring 1994. Although the college no longer had the Industrial

Editors Institute, it did inaugurate both a PR Day and an Advertising Day to bring faculty, students and professionals together in ways that promoted many of the earlier objectives. Moreover, the addition of Drs. Lynne Sallot and Karen Miller to the PR faculty brought its scholarly resources in line with increased demand for that major. At the center of all this change was Tom Russell, who had a unique blend of the personal and the private. He was the ultimate facilitator. He listened, found resources, and then got out of the way. His ego was never involved, perhaps because it never occurred to him to have one. The word most often associated with his administration was "integrity." He had a wonderful sense of humor that showed to special effect on public occasions from receptions to convocations to board meetings.

In March of 1999, the college hosted its annual PR Day. The featured speaker was Harold Burson of Burson Marsteller. In the audience was a future dean, who came over that day at the encouragement of Atlanta-based members of his board at Alabama, because, as they put it, "We love alma mater, but the best prepared student is a Grady grad." So unawares of the future, he attended the keynote event, visited with Russell to find out how it was done and was mightily impressed. He became a better dean for it, and the rest became the future.

## PEABODY REVISITED

The biggest outward change in the nineties came in the Peabody Awards, now under the leadership of Dr. Barry Sherman who was joined by Dr. Louise Benjamin (Ph.D. University of Iowa), a media historian, as associate director. For the first time entries exceeded 1,000, a number that holds today. In order to accommodate the increase, a decision was made to have the board meet twice before coming to Athens, once in Washington, D.C. in February and again in Chicago in early March. That screening process is still followed, only the Chicago meeting is now in Los Angeles. Making it possible was Director Sherman's request that all entrants submit two copies of their productions, one for screening and the other for archiving. Thus board members would have more time to screen in advance of the final meeting in Athens. Of course, today it is digital with board members having round-the-clock access and at meetings instantly on each screen. Still, board members find no substitute for the face-to-face exchanges they enjoy, however tense and tendentious these interactions sometimes become.

**LEFT:** Scott Williamson speaking at convocation. *Grady College Archives*; **RIGHT:** Tim Mapes receives first Dean's Medal from Dean Clark. *Courtesy Delta Air Lines*

A second change occurred when Coca-Cola, a major sponsor, stepped up to improve the production values of the New York awards event. Starting in the mid-nineties and under the leadership of Earl Leonard (ABJ 58) and Carlton Curtis (ABJ 72), Coca-Cola provided major funding for stage setting and multi-mediated presentations of the awards. Those who had attended previous events were much impressed and declared it "best ever." Moreover, the National Alumni Association under Dick Yarbrough's leadership (ABJ 59) sponsored a champagne reception for award recipients at the Museum of Television & Radio, now Paley Center. These significant changes continue to the present day with a later addition of a Coca-Cola-sponsored President's Reception in the Rainbow Room and more recently the University Club. Atlanta based Coca-Cola and Delta remain principal sponsors of this most prestigious award in electronic media. Scott Williamson (MA 92) of Coca-Cola and Tim Mapes (ABJ 86) of Delta are jewels in the Grady crown.

A corollary to the "big day" on May 16, 1994, was a meeting held three days earlier in New York to discuss fundraising for the Peabodys. The issue had long been present and remains on the agenda—how to conserve the world's third largest collection of electronically and now digitally produced media, because the University of Georgia Special Collections Library holds not just the winning entries but all entries presented for adjudication, meaning programming that producers considered their best work in entertainment, public service and journalism. Progress had already been made through selective computer archiving, but the cost of doing all entries was prohibitive. Approaches had been made to the National Endowment for the Humanities, which provided some $150,000 in funding but not nearly enough and every dean from Tom Russell to the present has considered it a priority. With current cost estimates ranging from fifteen to twenty million dollars, no donor, foundation or granting agency has yet come forward. Nonetheless, the group that assembled in 1994, led by Dean Russell, made it a priority if not yet funded. It will be one day. It is too important a national and international cultural treasure not to be. Even without digital preservation, the Peabody archives remain a rich source for students and scholars, and UGA archivists see to it that it is preserved in its present condition and that it is maximally available. The Peabody exhibit in Russell Special Collections is spectacular. Still, the issue of preservation and conservation remains urgent and unresolved. (It should also be noted that a lot of "paper" accompanies the archived recordings: reviews, notes from screening committees, write-ups by the entrants, all providing a body of testimony as to the value of the programming for scholars especially.)

But more than money and only at Grady, it's "Imagination." It took place on October 22, 1994, in the historic Morton Theatre in Athens, built in 1910 by freed slave Monroe B. "Pink" Morton, the only vaudeville theater on the National Register of Historic Places that was built, owned, and operated by African Americans. The featured attractions on that Saturday were Himan Brown and Mercedes McCambridge. Brown, who was born the year the Morton Theatre was built, made radio drama the phenomenal experience it became, beginning with "The Rise of the Goldbergs" and continuing through "The Thin Man," "Dick Tracy," and "CBS Mystery Theater." Brown was a benefactor of the college, having established the Himan Brown Audio Production Center. Although most known for her role in "The Exorcist," McCambridge was equally famous in radio drama and on Broadway in "Who's Afraid of Virginia Woolf." She was "the ticket" and it was a tickets-only event with a packed house. Of that day, Brown said, "I have never stopped believing that the spoken word and the imagination of the listener are infinitely stronger and more dramatic than anything television can offer." Brown died in 2010 at age ninety-nine. Imagination indeed.

Imagination reprised. In 2003, the Grady College launched the Robert Osborne Classic Film Festival. Osborne's signature Turner Classic Movies was already a hit, but now the show was on the road. Beginning with a single hit movie "Singin' in the Rain," the festival spread to more than fifty classic films over the next seven years. It soon grew to three days of packed houses at the Classic Center with presidential receptions and panels of Hollywood's most famous from years past: Patricia Neal, Mickey Rooney, Louise Fletcher, and a

## DEAN'S OFFICE

**ROW 1** Jeff Springston, Charles N. Davis, Alison Alexander
**ROW 2** Gabrielle Mason, Sean Polite, Parker Middleton, Debbie Sickles

## ADVERTISING & PUBLIC RELATIONS

**ROW 1** Jeff Springston, Michael Cacciatore, Kim Landrum, Elli Roushanzamir, Grace Ahn, Jennifer Griffith, Tom Reichert

**ROW 2** Karen Russell, Betty Jones, Joe Phua, Lynne Sallot, Elaine Lin, Joo Young Kim, Juan Meng

**ROW 3** Bryan Reber, Kristen Smith, Carolina Acosta-Alzuru, Jay Hamilton, Yan Jin, Kirsten Strausbaugh, Spencer Tinkham, Jeong Yeob Han

**ROW 4** Karen King, Maria Len-Rios, Nate Evans, Glen Nowak, Peggy Kreshel, Itai Himelboim

## JOURNALISM

**ROW 1** David Hazinski, Leara Rhodes, Sophie Barnes, Anettra Mapp, Pat Thomas, Keith Herndon, Tom Hudson, Ivanka Pjesivac, Dodie Cantrell-Bickley, Ann Hollifield, Laurie Anglin, Bart Wojdynski, John Greenman

**ROW 2** Tudor Vlad, Kent Middleton, Mark Johnson, Chris Shumway, Barry Hollander, Joe Dennis, Vicki Michaelis, Welch Suggs, Janice Hume, Bill Lee, Lee Becker

## MEDIA ARTS

**ROW 1** Andy Kavoori, John Weatherford, Emuel Aldridge, Hartmut Koenitz, Shira Chess

**ROW 2** Jeff Jones, Jeong Yeob Han, Itai Himelboim, Scott Shamp, James Biddle

NEW MEDIA INSTITUTE

Row 1. Scott Shamp, Deanna Wood, John Weatherford. Megan Ward, Emuel Aldridge

## ADVISING TEAM

**ROW 1** Kelly Meyer, Diane Miller, Sharon Shannon;

**ROW 2** Victoria Cooper, Beth Rector, Maria Cooper, Michelle McFalls, Carlo Finlay

PEABODY

ROW 1 Nate Kohn, Jeff Jones

ROW 2 Wes Unruh, Margaret Uhler, Matthew Shedd, Noel Holston

## EXTERNAL RELATIONS TEAM

**ROW 1** Diane Murray, Ryan Carty, Sarah Freeman, Stephanie Moreno

**ROW 2** Joe Dennis, Karen Andrews, Cecil Bentley

## BUSINESS & IT

**ROW 1** Don McClain, Janet Sharik, Cletus Stripling, Brooke Rooks, Terri Baker

**ROW 2** Jonathon Streetman, Kelly Meyer, Stephanie Martin, Denise Mattox

host of others. It was Osborne at his best. Central in all this was Nate and Pamela Kohn and Grady's external relations team. While on the faculty at Illinois, Nate was a producer of the Siskel and Ebert "two thumbs up" film review shows that became so popular. The Osborne Festival brought people from far and near. For example, Elderhostel made it a featured attraction for its members. In the end, the financial collapse and Turner's own decision to do festivals in L.A. and other cities made 2010 its last. But while it lasted, nothing equaled it.

**ABOVE:** Paul Hecht and Mercedes McCambridge play title roles in "Madeleine and Harry's Story," a radio drama done during first Himan Brown Audio Production Workshop, 1990. **BELOW:** Nate Kohn and Robert Osborne team up. *Grady College Archives*

Film, while synonymous with radio-tv-film, has always had an on-again, off-again experience in Journalism and Mass Communication education. At UGA today, it is in Drama, which itself originated in Grady in 1940, when Edward Crouse departed Grady to assume direction of the newly created department. Recent conversations encouraged by Nate Kohn, Associate Director of the Peabodys, have sought to bring film back into Grady. UGA's top faculty member in film, Dr. Richard Neupert, has supported it strongly, but for issues as technical as the turf battle over "which college gets the credit hours," it has been stymied in Franklin. Although collaboration can leap institutional barriers, the day will be bright when film links up with Entertainment and Media Studies (which is now a separate department in Grady headed by Dr. Andy Kavoori) in order to continue the storytelling tradition, both fiction and nonfiction, with the most exquisite audio-visual effects. The time has come, bureaucracy notwithstanding.

## THE ROARING MID-NINETIES

Success breeds success. Coca-Cola's Peabody re-make, secure funding for the Cox International Center and the Cox Management Institute, the Pew alliance for criticism in the performing arts, all were signs of success in external funding and made 1995 feel inevitable, although it is never that easy and always the result of cordial persistence and patience in connecting donors to opportunities. In January of 1995, Grady dedicated the William S. Morris Chair of Newspaper Strategy and Management, the first endowed chair in the college. Billy Morris, who had established a strong collaborative relationship between Morris Communications and the college through the work of Conrad Fink, Meigs and Regents Professor and a master of the business and economics of print journalism. Fink was first to hold the chair. Named for Billy's father, the chair highlighted the long suit Grady had developed in communication management studies across its disciplines.

The college also received a major gift from William I. Ray (ABJ 35), longtime Cox Executive and President of Atlanta Newspapers, Inc. It came in the form of a trust to support the college generally, effectively a discretionary fund to encourage faculty development, student programming and support, along with public service and outreach. In the years out, the fund grew so well that the college's operating funds that were never adequate, became less and less a drag-on operations. In fall quarter, 1995, the Georgia Chapter PRSA Suite, including the C. Richard Yarbrough Laboratory and Frazier

Billy Morris holds forth in Conrad Fink's classroom. *Grady College Archives*

Moore and Jasper Dorsey Offices, officially opened to benefit advanced public relations students. The aforementioned WXIA-TV gift enabled the refurbished broadcast suite to open, also in January. Things were cooking. The college topped the $10 million mark for endowment support.

Bill Ray, generous benefactor.
*Grady College Archives*

So it was on to the jeweled crown awaiting in New York, another celebration of the Peabodys. It was hard to top the year before when Bill Moyers emceed and Barbara Streisand, General Stormin' Norman Schwartzkopf, Alan Shepard, and Diane Sawyer were among thirty-one on hand to receive their awards. (One of the great things about the awards is that only winners, who have already been notified, are announced. So, no groaning or miffed nominees are in the house, contributing even further to the celebratory nature of the occasion.) Yet spring of 1996 brought a reminder that celebrated storytelling is often enough about tragedy. On that occasion, joining emcee Tom Brokaw and honorees that included Barbara Walters, Oprah Winfrey, Dan Rather, Peter Jennings, was also Frank Keating, governor of Oklahoma, there to accept for the Oklahoma City television stations that had covered the dastardly bombing of the Murrah Building, a manmade disaster that would remain singularly epic on continental American soil for another six years.

Wrapping up Peabodys that year, director Barry Sherman and development director Bill Herringdine travelled to Yaddo in Saratoga Springs, the Peabody estate acquired through George Foster Peabody's one-year marriage to Kate Trask. Peabody faithfully executed the will and wishes of Kate and her first husband, Spencer Trask, to convert the estate into an artists-in-residence program for writers, painters, and musicians. As Dean Russell noted, "The Peabody Awards look forward to renewing a direct association with Mr. Peabody's estate and its legacy to the arts and culture in America," fitting indeed, owing to Grady's long association with the arts, dating back to its beginnings.

'96 was also the year of the Olympics for Atlanta, a prize that like no other symbolized the city's arrival on a platform to match Henry Grady's aspirations for his expositions over a hundred years earlier. Indeed, it was the centennial for the Olympics, and Grady College was front and center in the person of Dick Yarbrough, who served on the organizing committee and handled all external relations for its leadership. It was a huge success, touching off a building boom in Atlanta and environs that became a sport-splex for thousands of world-class athletes and hundreds of thousands of visitors and tourists, the cumulative total being more like millions. It took years of planning and artful persuasion, but when Muhammed Ali touched off the Olympic flame, it symbolized, as nothing else could, Atlanta's arrival on the world stage, no longer a city "too busy to hate," but a city big enough to include all.

There did come a dark moment though. A crazed bomber by the name of Eric Rudolph touched off an explosion in Centennial Olympic Park that injured 110 and killed a mother, who had just arrived from Albany, Georgia, with her teenage daughter to take in the Olympic experience. A Turkish cameraman, rushing to cover the bombing, also died of a heart attack. It was horrible. Instantly, decisions had to be made, to continue or not continue the games being but one. Another UGA legend, Billy Payne, headed the Atlanta Committee for the Olympic Games and after conversations that included the president of the International Olympics Committee and President Bill Clinton, the decision was made to continue without suspension or delay of any event, this despite the fact that the bombing had taken place only hours before at 1:40 a.m. How to communicate the decision was left to Yarbrough, who had returned to the headquarters that overlooked Centennial Park just as Payne arrived back. The decision would be announced at 6:00 a.m. Yarbrough crafted a simple three-part announcement that ran roughly a page and a half expressing sympathy for the victims and their families, that the Olympic Movement would not yield to terrorism, and that the games would go on as scheduled. Despite some problems with credentialing the press that morning, by the end of the day arenas were at 95 percent capacity and 85 percent of volunteers had returned to their stations. (Rudolph, who was involved in at least three other bombings, including an abortion clinic in Birmingham, Alabama, killing a guard and mangling a nurse, went on the lam and was not apprehended, convicted, and sentenced until 2005.)

The Atlanta Olympic Games were not an unqualified success, at least looking from the inside out. IBM promised the national and international press instant results, print-ready from each venue but failed to deliver. The press started calling the Olympics the "Glitch Games." It took IBM five days to iron out the problems. The City of Atlanta failed to cooperate fully with unfortunate results that ran the gamut from vending to trash collection to snarled traffic—not a best foot forward. Worse still, the city actively competed against the Atlanta Committee Olympic Games for revenue. Although the games were privately funded at $1.7 billion, the city had set aside some funding for security and other necessities. It showed once again Atlanta's racial division: after all, metropolitan (white) Atlanta had long moved north, leaving a shrunken city of Atlanta, seventy percent black, downtown. Still, the games were memorable and memory often improves reality, as Henry Grady so well understood. (Grady's three expositions in the 1880s were beset but still served their purposes.) Atlanta proclaimed itself an "international city." Whether it was or not was debatable, but it was good for business to say so. And truth is, immigration since has improved the city's international flavor.

(Professor Bryan Reber, the first Yarbrough Professor in Crisis Communications, even before coming to UGA, used and continues to use Yarbrough's 2000 book on the Atlanta Olympics, *And They Call Them Games*. It is an excellent case study in public relations leadership and crisis communications management.)

There was one moment of genuine levity for UGA. Sanford Stadium was to serve as venue for both women's and men's soccer—in fact, the U.S. women's team won the gold medal in Sanford Stadium before the largest crowd at that time ever to view a women's sporting event. Yet, it all might not have happened but for the irrepressible Barbara Dooley. When Athletics Director Vince Dooley learned that the revered hedges would have to be removed to make the field soccer-eligible—what the rest of the world calls football—he had a message problem; to wit, convince the faithful that the current hedges were old, dying and needed to be replaced anyway, and that the job could be done before the opening of the season a month away. So Dick Yarbrough, then president of the National Alumni Association, set the alumni table. Vince was at his earnest best, when from the back of the room Barbara began to sing softly but audibly and to the tune of "Old Man River," "Those poor old hedges, those poor old hedges, they all are dying, they all are dying. . . ." Yarbrough reported not a dry eye in the house, because everyone was thigh-slapping laughing. He also reported that "coach" was not amused.[183] The hedges were removed, the games went on, the hedges were replaced, and the Dawgs didn't skip a beat.

The academic year 1996-97 brought another big announcement, the endowment by Charles and Lessie Smithgall of the Lambdin Kay Professorship to support the director of the Peabody Awards program. It, too, would become a chair. Thus with the Morris gift, the Ray endowment, and

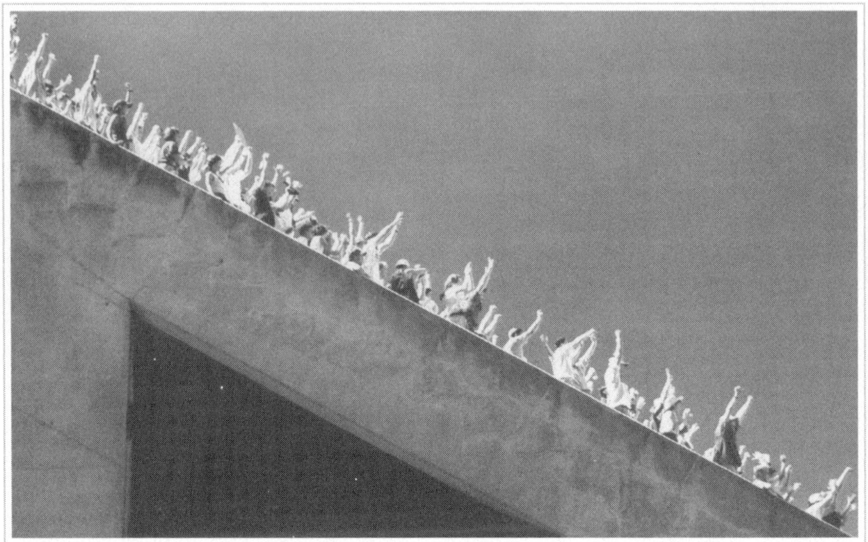

Northwest side of stadium, team USA has just scored against China on way to Gold in women's soccer. *Grady College Archives, photo by Shelly Campbell*

now the Smithgall endowment, Grady was hitting stride in the mid-nineties. 1997 occasioned another announcement that President Knapp was stepping down to become director of the Aspen Institute in Washington, D.C., where he also joined Heidrick & Struggles in their higher education practice that includes executive searches. Two years later he was back at Tulane's Payson Center and before long returned to UGA's Institute for Higher Education. His style and manner encouraged significant growth at UGA, including burgeoning student aptitude scores and first steps at building sustainable endowment support. The arrival of Michael F. Adams from Centre College in Kentucky heralded changes for Grady.

## TURBULENCE AT Y2K

The forty-nine year old Michael Franklin Adams was something of a surprise choice, although a handsome one with blond, silvering hair, penetrating blue eyes, and an excellent speaker. Born in Montgomery, Alabama, he grew up in Albany and Macon, finishing his high school days in Chattanooga as the family followed his father's business career. He received his undergraduate degree from David Lipscomb, a Church of Christ College in Nashville and later a master's and Ph.D. in political communication (a specialization within

President Michael Franklin Adams. *UGA Photographic Services*

Speech Communication) from Ohio State University. After a two-year stint teaching at OSU, he got his real start on Senate Minority Leader Howard Baker's staff in Washington as chief of staff, 1975-79, and also served as an aide to Tennessee Governor Lamar Alexander, 1980-82. He ran for a House seat from Tennessee's Fifth District in 1980 but lost by a wide margin to the Democratic candidate. From 1982 to 1988, he served as Vice President for University Affairs at Pepperdine University in Malibu, California, also a Church of Christ school like Lipscomb and Abilene Christian University in Texas. From there he went to a successful tenure as president of Centre College in Danville, Kentucky, an excellent private liberal arts college affiliated with the Presbyterian Church (USA). Centre had a student population of approximately 1,300 and faculty of about 150.

Adams's reputation among his peers burgeoned at Georgia. To his presidency of the National Association of Independent Colleges and Universities, he added presidential terms at the Association of Public and Land-Grant Universities and the American Council on Education, along with membership on the National Collegiate Athletic Association's Executive Committee. His numerous awards included the Knight Foundation Award for Presidential Leadership, the Pioneer Award for Leadership in Civil Rights, and leadership recognition from the Southern Association of Colleges and Schools. His sixteen years at the helm of UGA came during a period of remarkable growth in campus facilities, as the student population rose from 29,000 to near 35,000. However, his reputation among external and internal constituencies of the university was mixed. Even those who tout his success concede a confrontational edge and an administrative style that divided the UGA family. The Grady College was not spared.

On January 7, 1999, Tom Russell took a night call from the provost, Dr. Karen Holbrook. Her purpose was to advise Russell that Adams' "State of the University" address the next day would call for consideration of a consolidation of all communication units including the Grady College, the Department of Speech Communication in Arts and Sciences, and speech pathology and audiology in the Department of Communication Sciences and Special Education. Russell, who was caring for his dying mother on an

8:00 pm to 8:00 am basis, advised Holbrook that it would not go over well. Adams went forward anyway, unprepared as the ground was. The response was immediate and vocal from all affected units and their friends and supporters. On leaving Adams's presentation, Conrad Fink was widely quoted as being not only surprised but "sickened" by the announcement. Because among the affected units Grady had the most powerful and influential friends and alumni in media, the crescendo of opposition was deafening. They saw it as a diminution of one of UGA's national assets, its standing in journalism and mass communication education compromised. (Although rankings and surveys of Journalism and Mass Communication programs are viewed with suspicion by most faculty members, Grady often appears among the top three or four, as for example a 2014 ranking by the Radio Television Digital News Directors Association that listed Grady second behind the University of Missouri and a 2014 Yahoo poll that had it fourth, throwing in Northwestern's Medill and Columbia University, which because Columbia has only a graduate program is not comparable. Grady faculty members are more comfortable with research productivity studies and citation indexes, as noted elsewhere in this account. It is safe to say that Grady is comfortable with its "top five" aspirations.)

In fairness to Adams, his state of the university address included an "academic vision" for consolidating and strengthening multiple units. Also included was a call for a college focused on public policy, which eventually became the School of Public and International Affairs; another focused on ecology, which became the Odum School of Ecology; yet another on public health which became a college; and finally a first year medical school—each of which in one way or another became a reality. The catch for Grady was its surprise. That neither President Adams nor Provost Holbrook had broached the subject with Dean Russell or anyone else in the college prior to the night before is little short of amazing.

Of course Adams perceived Russell as fanning the oppositional flames, but perception was not reality. Russell had more important things on his mind, his mother, and knew the fire would need no fuel from him. Some members of the faculty did spur things along, but the sharp reaction from Grady alums and Atlanta media needed no encouragement. Moreover, Russell saw some merit in merger talks with Speech Communication but certainly not with a clinical program like speech pathology and audiology. The push-back led to Russell's being called to the presidential carpet a week later, where Adams did his version of a dressing down that more than a few among the university's academic leadership have experienced. In the end, the president's proposal for a communications college came to nothing but ill will. Russell, who was then in his sixteenth year of a remarkable run for the college, stayed one more year, announcing his resignation on February 15, 2000, effective June 30, in order to assume the Phil Landrum Professorship at Piedmont College in Demorest, Georgia. He couched it as a desire to return to teaching, which in part it was, and Adams expressed "regret" at his departure, all part of what one does.

One other feature of Adams' emphasis on the external dynamics of his role was an appearance to faculty of "remoteness." Perhaps it was only in contrast to the Knapp style, but it was noticed. In a letter to Claude L. Williams, Jr., a trustee of the UGA Foundation and influential alumnus, and others including State Senator Paul Broun, Grady faculty member David Hazinski summarized initiatives to equip adequately the broadcast news facilities, initiatives that already had netted $160,000 in equipment from CNN, matched by $78,000 from UGA. "That brings up our biggest problem," he wrote. "We're still not on President Adam's (sic) radar screen and don't know how to get on it." Williams forwarded it to Adams with an asterisk and a request for comment. Later he added, "P.S. Never got a response, CW."[184] Although only a year into his presidency and a relatively small matter at that, it was a harbinger of things that would boil over six years later.

* * * * *

Of course, change at Grady was set against a backdrop of impeachment proceedings against President Clinton, as a paltry land deal in Arkansas (Whitewater) transmogrified into the Monica Lewinsky scandal; of a dot.com bubble that was making start-up millionaires out of recent children; and fears of a Y2K digital implosion. The millennium was at hand, and special prosecutor Kenneth Starr of Whitewater fame would soon make his way to Pepperdine Law School as its dean. The appointment was earlier delayed when *The Washington Post* pointed out that billionaire conservative donor, Richard Mellon Scaife, whose *American Spectator* and other conservative organs busily hatched conspiracy theories about the Clintons, was a major backer of Pepperdine. To be sure, Scaife, as a maverick libertarian and conspiracist, considered Kenneth Starr to be a Democratic mole.[185] Imagine that.

The annual report for 1999-2000 was more proof that disturbance at the top often has little effect on academic enterprise. The only noticeable

Len Reid, acting dean, a position he would hold again. *UGA Photographic Services*

difference was that the report came out September 1 rather than the previous spring and acting dean Len Reid was its author. (Of course, such results are also proof of the good work Dean Russell had accomplished over the previous seventeen years.) Reid stayed in the acting role pending the outcome of a national search to determine Russell's successor. Reid also retained his portfolio as Associate Dean for Graduate Studies and Research—a most generous commitment of his time and talent. In addition to Russell's departure, there was considerable turnover in the dean's office. Dr. Melinda Hawley, Director of Public Service and Outreach, stepped down to take another position. Bill Herringdine in development went over to the UGA Foundation but remained part time with the college, and Ruhanna Neal, director of alumni relations, accepted a position with the College of Family and Consumer Sciences.

Reid's report found Ruth Ann Lariscy as co-investigator on a three-year, $750,000 project with the Centers for Disease Control titled "Communicating Genetics Information to the Lay Public." It also noted Jeff Springston in the second year of a $1.4 million project for the National Cancer Institute focusing on "Interventions for Breast Cancer Screening Behaviors." Both projects exemplified the college's burgeoning role in health and medical communication that would continue into the next century. *The Journal of Advertising* determined Grady to be number one in published research in advertising's major journals, a research tradition that continues into the college's centennial year, and a poll by the University of Texas placed Grady in the top ten nationally of Advertising and Public Relations programs. Finally, *Writer's Digest* ranked Grady's journalism program among the top five, a list that included Northwestern, Columbia, Missouri, and Ohio University. Top billing for sure.

And so the millennium passed with some turbulence at the top but with the college firing on all cylinders. 2001 was yet to come.

# THE 21ST CENTURY 6

2001 TURNED OUT TO BE MORE THAN A SPACE ODYSSEY PROGNOSTICATED IN STANLEY KUBRICK'S 1968 FILM OF THE SAME TITLE. It indelibly etched 9-11 in public memory as the horrific terrorist attacks of that day were exceeded by no other day in American history, not even December 7, 1941, the day that would live in infamy. The wars in Iraq and Afghanistan that proceeded from it, not to mention internal national security measures, would take a terrible toll in blood, treasure, and privacy.

Earlier that year the Grady College conducted a successful search for a new dean. John Soloski had been on the faculty of the University of Iowa's School of Journalism and Mass Communication since 1978 and its director since 1995. He had also served as director of graduate studies. Born in upstate New York, Soloski grew up in Boston where he earned a bachelor's degree cum laude in English and Political Science from Boston College. He tells the funny story of thinking he had applied for Iowa's renowned writing program only to wind up in its School of Journalism, where he received a master's in 1976 and a Ph.D. in 1978. A well-published scholar in media law and qualitative research methods, Soloski says he could not wait to get to the University of Georgia, in

Dean John Soloski with Greg Bluestein, highly acclaimed journalist for *AJC*, and his mother, Lisa Karesh, 2003 Homecoming. *Grady College Archives*

part because of the scope and scale of its programs in the Grady College. In 2003 he would be elected vice president of the Association for Schools of Journalism and Mass Communication and serve as its president in the following year. Like a number of Grady deans, he was a figure to be reckoned with in national circles.

It seemed like a perfect fit, and it was in the early going. "I came to UGA for one reason: it ha[d] the potential to be one of the premier public universities in the nation. Few universities had increased their overall reputation in such a short period of time as UGA."[186] The college began developing a strategic plan, while establishing near-term objectives for student "core competencies," promotion and tenure guidelines as well as post-tenure review, technology needs and laboratories, and undergraduate admissions. Facility renovation became a priority and during Soloski's tenure the college built out a new, handsome Peabody Suite on the third floor. (Previous quarters for the Peabody Awards were not much larger than two offices and two closets on the ground floor and were the subject of wincing embarrassment and bad jokes.) Soloski also set about courting the college's external constituencies and asked Dean Krugman, who at the time was Department Head of Advertising and Public Relations, to serve as Associate Dean for Academic Affairs so that Soloski could be on the road for at least two days a week. Karen King became department head in AdPR, joining Kent Middleton in Journalism and Alison Alexander in Telecommunications to form the academic leadership team, along with Jeff Springston who had been appointed Associate Dean for Graduate Studies and Research in 2003—a formidable team indeed.

Jeff Springston, Associate Dean for Graduate Studies and Research with student Hannah Bause. *Grady College Archives*

Dean Soloski remade the advisory board by combining the alumni board with it and calling it a professional advisory board, and with a director of alumni relations, he began expanding events, such as hosting Peabody announcements as well as alumni awards in Atlanta rather than in Athens. Of course the presentation of the Peabody Awards continued in the Grand Ballroom of the Waldorf Astoria. There is no doubt that in reaching out, Dean Soloski won the confidence of many of the college's most influential leaders and supporters.

When Soloski arrived, he believed a number of issues needed early attention; no identifiable external relations team, only two endowed professorships filled by eminent faculty members but not fully funded, nothing that defined the college, "no core competencies that every student had to master," "no strategic plan," "outdated bylaws," faculty members identifying "by their departments and not by the college," even business cards that lacked standardization. In addition, the threat Adams posed of combining "communications" units in the university festered. (Although Adams had signaled quickly in the upsurge of faculty reaction, along with that of their allies in the professional community, that nothing would be done without faculty buy-in, the question remained open, at least from the standpoint of discussion.) Soloski was on the national accrediting council when the college went through its most recent review and believed it had headed perilously close toward either provisional or outright failure to be re-accredited, the major exposure being on the standard of "diversity." (He was right. It was common in the 1990s and early 2000s for colleges to fail what was then Standard 12, although most of them were re-accredited in any event. Acting Dean Len Reid, Provost Karen Holbrook, and President Adams appeared before the Council, with the result that the college was in fact re-accredited.[187]) So clearly, Dean Soloski believed his work to be cut out and instituted a planning and re-visioning process, and hit the road, cultivating alumni, friends, and donor support.

Soon there emerged core competencies for students—communicate effectively; acquire knowledge of standards of ethical inquiry and professional codes of ethics; gain an understanding of mass media history; engage First Amendment principles; evaluate the structure, function, operations and economics of mass media institutions; understand communication theory and research; learn how communication affects and is affected by diversity; and finally, develop critical thinking and creative problem-solving skills. New bylaws, an important concern for Soloski, sought transparency in decision making, a new promotion and tenure document, and significantly a new diversity plan and a standing committee focused solely on diversity. All good things and all completed.

The diversity agenda deserves special attention. From his position on the Accrediting Council, he knew the college was vulnerable, even as it navigated a cultural/political environment that in Georgia was generally hostile to "affirmative action." Designating a standing committee of the college to the issue of "Diversity" was a crucial first step. It gave the faculty direct responsibility for developing, evaluating, and reporting on a diversity plan and a series of steps that has moved the college forward. By 2005 the college could report an increase in minority faculty of 38 percent (from 3 to 8 members) and minority staff grew from 1 to 3 members.

The work in the Soloski years was built to last. From 2008 to 2011, of seven junior hires six were international: two from Korea (Jeong Yeob Han and Sun Joo "Grace" Ahn), one each from Singapore (Joe Phua), Israel (Itai Himmelboim), Nigeria (Tayo Oyedeji), and Germany (Hartmut Koenitz). These global hires enriched the curriculum and intellectual environment and were indicative of the future. Grace Ahn, for example, a Stanford Ph.D., was the first Grady faculty member to receive significant "start-up" funding from the Office of the Vice President for Research. The result was a Virtual Reality Lab for her work in health communication. At this writing only Tayo, who took a year's leave to obtain an MBA at Oxford University then returned to Nigeria, is no longer with us.

Grace Ahn leads the way. *Grady College Archives, UGA Photographic Services*

The college also appointed a diversity officer for student recruitment. Joe Dennis, who is also Director of the Georgia Scholastic Press Association, developed outreach programs that take Grady into high schools with significant minority enrollment with excellent results. The summer Journalism Academy for high school students has also seen dramatic improvement in minority representation. Scholarships help, and Richard "Rick" Davis and Richard Griffiths at CNN have played an important role in securing funding. Griffiths has also taken an important lead on the college's advisory board; for example, helping set the agenda for board contributions to both curricular and extra-curricular activities.

Joe Dennis with Savannah Brown of Martin Luther King High School, top student in 2010 Journalism Academy. *Grady College Archives*

Another instance of diversity programming was the college's partnership with Berkeley-based New American Media (NAM) to put a spotlight on minorities working in media, both regionally and nationally. Knight Chair Pat Thomas was instrumental in developing the partnership. One result was Grady's co-hosting with NAM the National Ethnic Media EXPO & Awards in Atlanta. Held in June 2009, it attracted over 450 ethnic media professionals and supporters from across the country. It was the largest gathering of ethnic media professionals before the 2010 Unity gathering in Chicago, where Grady also had a highly visible presence. No one could doubt Grady's commitment or results, and the college's 2012 re-accreditation team's recommendation found it in "compliance" on all standards. It did note a need to improve what it terms "domestic diversity" but was impressed with the overall results, especially the globalization of its faculty and burgeoning study-abroad programs.

Resource development, especially endowment, was equally important in Soloski's plan. By 2004 he could announce two significant gifts that would lead to chairs. First was the Carter Chair for Journalism Excellence. John Greenman, former publisher of the *Columbus Ledger-Enquirer*, became the first Carter Professor in 2004 and joined the faculty in August. Since that appointment he has reached out through the Southern Newspaper Publishers Association and the American Press Institute to develop training programs that nimbly match the technological and readership challenges of journalism with new ways forward. He has also developed the McGill Lecture into a focus on journalistic courage, with student fellows who actively participate in

**ABOVE:** John Greenman, right, with Frank Denton of Morris Communications talking with McGill Fellows. *Grady College Archives*; **BELOW:** Pat Thomas, health and medical journalist and leader of Knight initiative. *UGA Photographic Services*

the selection process through research and by active engagement with the named lecturers. Separate and apart, Greenman created and developed a travel writing program that has taken students to Cambodia and Prague.

The second gift was $1.5 million from the John S. and James L. Knight Foundation, matched by $1.9 million from UGA. It was an unusual financial arrangement, but one that resulted in a significant step forward in Health and Medical Journalism. It envisioned a partnership among medical schools at Emory and Morehouse and with UGA's new school of Public Health to improve media coverage and to address the flow of health information to the Black Belt—that underserved region of the American South, named for its rich alluvial soil, but also containing a majority African-American population. The college was fortunate in recruiting Patricia "Pat" Thomas, a Berkeley graduate and an award-winning medical and science writer with stints at Harvard and MIT. Today her collaborative ventures involve UGA's own start-up medical school, which is part of the Medical College of Georgia, one of President Adams' more prescient visions for UGA.

The Knight Chair also complemented huge strides forward in Grady for interdisciplinary research in health communication. For example, Jeff Springston was a principal in a $3 million grant from the National Cancer Institute that followed on his earlier $1.3 million award on breast cancer research. Springston was also involved with a $196,000 grant from the Georgia Cancer Coalition focusing on digital delivery systems for health care information. Then with Provost Holbrook playing a most constructive role, Vicki Freimuth, former director of communication for the Centers for Disease Control, accepted a joint appointment between Grady and Communication Studies (formerly Speech Communication) to develop a

Center for Health and Risk Communication. All of this, not to mention Krugman's research in cigarette warnings and tobacco messaging as well as Lariscy's and Wendy Macias's work in addressing the needs and necessities of the nation's health communication officers.

Soloski also worked with the Dean of the Law School in approaching Otis Brumby, Jr., owner and publisher of the *Marietta Daily Journal*, an influential figure in Georgia press and politics, about establishing a chair in First Amendment Law. A graduate of The University of the South, Sewanee, Brumby later took a law degree from UGA before settling into publishing and community leadership. He was a mover and shaker in Cobb County and a forceful advocate for open government. When *The New York Times* offered millions for his paper in its effort to grab North Atlanta, he spurned it. Ironically and somewhat humorously, his family business was also famous for the Brumby Chair, an oak-slatted, high-back rocker so familiar on southern porches. Brumby agreed to fund a chair in the Law School at $600,000 that would benefit both Law's and Grady's interests in First Amendment issues. The fund was created in June 2007, two years after Soloski's departure as dean, even as he helped develop it. Because it has not been augmented since, its proceeds are used for speakers, lecturers, and visiting professors.

As all these things moved forward, Grady faculty were winning top awards. Len Reid became a Fellow of the American Academy of Advertising (AAA); Dean Krugman won AAA's top research award, one that Reid had earlier received; Conrad Fink, who was already a Meigs Professor, was named a Regents Professor, the top teaching award within the University System of Georgia; Grady was once again the top research program in advertising; Lee Becker received the Presidential Award from the AEJMC for his invaluable surveys; and soon Lynne Sallot would receive PRSA's top honor for scholarship (she had already been inducted into Georgia PRSA's "Order of the Phoenix"). More proof that the engine that "could" was Grady's faculty.

Lynne Sallot, Meigs Professor. *UGA Photographic Services*

Yet faculty must also inspire and that happened as well. The broadcast news faculty and their students organized and produced "Athens Reacts," a journalistic/documentary look at how Athenians experienced 9-11. It was a huge success for those who suffered a thousand miles from the Twin Towers. One thing that can always be said for Grady's investment

Left to right, Steve Smith, David Hazinski, Michael Castengera, and Dan Keever, 2006. *Grady College Archives*

in broadcast and now digital news is its passion. David Hazinski, Steve Smith, Michael Castengera, and recently retired Dan Keever, all are consummate professionals and teachers, driven by news and its obligations. They have not shied at being an "open records" and "open meetings" thorn in the side of the university's administration. The result is one of the most intense experiences students can have at UGA. If you graduate from the Broadcast/Digital Journalism sequence, you have shed blood and are forever grateful. And always in the shadows to make sure the lights and cameras are ready for action are the engineers and technicians, Glenda Smith and Sonny Dixon.

The tradition continues with the additions of Chris Shumway and "Dodie" Cantrell-Bickley, remarkably gifted and inspirational teachers and professionals. Former television journalist and Dowden Professor, Ann Hollifield, has lent her expertise and long suit in management research to enrich the sequence as Department Head from 2007-2014. Not to be forgotten is Bob Furnad, former President of CNN News, a brilliant television journalist who gave unstintingly of his time to our students, or as Dean Clark observed on Furnad's acceptance of the DiGamma Kappa Award, "Furnad did not come over from his home in Newton County to chat with the dean. He went straight to the First Floor to engage students." And who will ever forget Dan Keever, an academic professional who brought years of experience at WAGA-TV and handed it off to Grady students. The consummate cameraman, he even shot the 1968 Democratic Convention in Chicago, where the other "Dan," Rather that is, got punched in the gut.

## CONTROVERSY IN THE ADAMS YEARS, CHICKEN OR EGG?

Behind the scenes not all was tranquil and seldom is. Fissures developed that tore at the UGA tectonic plate. Adams decided that legendary coach Vince Dooley had to go as Athletics Director. He had support from an influential Regent. Dooley wanted more time; i.e., a year's contract extension for a total of four years. Adams gave it some thought, but in the end did not agree to Dooley's terms. Overlaying this tempest was growing restiveness among trustees of the UGA Foundation, who saw Adams' personal use of foundation money as at one end "extravagant" and at the other end "impermissible." Expenditures from a foundation whose fiduciary was to protect the intent of private gifts, some of which were to be sure "unrestricted," went to salary supplement for the president, stipend for his wife, party for a son, end-around on an otherwise worthy project in Costa Rica, an apparent insider deal with an architect, and a big severance agreement for a football coach (Donnan), each of which the Foundation either signed off on, looked the other way, or did not know about.

Towering figures among Georgia alumni, former Attorney General of the United States Griffin Bell and Billy Payne, to name the most towering, thought that Adams was unnecessarily over-reaching in the Dooley case and were deeply distrustful of Adams's use of foundation money. The conflation of the two was toxic for the university, especially when it became known that the foundation had commissioned a Deloitte & Touche forensic audit by way of Griffin Bell's law firm, King and Spalding. The audit confirmed a series of questionable uses of gift funds by President Adams. Additional trouble was that the audit also revealed lax oversight by the trustees. So, both could be blamed. The real problem was that it was the Regents, presiding over thirty-four other institutions in the state as well, who hired the president. Thus, a handful of UGA-affiliated regents, one of whom was an Adams backer with extraordinary influence, came to resent one institution's foundation trustees backing them into a corner with a foundation-commissioned audit. After all, the Regents were responsible for the whole UGA budget, not just the comparatively small fund of private gifts for UGA. They also were responsible for hiring and firing a president.

Thus assured of regents' support and that of the new and first Republican governor since Reconstruction, Adams moved into this vacuum of push and pull and made it a contest between Dooley and him, at a more exalted level, Athletics vs. Academics. Months before the audit report, Soloski wrote a letter of praise for Adams' sticking to his guns, telling Adams that his stand on the Dooley issue re-affirmed his reasons for coming to Georgia.[188] Later, as events unwound and Soloski came to understand the full extent of the controversy and on reading the release of the Deloitte & Touche audit almost four months later, Soloski's support for Adams lessened significantly.

The result of the confrontation was not predictable. Enough UGA supporters accepted the Adams's position that the controversy centered on Academics versus Athletics and followed his lead. After all, it was a long-standing given that football reigned supreme among Southeastern Conference schools, Vanderbilt always excepted; and more thoughtful alumni and most faculty were at least slightly embarrassed by that truth. The iconic Dooley, of scholarly bent himself and author of Georgia's greatest success in football, had to go. It was certainly the president's prerogative. However, one huge result was a break-away from the UGA Foundation, with a group following Adams' and the Regents' lead in creating the Arch Foundation in order to support a capital campaign that was getting underway.

Thus did UGA come to have two foundations, both supporting the university through the endowments and gifts they held, but at odds. It was a remarkable controversy because of the divisions it created, leaving most alumni perplexed, because it seemed so unnecessary, rallying fans to coach Dooley who only months before they had criticized, at least in private, for increasingly poor results in the football program, the nascent Mark Richt turn-around notwithstanding. In all this contretemps Adams retained support of the Regents, but lost key and eminent supporters of UGA itself. Many said they would not give to the university as long as he was president, and all deans experienced some difficulty in fundraising as a result. (Deans are at point in fundraising, because most alumni, especially those who associate with the academic side of the house, identify through their colleges.)

To be sure, many of these same supporters wanted to believe the president. They knew that Athletics had too much power, and their days at Georgia and their professional lives benefitted from its academics. But as artifice, and that is the way it felt to many, athletics versus academics was thin veneer. There was even a vote of "no confidence" in Adams taken by faculty in Arts and Sciences, in part over whether his support was truly for academics as he claimed, but also the audit, which was released before the vote. Of the over 720 faculty members in Arts and Sciences, 64 percent participated and 70 percent of those voted "no confidence" in Adams's leadership. Fifteen percent voted "confidence" and the other fifteen percent abstained. President

Adams who was in Miami for a meeting of the American Council on Education pledged to learn from it and engage the faculty meaningfully over its concerns.

(The reader may recall that thirty years before President Davison had a similar experience when a faculty revolt started in Journalism, spread to Commerce, and wound up in Arts and Sciences. He also was just over six years into his presidency when it happened, and he, too, set up mechanisms to engage better with faculty. In fact, comparisons are made between the Davison presidency and that of Adams, which covered thirty-five of the last fifty years of the university's history. Their administrations were intersected by the ten years of President Knapp, who had a very different style that faculty viewed as more engaging. That said, all three deserve credit for significant accomplishments, however they went about it.)

It was in this time and under these circumstances that Adams asked for letters of support from the deans for the establishment of a new foundation. (Given support from the Regents and the governor, he did not need them.) Soloski said he would not sign any letter that supported Adams in the controversy. The situation had changed markedly. With the Deloitte & Touche report out, key alumni were weighing in. Eventually Soloski joined with a few other deans to draft an innocuous, noncommittal letter that all other deans signed—five sentences, completed just in time and picked up by newspapers. Soloski believes Adams's developed an animus over this perceived disloyalty that eventually led to his resignation.[189]

Of course in an event like this one, it is never just one thing, and there were internal problems in the college. Conflicts within the external relations team led to breakdowns in communication, such that the dean turned to Human Resources for an evaluation of the unit. The Senior Director for Faculty Staff Relations undertook the assignment. In the meantime, Soloski had hired a new director for the unit and sped up her assignment to help relieve some of the problems. When she asked for permission to prepare a formal reprimand of the Director of Alumni Relations, he agreed and at her request also agreed to join the meeting. As the meeting began, the alumni director handed the dean a piece of paper and asked that he read it. The first paragraph alleged that he had sexually harassed her. Soloski immediately ended the meeting and, as dictated by university policy, called legal affairs and faxed a copy of the complaint. Soloski described what followed as a six-year battle to clear his name and "the worst period of my life."

There were never any allegations of touching or anything more, and Soloski had explanations for the two comments the alumni director was now alleging as "sexual harassment." The two comments had been made six months apart with the last one a month prior to the complaint. He had explanations for each and felt certain the process would allow for that additional context. It did not. Soloski was handed the complaint on May 18. On June 16, while attending the annual gathering of the Georgia Press Association, he received a call from an *AJC* reporter who was doing a story on the allegation.[190] Clearly there had been leaked information, source unknown. The confidentiality that by policy was supposed to be guaranteed thus blown, events quickly spiraled toward his resignation, effective June 30, 2005.

Eventually Soloski sued to clear his name, first in Fulton Superior Court and eventually in U.S. District Court. He won complete vindication from first a magistrate judge, and finally the senior district judge who ordered restitution of $75,000 (Soloski says the suit cost him $400,000), an apology and expungement of the allegation and any record of sexual harassment in his personnel files (meaning it never occurred). The judge said the university, meaning Adams, Provost Mace, and its Office of Legal Affairs, had "grossly abused discretionary authority" and wrongfully applied the law of sexual harassment under Title VII. The court concluded, "Plaintiff's (Soloski's) conduct was so far from constituting sexual harassment that to conclude otherwise, while claiming to apply the applicable law, deprived the plaintiff of due process and was a gross abuse of discretion on the part of Defendants." It was as complete a vindication as one could receive, but the cloud did not dissipate. Forever after the disproportionality between complaint and outcome dog this case. Soloski's career options were ruined. It gave rise to suspicions that the university operated from animus, poor judgment, or pretext. How else to explain what happened? In any event, the university looked bad.

It had taken over four years to get this far. Although some highly respected members of the faculty stood by him, Soloski did not find the faculty rallying. He said, "Alumni and faculty members with whom I had been friends shunned me,"[191] a sign that sour conditions in external relations may have spread to the college more generally. In court, he said that being labeled a sexual harasser in a university was the equivalent of being labeled a pedophile. All converged to condemn him to a lonely exile in the Journalism Department, as he continued on the faculty, teaching a couple of classes, one of which was a large lecture section, and trying to re-start a research program.

By earlier having negotiated a severance agreement with former provost Karen Holbrook, he received a better compensation arrangement than most.[192] Although the truth prevailed in a federal court, the personal toll on Soloski was grueling, and he found himself suffering severe depression. One of his admirers and supporters, the famously successful journalist, White House aide, publisher of the *LA Times*, head of CNN News and Grady alumnus, Tom Johnson, suffered a similar condition about which he was open and candid in order to advance the cause of treatment. Johnson helped Soloski get into Emory's renowned clinic led by Dr. Charles Nemeroff, a noted figure in the study of depression. To his credit, Soloski stoically endured the years that followed and never imposed on successor deans. Students also commended him for not bringing his troubles into the classroom. When asked what he might do next, he said he would like to advance the cause of the Center at Emory that his friend Nemeroff founded. (Clearly much has changed since those days and Soloski appears happier and healthier than in many a year, but nothing can make up for the years lost.)

The trials and travails of this period: the Dooley controversy, Deloitte & Touche audit, Arts and Sciences vote of "no confidence," the forced resignation of Soloski—all covered a two-year period, spring 2003 through spring 2005, but had a long shelf-life. They were chronicled in a book published by Rich Whitt, former *Louisville Courier-Journal* Pulitzer Prize-winning reporter, who had recently retired from the *AJC* to pursue writing. In his book, *Behind the Hedges*, New South Books, 2008, he lays out the case for a flawed presidency, which is repeated in Vince Dooley's recent illustrated history of the University.[193] Layered in were the District Court ruling for Soloski, 2009, and a 2010 national story in the *Boston Globe* that echoed all of the above.

Despite the revelations that in their time were dealt with one by one by the administration, Adams had a sixteen-year run of considerable success, and even his detractors concede that much. A billion dollar boom in bonded construction transformed the campus, although state funding for higher education from 2003-on dwindled and imperiled its flagship university. Its faculty and staff paid the price and students were saddled with ever-higher tuition. Adams' ability to be pitch-perfect whether addressing anniversary celebrations of the university's desegregation or assemblages of senior administrators was remarkable. No one in those gatherings doubted that he "got it" or assumed that he was miscast. He never missed the point of it all. And near his retirement, the *Athens Banner-Herald*, May 18, 2013, ran a story "Michael Adams leaves presidency with big imprint on UGA sports" in which athletic administrators and coaches were uniform in praise of his leadership. Adams and his wife were devoted fans and followers of UGA's athletic teams. One observer of the Athens and university scene for the last forty-five years, when asked his opinion of the Adams presidency, thought for a moment and said, "Ask me in twenty years." Indeed, future generations will judge better, even beyond "survivor" explanations, his successes. It all matters.

Who knows what frailties inhabit those who would be leaders and the parade of Grady deans exhibit a wide assortment, including this author and former dean. The same is true of faculty members, who are the engines that drive a college forward, whatever trust individuals may place in deans, or for that matter, presidents. More important, each faculty member plays a role in the memories of students, who as alums have affectionate ties, most of them at least, to their days at Grady, and all of them to particular faculty members who inspired, challenged, gave a helping hand and consoled as needed.

In 2012, those former students turned out for a memorial service in the Chapel for Conrad Fink. Amy Glennon (ABJ 90), publisher of the *AJC*, and Steve Sears (ABJ 90), columnist for *Barron's* and author, spoke for the rest, remembering the man all feared, at first, but all came to love for the unstinting way he improved their performance and the confidence they developed through his gruff, affectionate way. At the close of formal comments, those students, now accomplished professionals, came to the well of the Chapel to share their memories and salute their mentor. To this day, copies of student papers he marked in red pencil have been framed and hang on walls as reminders. The injunction "come see me" at the bottom of a paper was an invitation to a new way of thinking and writing. To be called "pal" by Professor Fink was to become for life a "Finkite" or "Finkster" as they will ever refer to themselves, his passing notwithstanding.

## CLARK LEANS INTO THE CENTENNIAL

When a search firm contacted me, I was then completing ten years as dean at the University of Alabama. I decided to change retirement course and make application. The opening sentence of my letter of interest read, "It is not that I was born and grew up in Grady County, Georgia, or that my master's thesis was on Henry Grady, or that my first published article was on Grady." Surely that made me the sentimental favorite. In any event, I got the job. I received all my degrees in history from Emory University and The University of

North Carolina, focusing on the South since the Civil War. One book, *The Schoolhouse Door: Segregation's Last Stand at the University of Alabama*, published by Oxford University Press, was named a "notable book" by *The New York Times Book Review*. Another was a political biography of the founding editor of the *Charleston News and Courier*, Francis Warrington Dawson, who was Henry Grady's chief rival as architect of the New South. I served as executive assistant to a University of Alabama president, which included a stint as faculty athletics representative. So, I was familiar with the ins and outs of university administration. Besides, we had already purchased a home in Stone Mountain to be near grandchildren. For me, the stars were lining up. (Interestingly and before knowing I would be a candidate, I had wanted Grady's own Dean Krugman to be my successor at Alabama, but Krugman withdrew. Dinner at Kozy's in Tuscaloosa cemented a friendship for life. At that time, Krugman and Len Reid had undertaken responsibilities of the dean's office at Grady on an interim basis.)

During the interviews, I promised President Adams a full five-year term and wound up extending it to seven. I was elated by the opportunity. For me it was truly a "dream job." I remember vividly one faculty member, Lynne Sallot by name, saying there was something special about the Grady spirit. "Don't screw it up," she said, or words to that effect. So, Mary and I endowed the Darwin-Davis Award to honor that spirit. And in that spirit I decided to make my first act a popular one. I asked Dr. Karen King to serve as department head of Advertising and Public Relations, a position she had previously held. Fortunately she acceded to my request, thereby getting me off on the right foot.

I had a problem. Although I knew a great deal about Henry Grady, I did not know much about the University of Georgia, other than to have rooted for the football team growing up (playing Zeke Bratkowski in the back yard) and having envied UGA's academic rise, much as had Soloski. I remember vividly, having walked into the Classic Center before the inaugural football game of the 2006 season and seeing 500 of President Adams' closest friends. I did not know a one—oh, maybe three—and of course a few administrators with whom I had interviewed. By contrast, on becoming dean at Alabama ten years before, I would have known 430 with the others being children and grandchildren, the result of having been six years in the president's office there. Soon, however, with my assistant dean for enterprise and development, Dr. Parker Middleton's orchestration, that liability evaporated. Even an introverted dean must seek out and find energy from those passionate about the college and wanting to infuse it with their own energy. And yes, those contributions came in full measure of time, talent, and treasure. Sooner than one might think, I had my own 500. To identify any among them is to risk the affection I have for all others, but the names that follow represent all and to attempt all would defy the confines of this book's covers. So a few must now stand for the many.

Perhaps one starts with the Julies, Winskie and Moran that is. From Statesboro, Winskie (ABJ 84) presided over Porter Novelli's North American empire, providing leadership for an agency that started with social causes and nonprofits and is now comprehensive and global. To take Winskie's measure, you would have to observe her interacting with Grady students at New York headquarters—then you would know how she got where she got. She explained with exceptional clarity what the business involved and what first steps were necessary. Julie Moran (née Bryan) (ABJ 84), pioneering sideline reporter and later host of ABC's Wide World of Sports, a native of Thomasville, Georgia, got a leg-up as America's Junior Miss in 1980. She covered the Super Bowl, figure skating, and horse racing, including the Triple Crown. Moran left her fifty hour-a-week job with Entertainment Tonight for more time with her two daughters and husband, actor Rob Moran. Success is always about family, if occasionally purchased at its expense. Not for Moran. Both Winskie and Moran are Fellows of the Grady College.

**ABOVE:** Julie Winskie. *Grady College Archives, courtesy Julie Winskie;* **BELOW:** Julie Moran in front of the hedges. *UGA Photographic Services*

In making friends, I learned a lot. While working D.C., Parker Middleton and I always walked wherever we were going, memorably one six-miler in freezing snow, but at the end of another hike was Chris Decherd (ABJ 90) at Voice of America's Cambodian Bureau. I had typical suspicions of VOA as propaganda but soon learned what a news bureau can be. Comprised mostly of native Cambodian journalists, the bureau serves as a link between that country and colonies of Cambodian immigrants in the U.S.; for example, Long Beach, California, and Lowell, Massachusetts. Altogether they make up 1 percent of the U.S. population.

**LEFT:** Chris Decherd. **RIGHT:** (from left to right seated), Elaine Lin, faculty member, Karen King, department head, and Dana Todd. *Grady College Archives*

Selwyn Crawford lectures. *Grady College Archives*

Watching these journalists work, I noticed a scar on the back of an older journalist's head. Decherd explained that by winding up on the bottom of a pile of dead bodies in Cambodia's awful "killing fields" of the 1960's and '70's, he had survived. Neither Parker nor I will ever forget. Decherd, too, is a faithful member of the Alumni Board and loyal "Finkster."

Dana Todd (ABJ 91) not only came back to serve on the Alumni Board, but as Senior Vice President for Marketing at Chicago-based Performics created a special program for Grady students. Todd, a nationally recognized leader in Search Engine Optimization and Search Engine Marketing, now puts that talent in service of students through the Google Performics Scholars program, where Grady students get training in Google advertising, display advertising, search advertising, as well as reporting and analysis. Each participant becomes Google Adwords Certified. Another member of the alumni board, Selwyn Crawford (ABJ 81) is assistant metro editor of the *Dallas*

Katherine Strate in deep thought. *Grady College Archives, UGA Photographic Services*

*Morning News*, but is better known among Gradyites as a stalwart in the Cox Institute's summer program for college news editors where his experience is valued by "democracy's next generation."

Katherine Strate (ABJ 09) was an instant favorite of mine and of Jackson Spalding, the agency to which I outsourced the PR function of the college in my last year. Indefatigable, funny, and focused characterize her commitment. A member of the Alumni Board, she took the lead in that society's initiative to start a Young Alumni Association which is up and growing with immense vitality, thereby completing the alumni loop. But the loop is never complete without those who came before, especially those who are forever young, in this case Neely Young. Highly successful in Georgia newspaper circles and currently editor, publisher and owner of *Georgia Trend Magazine*, Young accepted my request to serve on the Board of Trust and engages actively in that capacity, bringing the wisdom of years to succeeding generations. A (1966) graduate of the business school, he is really a Gradyite and generous at that.

July 1, 2006, my first day, was a Saturday. Knowing no one would be in the building that day, I arranged a reception at the *Cairo Messenger*, my hometown newspaper and still favorite read. The purpose was to proclaim the *Messenger* an official campus of the Grady College—deans do proclamations. It was a small gathering (few remembered me) but all the more intimate and meaningful for it. Its editor, publisher and owner, Randolph H. "Randy" Wind, continues a long family tradition dating back to 1904. In fact, the year of my appointment, 2006, was the centennial year of the establishment of Grady County and Wind was president of the Georgia Press Association, so the stars were truly aligning. Wind's wife Mesha (ABJ 90) was a television reporter and anchor for WALB (Albany, Georgia) when they met. She is currently a member of the Grady Alumni Society Board, a graduate of Leadership Georgia, a principal in UGA's Archway Project with Grady County, and Grady County Woman of the Year. The point here is that I knew from day one that others would determine whatever success I enjoyed, and so they have. Besides, Mesha would bring me "pure Georgia cane syrup" from Grady County. My cup overflowed.

Drewry Room re-make. Seated left to right, Cindi Johnson, Brian Begnaud, Kirsten Strausbaugh, Booke Rooks, Janice Hume. Standing left to right, Jane Worley, Karen King, Lynne Sallot, Sean Polite, Debbie Sickles, Ann Hollifield, Donna Lord, Michael McNiven, Louise McElroy, Terri Baker, Jenn Smith, Parker Middleton, Karen Andrews, James Biddle, and Donna LeBlond. *Grady College Archives*

I tell any and all that "luck" is my companion. For example, on arriving I thought the interior walls of Grady looked a little drab and the wall hangings a little dated and quite frankly not representing the college's diversity. So, I said, "We own our walls," which in my limited imagination meant re-arranging the pictures or some such. Well, a faculty and staff group quickly formed, spearheaded by Kirsten Strausbaugh-Hutchinson, a member of the advertising faculty and a designer par excellence. Then Brooke Rooks, head of the business office, found resources, and suddenly all walls in the building were painted in vivid colors adorned by geometric design elements in relief. Moreover, this group single-handedly took over the Drewry Room and again based on Strausbaugh's design plan, transformed it into an aesthetic marvel, all done on weekends and off-hours. That experience became a mantra for my administration, or as I put it, "I intended less and got more," which on reflection is the way I characterize my seven-year tenure.

That tenure, 2006-2013, was marked by significant faculty and student achievement, one major failure, and one letter of resignation; in short, a tenure like most. Grady had recently adopted a strategic plan that amounted to generalizable if important aspirations. My first step was to develop an "action agenda" that emerged from my candidacy, and accordingly asked faculty and staff focus groups to develop each emphasis of the agenda, which they did in the fall of 2006. Quickly there emerged a proposal for a media studies major from the college's arts and sciences heritage, which in turn harked back to the 1950's discussion of journalism's "communications" roots. Faculty also developed action plans for facilities, diversity and other emphases—in all, seven.

One in particular drew special scrutiny and attention: an investigation into securing a commercial license for television. Based on a "teaching hospital" model that I developed at the University of Alabama in 2000, it found favor among the broadcast/digital journalism faculty, which had depth experience in television, including international start-ups. Together, we began investigating options from low power to full power commercial licenses. Eyes quickly fell on WNEG-TV, a CBS-affiliate owned by Media General and operating from Toccoa—NEG standing for Northeast Georgia. A trip to Richmond, Virginia, that included then former UGA Senior Vice President for Financial Affairs and now Chancellor, Hank Huckaby, resulted in an offer by Media General to sell but at a number I thought too high to recommend. When President Adams said he did not think so, we returned to the negotiating table and in fact got the number down to what I regarded as reasonable.

We then undertook a campaign to inform all constituencies of the value of such an undertaking. We made an alliance with the North Georgia Community Foundation (NGCF) and sought support from the Knight Foundation to establish community information centers, qua bureaus, throughout Northeast Georgia. I went to Miami, along with Jim Mathis of NGCF, where Knight had convened a gathering of community foundations to discuss what Knight might accomplish by working through them. In turn Knight sent a deputy to Athens who reported favorably but in the end Knight did not accept UGA's commitment of $5 million (the figure it had in the station) as a match in lieu of the match required of the North Georgia Community Foundation (which it could not afford), although initially officers at Knight seemed favorably disposed to such an arrangement. I continued spreading the word to civic clubs throughout the service area, to fellow deans encouraging them to develop educational and outreach programming. Already the UGA Research Foundation had committed $5 million for purchase and start-up costs, which eventually reached $5.8 million.

The university signed the purchase agreement in June of 2008 for transfer in October. The ink had not dried, when other pens were inking deals between the Southeastern Conference and ESPN and CBS, effectively precluding WNEG from access to UGA athletic programing, even delayed broadcasts, and thereby instant UGA branding for the station. Among other things, the agreement ended the possibility of a deal with Comcast that would have paid UGA $8 million for athletics programming—45 events a year for five years, produced by Grady students with staff assistance—and would have given UGA a statewide channel valued at $4 million a year. UGA could have recorded the total value of the Comcast proposal under CASE standards at $28 million. Then in September, before taking possession of WNEG in October, Lehman Brothers collapsed, portending the Great Recession.

We pursued partnerships for the commercial television venture with Cox Enterprises (Grady alum and vice chair of the Cox Board, Dennis Berry, thought well of the idea), Turner Networks, and Raycom Media. Raycom proposed locating a digital media hub in the station that had been built out on the ground floor of Grady. Its purpose would have been to locate approximately a dozen journalists, who, working with Grady students, would re-purpose content from Raycom's forty-seven stations that reached 12 percent of the U.S. market. Additionally, they agreed to work with WNEG to obtain Raycom content, including sports. A number of faculty members were understandably suspicious of such an arrangement, but working with Raycom's senior executive leadership, who came to campus on several occasions, questions were addressed and most answered. Department Head Ann Hollifield, with Michael Castengera and Steve Smith of Digital Broadcast News were especially helpful in these discussions. A deal seemed within reach in January 2010.

Then the provost believed that he had reliable information of widespread faculty opposition to the agreement. When I said it was my job as dean to determine the level of faculty support and asked if I could put it to a scheduled vote, the provost said, "no," whereupon I resigned, effective June 30, 2010. It was a question of process. The faculty and Raycom executives had spent a lot of time debating, discussing, and developing a proposal. I reported these meetings and discussions to senior administrative leadership on a regular basis. The faculty should have had a formal say on whether it wished to recommend it, the dean then forwarding it with his own recommendation. The administration later talked me out of the decision to resign, but of such inner workings are deanships made and occasionally broken.

Ultimately WNEG failed financially, and the university decided to convert it to a public station under the call letters WUGA-TV. It was a case of back to the future as UGA had transferred an earlier public television license to Georgia Public Broadcasting in 1982. (Cox "gifted" the license to UGA in 1958, but it did not go on air until 1965.) Grady alum and Senior Vice President for External Affairs, Tom Landrum, played a significant role in the conversion to public. That action kept in play opportunities for students to experience real-world television and for UGA to broadcast its content. Tom Jackson, Vice President for UGA Public Affairs, says that "with satellite and cable carriage across the Atlanta DMA to the Alabama line, and the over-air signal from Gwinnett (County) to Greenville (S.C.), it's the largest coverage area of any Georgia station." (It may be that the time has passed for universities to optimize legacy media but in combination with social media, it could still work.)

I can be faulted for asking the college and university to accept the risks and freely accept responsibility, but the retained assets, including spectrum, and opportunities that were re-purposed as WUGA-TV have significant value. Moreover, in an arrangement worked out by me with a New York broker the university received at least two offers to "buy" that would have covered costs of the agreement (with retained assets) made with the Research Foundation. Michael Castengera and Parker Middleton also were keys in negotiating this possible way forward. To its credit, the university determined not to accept the offer and to pursue the public option. Also of note were the enduring and lasting relationships that were built between the college and leadership at Cox, Turner, and Raycom, each of which has paid significant dividends.

Indelible, too, for me, was an "open mic" meeting with students. These meetings were scheduled from time to time by Grady Ambassadors, who in addition to representing the college before its external constituencies also represent its students. This particular session came in the wake of WNEG's acquisition and changes it portended in the broadcast journalism program, changes that students in that curriculum found unsettling, at least as they understood the situation. Just before the session I got word that it might be a bit testy, so fortunately Ann Hollifield and Michael Castengera, who understood most how the directional changes would affect students, made themselves available. Still, it was an intense exchange, but from it came one relationship that lasts.

Katie Barlow, who was president of UGA's Student Government Association, took a lead role in framing student questions, some rather sharp. Later, feeling a bit apologetic, Barlow visited me. I assured her no apology was needed and that she and her fellow students were on an important mission and rightly expected answers. From that episode came a lasting friendship. I had the privilege of writing a recommendation letter for Barlow to Georgetown Law School. There she became a National Champion in the

Katie Barlow stands and delivers. *UGA Photographic Services*

American Bar Association's 2014 National Appellate Advocacy Competition and serves as an assistant to NPR's Nina Totenberg. I now know why I felt overmatched in the "open mic" meeting.

## BUILDING ON STRENGTH

In 2008 the college launched the Centennial Campaign for Grady with a Tribute Gala at the Classic Center where over fifty leading alumni and friends of the college were inducted into the inaugural class of the Grady Fellowship. It also announced a commitment to increase the asset value of the college by $100 million by 2015. Included in that appraisal was the estimated value of a successful commercial television venture and a new building for Grady, neither of which obtained, at least in the way originally planned. The value of a new building was estimated at $37 million, a figure comparable to what Texas achieved through the Belo Foundation and Missouri with

Donald Reynolds generosity. However, Grady had no similar friend or foundation step forward, in part because of the crushing weight of the recession. A new building had also been a priority for Dean Soloski, who developed with faculty and staff a handsome prospectus.

Where Grady succeeded was in major gift activity that enabled it to go from four endowed and named faculty professorships and chairs to fifteen. My work in that arena was done in partnership with the college's chief advancement officer Dr. J. Parker Middleton. A remarkable executive assistant, Cindi Johnson, enabled and coordinated our work. With their help and that of others, especially Diane Murray and Shanna Sheats, an alumni advisory board was re-established with the exclusive purpose of reaching out to the over 23,000 alumni who represent the college. The alumni awards event provides the occasion for the college to recognize young alumni who are off to a fast career start with the John E. Drewry Early Career Award; mid-career achievement, with an award named for Henry W. Grady; and finally life-time achievement, with an award named for John Holliman of CNN Gulf War fame who tragically lost his life in a 1997 automobile accident. The event moved back to Athens from Atlanta and is now held as a brunch at the Georgian Hotel, with the award recipients and the President of the Alumni Society then proceeding to the Classic Center for Grady's spring convocation that recognizes well over 400 graduating students and their families and friends.

It is quite a ceremony. Just imagine, over 400 graduates on stage, over 2,000 family members and friends in the Classic Center's main concert hall. The platform party emerges on stage with the assembled graduates seated behind a massive, elegant curtain, the dean asks the audience to rise for the meditation, a piano rendition of James Weldon Johnson's, "Lift Every Voice," in turn yielding to a crescendo of Brahm's "Academic Festival Overture;" then parents and all, many expecting a processional, are greeted instead with a rapidly ascending curtain, revealing all on stage, the dean proclaiming, "Families and friends, behold your graduates!" The audience bursts into a frenzy of shouts and applause. No one forgets the moment. The alumni event and convocation has an impresario, Karen Andrews, Grady's incomparable director of events.

Spring convocation 2011 had a special moment. The speaker for the occasion was Ed Bastian, President of Delta Airlines. His daughter Brittany was among the graduates, but he also had another reason for being there. We were to name our 20,000th graduate. At the conclusion of his remarks, a

**ABOVE:** Convocation with alumni award winners at right. *UGA Photographic Services*; **BELOW LEFT:** Karen Andrews with Grady Ambassadors Serra Stalling, Francesca Pefianco, and Helen Farmakis. *Grady College Archives*; **BELOW RIGHT:** Ed Bastian, President of Delta and friend of Grady. *Grady College Archives*

drum containing the names of all graduates in that class was rolled, accompanied by 800 thrumming feet on stage. A card was pulled. The dean read the name on it. A stunned silence followed before Kristyn DeMaeyer of Lawrenceville, Georgia, rose, a little unsteady, to accept applause and congratulations as the 20,000th graduate of the Grady College. There was more. She stood by President Bastian who announced that Delta had two tickets, first class, anywhere in the world in her name. The dean then pronounced all 2011 graduates eligible to claim status as Grady's 20,000th. It was a Twenty Grand occasion indeed.

Grady needed a leader to spearhead the alumni charge. While still dean-in-waiting, I found her across a crowded room high atop New York's Rockefeller Center. With a business card that read: Consul: Head Political/Economic Relations and Public Affairs, the Consulate General of

Canada, New York, NY, Jennifer Sloan (ABJ 86) had previously chaired the college's Alumni Board. So, I thought, "Strike now, don't wait, ask now!" In progressive steps, "Jenn" led the re-formed board through several iterations until its present configuration that provides dynamic leadership for the college. During that same time she became Executive Vice President for one of the world's three largest diversified mining companies, Toronto-based CVRD Inco. Before she was done, she took the inaugural Communications portfolio for York University, Canada's third largest and considerably bigger than UGA, and is now Director of Governmental Affairs for Target Canada—and through it all kept Grady on her mind.

Jenn Sloan on target for Grady. *Grady College Archives, courtesy Jennifer Sloan*

Another change that we considered more than symbolic was renaming the Advisory Board to Board of Trust, following a decision to label the college "A Tradition and a Trust," in order to anchor its mission against a background of digital turmoil in the industries it serves. We also decided to call its students "Democracy's Next Generation," which appears in gold lettering above the entrance to the Journalism Building, and all graduates are "pinned" into the Grady Society at convocation. These were small but important steps in re-asserting the college's brand. The final makeover in these years was the Grady Fellowship, established when I visited Tom Johnson, who quickly announced that he would support any dean of Grady and "shoot a bullet" for the college but was beyond board service and like involvement. Although I was not with Johnson for other than introduction purposes, I realized how valuable Johnson and others like him were to the college's mission. Thus I declared the Thursday before Thanksgiving to be All Fellows Day and the occasion for inducting into the Grady Fellowship individuals whose lives and careers have brought lasting fame and support to the college. Most but not all are alumni of the college, and a Sanford Circle recognizes posthumous Fellows and those Fellows who have passed in the year ending.

The Fellowship Gala reflects Peabody production values, as Jody Danneman (ABJ 88), who produces the Peabody Awards Show in the Grand Ball Room of the Waldorf Astoria, serves up an audio and visual feast in tribute to new inductees and a salute to all Fellows of the College. Danneman formed Atlanta ImageArts in 1997 and became executive producer of the Peabody Awards in 1999. Danneman is ably assisted by another extraordinarily talented Gradyite, Shannon Sullivan Callado (ABJ '10), who joined Atlanta Image Arts as an intern before accepting the permanent position. Danneman has also chaired Grady's Alumni Society Board and in 2011 became the college's third recipient of its Dean's Medal.

**ABOVE:** Tom Johnson DiGamma Kappa Award recipient, interview by student. **BELOW:** Shannon Sullivan Callado and Jody Danneman, producers extraordinaire. *Grady College Archives*

Each Fellowship Gala also featured a theme that drove development initiatives in the college. Memorable was the evening devoted to sports journalism. Not only did the gala feature a star-studded panel of sports journalists led by Conrad Fink, I also invited UGA sports legends from Grady County: Hall of Fame football players like the "Big Toe from Cairo," Bobby Walden; "Big Bill" Stanfill of Miami Dolphins fame; track and field great and also UGA coach, Lewis Gainey (my high school classmate); and most legendary, Teresa Edwards, who won five Olympic medals in basketball (four Gold) and seventeen international golds before losing a game—clearly as I boasted, "Edwards is UGA's greatest ever athlete."

Present that evening, either as panelists or honorees, were sports journalist legends Tony Barnhart (ABJ 76), Mark Schlabach (ABJ 96), and Senior Associate Athletic Director Claude Felton (ABJ 70, MA 71), a.k.a., the "Claudefather of Sports Information." Current UGA Athletic Director, Greg McGarity (ABJ 73) is a Grady Fellow, and the recent passing of Grady Fellow Dan Magill (ABJ 42), a legend in sports information and unsurpassed in the world of intercollegiate tennis, places him in the Fellowship's Sanford Circle.

The developmental theme that evening led to the John Huland Carmical Chair in Sports Journalism, currently held by Vicki Michaelis and an Athletic Association Professorship held by Tom Reichert, also department head in Advertising and Public Relations. Also instrumental in developing that

**ABOVE:** Welch Suggs and Vicki Michaelis. **BELOW:** Chip Caray and Greg McGarity. *Grady College Archives*

initiative was Welch Suggs, who joined the faculty after serving as an assistant to President Adams with special assignment to Athletics and as a staff officer to the Knight Commission on Athletics. Also of note, Jimmy Alston (ABJ 66), who heads the Carmical Foundation, worked tirelessly with Dean Clark and the Grady team in creating the chair.

(While on the subject of sports journalism, I must establish my own sports "creds." Playing pitch and catch, using green tung nuts in the absence of a baseball, all the while listening to Red Barber announce Brooklyn Dodger baseball on the radio in the early fifties, I was alternately Preacher Roe or Carl Erskine or Don Newcombe, and Barber was calling my fireball. In that way I came to appreciate, even jury, baseball announcers, using the Peabody's sole criterion of excellence. Sixty years later, I am prepared to name the greatest announcer of all time, and it is a Grady grad, Chip Caray (ABJ 87), son of the inimitable Skip Caray and grandson of legendary Harry Caray. As great as his predecessors were, none has called a game with more concision and clarity or put the spotlight on guests in the booth with such consummate interviewing skills. He has even been known to have his daughter, Summerlyn, in the booth with a transparent fatherly affection that never yet obscures the game. "He is the best," so says a former hotshot pitcher, now dean emeritus. Caray is also a member of the Board of Trust.)

I continued to reside in Stone Mountain to be near grandchildren and commuted daily. Walking into the building each morning with staff members like Donna LeBlond, Sophie Barnes, Debbie Sickles or Cheryl Christopher, I was reminded continually how much I owed to them and to faculty and academic leadership: to Conrad Fink for the Carmical Sports Journalism Chair and to Kent Middleton for his role in drafting and developing same; to Lee Becker who received AEJMC's Deutschman Award for lifetime achievement in research and who took me on a memorable Cox Center venture to Belgrade; to Tom Reichert for Cannes Lions and a joint venture with Creative Circus, a portfolio school in Atlanta; to Betty Jones for memorable PRSSA trips with students to Washington, D.C.; and to all others, Kristen, Peggy, Carolina, Mark, Biddle, Jenn, and to Juan Ming for indulging my naming her first born "baby Cullie" (the female spelling of my nickname), each of some 100 individuals remembered by me in such particular ways and each evoking gratitude.

**ABOVE:** Jim Cox Kennedy. *Courtesy* ***Atlanta Journal-Constitution***; **BELOW:** Kennedy Professors, Scott Shamp, Karen King, Karen Russell, and David Hazinski. *Grady College Archives*

Other chairs and professorships included four Jim Kennedy Professorships in New Media, donated by James Cox Kennedy, chair of Cox Enterprises, Inc., two Charlayne Hunter Gault Distinguished Writers in Residence, supported by endowment and a gift from *The Atlanta Journal-Constitution*, the aforementioned Yarbrough Chair in Crisis Communication and Tieger Chair in Public Affairs Communication, as well as an Athletics Foundation Professorship. Together with the Dowden Professorship, they built support for faculty in an era of severe economic recession.

State funding for higher education topped out in 2003 and began a steady decline through 2014 thereby ending general compensation improvement for faculty and staff. The last increase was January 2008, based on 2006-07 performance indicators, even as employee contributions from health insurance to parking rose steeply over those same years. Targeted improvements helped, such as counter offers to faculty who were sought by other institutions and stipends for research productive faculty, plus professorships and chairs, but for public higher education generally, especially for staff, it had been downhill since 2007. The remarkable thing is despite the crushing weight of the recession and decisions in Atlanta, faculty and staff maintained Grady's vaunted spirit.

**LEFT:** Charlayne Hunter-Gault and Valerie Boyd, gifted writers. *UGA Photographic Services*; **RIGHT:** Cynthia Tucker with Mary Frances Early, UGA's first African-American graduate. *Grady College Archives, photo by Nancy Evelyn, UGA Graduate School*

In my last year the Regents approved a Master of Fine Arts in Mass Media Arts that included narrative nonfiction and documentary production, which is scheduled to launch in the college's centennial year. Spearheaded by Valerie Boyd, former book critic for the *AJC* and author of *Wrapped in Rainbows*, a biography of Zora Neal Hurston that, when reading it while interviewing for the deanship, convinced me that I was coming to the right place. Boyd was the inaugural Charlayne Hunter-Gault Distinguished Writer in Residence. Also in the lead on the MFA initiative was Nate Kohn, professor and associate director of the Peabody Awards who led from the media side. Associate Dean for Graduate Studies and Research Jeff Springston successfully navigated the proposal through the university and on to the Regents. Springston's leadership was key. Joining Boyd as a Hunter-Gault Distinguished Writer was 2007 Pultizer Prize-winning columnist Cynthia Tucker, who proceeded from a long line of great opinion writers in Atlanta going back to Henry Grady himself and continuing through Ralph McGill and Gene Patterson. Working with leadership at the *AJC*, especially its editor Kevin Riley, to make that possible was a high moment for me, a great admirer of Tucker's work.

Serendipity has a name: Monica Kaufman Pearson, the most recognized name and face in Atlanta broadcast journalism. Longtime WSB anchor, recipient of over thirty local and regional Emmys, and member of the Atlanta Press Club Hall of Fame, Pearson "retired" to Grady to pursue a master's degree, a program she began in 2012. When asked why a veteran of such

Monica Kaufman Pearson, most recognized anchor in history of Atlanta television and Grady great. *Grady College Archives*

experience would return to study journalism, she said, "My mind was just opened so much. I was a good reporter. I would have been a better reporter if I had gone through this (program) earlier." Inspired by media history professor Janice Hume, Pearson did her thesis on Reconstruction era news coverage of Georgia's first African-American congressman. Pearson wanted qualifications to teach, but she was already a "student teacher" by her very presence in the classroom—reminiscent of the way a far younger John Drewry got into teaching all those years ago. Pearson received her degree on August 1, 2014, and is considering a terminal degree, either Grady's MFA or Ph.D. (Imagine an event featuring Pearson, Cynthia Tucker, and Charlayne Hunter-Gault talking about journalism and moderated by Valerie Boyd. It will happen.)

In addition to the MFA, the university also recommended a move of the Center for Health and Risk Communication to the college in recognition of its heavy investments in health communication. Dr. Glenn Nowak, first hired out of the University of Wisconsin in the early nineties, then joining the Centers for Disease Control as a chief communications officer, returned to Grady to head the center. However, he may best be remembered as # 2723, his number in the 1994 New York City Marathon, a study in pain itself. (Grady faculty members do all sorts of wonderful and weird things.)

Although the college did not get a new building, it began converting each and every floor to new purposes. It started with faculty and staff's determination to redesign the interior, especially on the Second Floor, and continued with conversion of the First Floor for television programming,

Glen Nowak, 1994. *Grady College Archives*

along with gaming and virtual communication research labs, to the Fourth Floor, completely outfitted for the New Media Institute and the Cox Center for International Research and Training in Journalism and Mass Communication, plus classrooms, labs and commons space. Moreover, with construction cost-savings from the economic downturn, brick turned to glass in modernizing the face of the college. The college has designs on the Fifth Floor and will sooner rather than later get it. So, even without a windfall donor, the college is improving its facility assets measurably.

Jay Hamilton. *Grady College Archives, photo by Center for Teaching and Learning, UGA*

Faculty and staff made this happen. Dr. Jay Hamilton, now a Meigs Professor, a superb scholar and an even better human being, took charge of the planning committee that saw to a conclusion these critical improvements to a forty-five year-old building. Even his committee's herculean efforts would not have succeeded without the incomparable Brooke Rooks, chief financial officer of the college, whose charge includes facilities. She comprehends and makes everything happen, especially when it requires creative resource combinations. She and her staff of Terri Baker, Erin O'Hare, and Denise Mattox are unbelievable and irreplaceable. These plans were an elaboration of those developed under Soloski's tenure, proof that nothing starts or stops, academia is a continuously unfolding realization of its possibilities.

A recent report on facilities, developed by a faculty focus group in 2014 under Dean Charles N. Davis's direction and led by, you guessed it, Jay Hamilton, came to similar conclusions a focus group reached in 2007; to wit, the building has "three main problems: 1. It inhibits collaboration among faculty both within and between departments and campus-wide, and between students, 2. It embodies working conditions that inhibit optimal productivity, and 3. It does not present to visitors an impression of the college that corresponds to its current strengths, or to its vision and mission. " Proof that the more things change. . . . Yet the report is right and not far off the criticism offered soon after the building opened in 1969. Time is always the enemy and a new building is highly to be desired, but until that day, one should also remember that dreams and opportunities have been built in the present edifice.

Brooke Rooks gets it done. *Grady College Archives*

## THE GRADY WAY

All great Grady traditions continued into the 21st Century but a number were transformed. The "institutes"—press, broadcasters, and industrial editors—had been discontinued, but Grady remained engaged with the broadcasters association, the press association, and advertising and public relations professionals. Engagement strategies developed as "learning alliances" with agencies and corporations such as Turner for everything from television programing to digital outreach in the form of new apps and research. Parker Middleton played the instrumental role in developing those alliances. A special relationship developed with Steve Koonin, Jennifer Dorian, and Jeff Gregor, the executive team at Turner Entertainment. It provided funding for faculty and student research and focus groups centered on new programming for the network. For example, one Grady team did a "digital roll-out" proposal for the popular late night Conan O'Brien program. When integrated into Turner plans, the O'Brien show now boasts a whopping 10.7 million Twitter followers and another 2.5 million Facebook fans.[194]

Steve Koonin and his wife Eydie also made a generous gift to support scholarships for Grady students. Their son, David, was a regular in the dean's office, much to my pleasure and instruction. So was young Jeffrey Gregor, who made an unfortunate wager with his dean and lost. (It was Cairo High School, 21, St. Pius, 0, in a state football championship playoff game.) Memorable for me were meetings with Steve Koonin at Oceanaire in Atlanta where we talked college business, especially the commercial television

Steve and Eydie Koonin flanked by first Koonin Scholars, Cody Nichelson, Whitney Jinks, and Tukio Machini. *Grady College Archives*

venture. Koonin's counsel was like "drinking from a fire hose," so developmentally sound were his thoughts. Although not a Grady graduate, Koonin is a Fellow of the college and recent recipient of the college's DiGamma Kappa Award that lists among its recipients Walter Cronkite, Barbara Walters, Ted Turner, Bernard Shaw, Tom Brokaw, Leslie Stahl, Katie Couric, Wolf Blitzer, and now Steve Koonin, now president of the Atlanta Hawks—who at this writing are on a miracle season.

Grady's relationships with Atlanta's major brands continued: Delta with Tim Mapes (ABJ 86) and its president, Grady Fellow Ed Bastian. Coca-Cola with Scott Williamson (MMC 92); Lockheed with Brian Johnstone (ABJ 68); and Verizon with Chris Jones (ABJ 73), all created the most envied internship programs for Grady. Scott's time in the halls of Grady made it hard to distinguish him from a faculty member; Chris extended his time as chair of the board to complete Clark's term as dean; and Brian worked with Lockheed's Dallas Office to assure that Grady was always represented in its signature internship program. Brad McAfee, President of Porter Novelli North America and Manager of its Atlanta Office, has made himself maximally available to students, faculty, and deans of the college. Previously noted in context of board leadership was Mark Smith of Smith Communications, Inc., who remains the longest serving board chair, Swann Seiler with Georgia Power, and current board chair Melissa Libby (ABJ 85) of Libby and Associates, a food PR agency in Atlanta. Melissa also has been an invaluable sounding board for Grady deans. (Get Melissa to tell you about taking Julia

**LEFT:** Melissa Libby, center, with Julia Child and wine legend Robert Mondavi in Atlanta. *Grady College Archives, courtesy Melissa Libby*; **RIGHT:** Dink and Eric NeSmith, father and son, and dedicated to Grady. *Grady College Archives, courtesy Dink NeSmith*

Child for lunch at a McDonald's drive-thru in Atlanta. She swears it was Child's idea.)

Through the years Grady alums have given back generously of their time, talents and treasure—none more so than William H. "Dink" NeSmith (ABJ 70), recent Chair of the University System of Georgia Board of Regents, and true friend of every Grady dean since 1970, his graduation year. Dink had to have been the youngest chair of the Grady Advisory Board (1982), the youngest president of the Georgia Press Association (about the same time), the youngest trustee of the UGA Foundation, and the youngest chair of the regents. If not, it is a razor's edge. His son Eric (ABJ 02) follows in that tradition as current President of the Grady Society Alumni Board. One measure of the Bulldog nation's health is how many NeSmith feet are under Dink and Pam's holiday table. Grady is truly a big intimate family. All Gradyites know it.

Under Lee Becker's leadership, the Cox Center will reach thirty years in the college's centennial. Becker took Al Hester's accomplishments and has continued to elaborate them for journalists around the globe. The grants garnered for these opportunities now have reached millions of dollars. Tudor Vlad, a Senior Research Scientist in the college, has been instrumental in the Center's success. As dean, I especially enjoyed visiting with international delegations, often asked on those occasions to explain the American South in the politics and culture of the nation. As noted earlier, all who participate in Cox Center programs come away feeling that they have learned more from their

**LEFT:** Lee Becker makes a point in Belgrade. **RIGHT:** Carolina Acosta-Alzura and Tudor Vlad in Belgrade with Serbian Journalists. *Grady College Archives*

guests or host countries than they have given, lessons in journalism and mass communication that they pass on to Grady colleagues and especially students.

The Cox Institute also enjoyed a renewal. It changed its name from Newspaper Strategies and Management to Journalism, Innovation, Management and Leadership. My penchant for "luck" held. Well, make that Grady's luck. It came in the form of Keith Herndon (ABJ 82), who managed Cox digital media strategies from the mid-nineties well into this century. He also performed due diligence on Cox new media investments. With a master's degree from Oklahoma and a Ph.D. from Australia's Curtin University of Technology, he came to Grady with the business savvy of a Conrad Fink, an unmatched experience with the digital future, and a book on the same. To join Grady, he gave up most of a lucrative private consulting practice. His love of Grady, its students, faculty and staff was compelling. Moreover, Kent Middleton's willingness to accept the portfolio of the Morris Chair in Newspaper Strategy and Management, which includes direction of the Institute, previously held by Fink, made the transition both possible and seamless. That Conrad had gotten to know and value Herndon's work prior to his passing made the handoff perfect. Among many other things, Herndon has established a partnership with Poynter to offer a Certificate in Media Leadership to select Grady students.

Making the transition possible was Janice Hume's willingness to step up as Department Head in Journalism, following Kent Middleton's most successful thirteen-year run in that position. A fourteen-year veteran of the department, Hume had just completed her third book, *Popular Media and*

**ABOVE:** Cecil Bentley, Keith Herndon, and Kent Middleton. **BELOW:** Janice Hume with student, 2002. *Grady College Archives*

*the American Revolution: Shaping Collective Memory* that extends her leading role in the scholarship of public memory. She brings with her scholarship a significant record of professional experience and becomes the first woman to head the department and now holds the Carter Chair.

Early in my tenure the New Media Institute returned to Grady. It had previously been designated a university institute and was quartered downtown. Although it maintains its interdisciplinary approach, its return to Grady both physically and programmatically was a boon for Grady students. A New Media Certificate is a real asset in any job search. Founded in 1999 by Scott Shamp, a Kennedy New Media Professor, it is a hive of activity as students swarm around Shamp, Clate Sanders, and Emuel Aldridge on

Shamp and NMI students in front of President's Office, 2013. *Grady College Archives*

projects that develop digital skill sets and problem solving approaches for real world applications. The Institute's Advisory Board has assembled major players, especially in the Atlanta market, and it has pursued projects jointly with the likes of Coca-Cola, Turner, UPS, and First Union. The academic year always concludes with the "SLAM," where students wow a packed auditorium with examples of their work, which have merited the Shamp of Approval, otherwise known as "Cool!" Shamp emcees the event, and it is "Awesome!"

*(Grief comes to Grady. On April 25, 2009, as parents and friends gathered for another grand SLAM, spirits were exceptionally high. Then, shortly after noon Blackberries began to buzz with news that a shooting had occurred somewhere just off campus. I tried urgently to get through to campus security, who when reached, expressed some exasperation because of the number of calls, but said the campus was not on lock down. Still, as information accumulated, it was clear something terrible had happened, so Cecil Bentley, director of career services and assistant director of the Cox Institute, and I closed the doors to the auditorium and stood watch. The Cox Institute for college newspaper editors had only recently had staff of the Virginia Tech Collegiate Times recount their experience covering the horrific shooting there only two years before. The SLAM continued but everyone worried. No one knew where the shooter was, but word began to spread as to who it was.*

*(George Zinkhan was a highly respected professor of marketing in the Terry College. He held the Coca-Cola Company Professorship and was a colleague and collaborator with Grady faculty and graduate students, especially in Advertising. In fact, he received the American Academy of Advertising's top research award and served a term as its president. We considered him a colleague and friend. Now he was the presumed killer. In an apparent jealous rage, he, with his children in the car, drove to where the Athens Town & Gown Theatre was holding a reunion picnic. Leaving the children in the car, he got out and proceeded to kill his wife and two others. Seated directly across from the first victim was Sean Polite, who had recently taken a position as an assistant in the Dean's Office. Heavily involved with the community theatre was Leara Rhodes, a much admired and longtime*

*faculty member in magazines and a dedicated community volunteer. At the scene also was Michael Castengera's daughter. The Grady family was there. It was devastating, but in the days and months ahead, all experienced what it means to be in "the arms of Grady," an emotional time relieved only by shared love and affection and that too should never be forgotten.)*

Equally spellbinding among student presentations is Gradyfest where media arts students show their best, Grady's own film festival. It shows on the same Saturday evening in April that SLAM takes place during the day. Featured are student productions that range from fiction to nonfiction, cartoons to animation, student imagination unleashed. With the coaching of award-winning filmmaker and narrative and documentary specialist Jennifer Smith and digital artist extraordinaire James Biddle, the energy in the theatre is palpable as parents and friends flock to see the show and no one is disappointed. Turner's Dennis Adamovich juries the Turner Prize and Grady Fellows Carolyn and Randall Abney determine the Dean's Prize. Numerous other awards are handed out, a truly special evening. Smith also developed a domestic study abroad program, called L.A. Summer Study, and if you have never witnessed Biddle announce the graduates at Grady's convocation, you have not heard anything yet, basso profundo indeed.

Gradyfest and SLAM begin to explain why the Grady spirit is so jubilant at convocation and at commencement exercises in Sanford Stadium or Stegeman Coliseum, but it does not end there. A final overarching element is the "service learning" and "team learning" that are hallmarks at Grady. Nowhere is this more evident than in Grady's campaigns classes in advertising and public relations. Students in those programs even have their own agencies, Creative Solutions in PR and HBS in Advertising, agencies that

James Biddle, maestro. *Grady College Archives*

Beverly Surowiec, Jackie Reed, faculty adviser Ron Lane, Barbara Busey, Dennis Shelton, as winning ad team, 1982, part of the Grady tradition of team learning. Jackie Reed Herr is now a Board of Trust member. *Grady College Archives*

have their own client lists separate and apart from formal classes. Every campaigns class has a client, be it nonprofit, governmental, or in some instances for profits. It all depends on the case; for example, a greener campus, public safety, at risk schools, healthier choices. In the end each client receives a "book" to rival that produced by an Atlanta agency.

Another learning alliance is with Ryan Seacrest. The phenomenal entertainer wanted to establish a foundation, a major purpose of which would be to relieve and inspire children confined to hospitals. His father, Gary, recalled how as a kid with a mic in hand Ryan acted out his future. Why not give the same lift to youth generally but especially for those in Children's Hospitals. Naming his sister Meredith (ABJ 2003) president of the foundation, they decided to launch in his hometown of Atlanta. With Grady College as partner, the first children's broadcast media center opened in Emory's Eggleston Hospital. Assisted by Grady student interns, information and entertainment programming focused on children through closed-circuit television. The focus on children included their own participation. The excitement has now spread nationwide, with another center at Scottish Rite Children's Hospital in Atlanta. Ryan may have been only a UGA matriculate before heading for Hollywood and destiny, but his current roommate is a black lab named Georgia. It is clearly on his mind. His mother, Connie, says

Seacrest family, Connie, Ryan, Meredith, and Gary. *Courtesy Meredith Seacrest*

that as he turns forty, he is about ready to settle down, but then why, if your aspirations were to become the next Dick Clark and Merv Griffin. His multimedia empire combines the best of both his idols.

One recent project had Grady Students joining an Archway Community, so designated by the UGA Office of Public Service and Outreach that adopts counties throughout Georgia, which demonstrate they can benefit from UGA's planning resources. In this instance the Archway team determined that Grady County had the ingredients to make those resources work and that among the county's most important needs was a communications plan. Since it was the dean's home county and the one named for Henry Grady, he joined the work in progress and was hugely impressed by the final presentation by Grady students. So was the leadership in Grady County. The result is a new lake in Grady County that had been an aspiration of the county for well over fifty years. As important a leave-behind was a new understanding by residents about how they can communicate more effectively and use media to advance common interests.

Working 250 miles from Athens, Grady students did the research, mapped the available communication assets, and devised the implementation plan. It is the kind of teamwork, service learning, collaborative critical thinking, and execution such as few other educational experiences can offer.

**ABOVE:** Team Grady works for Grady County. *Grady College Archives, photo by UGA Office of Public Service and Outreach*; **BELOW:** Dean Clark urges calm. *UGA Special Events*

The result is that students who graduate from Grady, and over 99 percent of those admitted do, share a bond like no other. From media arts to magazines, from journalism in all its forms to campaigns that influence public policy and human behavior, students learn by doing. As Oliver Wendell Holmes put it and they discover, "To act is to affirm the worth of an end. To persist in affirming the worth on an end is to make an ideal." So it is with the Grady experience, and so goes it at graduation.

**ABOVE:** Grady graduates ignore their dean, faculty member plugs ears. It is wild and loud. *UGA Special Events*; **BELOW LEFT:** George Abney with PR senior Catherine Kelley Caruthers. *Grady College Archives*; **BELOW RIGHT:** Diane Miller. *Grady College Archives*

There is a glue that holds. Often forgotten are the "lost," and there are varying degrees of being lost, but to be a brand new student, even a graduating senior, for most is at least to be uncertain. Yet to be experienced by a freshman is a large lecture section or an intimidating faculty member, whatever the good that comes from it. Questions abound: what are the course and performance requirements, how does one gain the insouciance of an admired senior in the sorority? Many if not most students enter feeling alienated, not belonging, and that's where the A-team comes in. Of course some students were so plugged-in in high school as to affect a certain swagger. But when alumni pinch themselves, they remember how lonely they could be in a crowd. The "A" stands for advising, but it also means "crack" team. The college depends on it. They are the gyroscopes for students.

From the sixties into the eighties, advising meant George Abney. No one ever gave students more attention. He was beloved. Vera Pen followed Abney as Director of Student Services and the college named its top staff award in her honor and memory. Dr. Parker Middleton followed Pen, and when Middleton took the advancement portfolio in Dean Clark's first year, the college was fortunate when a search resulted in Dr. Diane Miller coming over from the UGA Honors Program. Her equanimity is sublime, whether handling academic misconduct cases, grade appeals, or supervising the admissions and enrollments process. Dr. Miller works with a superb advising staff, six in all. They are called the A-team for a reason. Moreover all the details of graduation and convocation are hers to manage, and she handles it with characteristic aplomb. Her sense of humor is unequaled, always subtle and supportive. Dr. Miller prepared for the life of a scholar and added to it advanced work in counseling. Although she maintains the inquisitiveness and insightfulness of the scholar, it is in the latter role that she served our students best.

Of course, no Grady tradition gives it greater national and global recognition than the Peabody Awards. It will be a year shy of its 75th when Grady celebrates its 100th, although if one marked its original chartering in 1940, there is complete symmetry. In recent years, the dean, as ex-officio member of the Peabody Board, joins the board in L.A., D.C., and Athens. Sitting in on deliberations based on total immersion by board members in the entries they jury, I observe the most intense intellectual and artistic engagements. Because of this sequestered give and take, past members of the board count their service among life's highest rewards. The friendships and conversations I enjoyed are indelible, and so it was for the deans before me and will be for those to come. To mention but one evening's engagement is unfair to all others, but exemplary was a New York dinner with Neil Aronstam (ABJ 66), former board chair, exceptional innovator in advertising and brilliant conversationalist, and with Horace Newcomb, the consummate Peabody director. On that occasion, a symphony of blended thoughts emerged around the challenges and opportunities of meshing Grady's opportunities with the University of Georgia's leadership. Insights over dinner that evening were sustenance for the challenges ahead.

As the 75th approaches for the Peabodys there is perfect symmetry. The hand-off from Horace was to one of his students, Jeff Jones. At the University of Texas, he had been a student of Newcomb's, but that's not what made him

**LEFT:** Neil and Vicki Aronstam with Horace Newcomb. **RIGHT:** Jeff Jones. *Grady College Archives*

the natural. Jones had an innate understanding of how to promote the awards, something that on first blush needed no promotion. Yet it did. Jones inked a deal with Pivot, a pioneer in participant media, to join the oldest award in electronic media with the newest form of audience aggregation to broadcast the Peabody Awards. Never before had the Peabody Awards event been able to reach such a broad audience. Sequestered in the Waldorf Astoria, it was elegant, but never as other events, Emmys, for example, available live. Jones is another example of Grady's future. His only drawback is two Auburn degrees, but he has surmounted that in pointing Peabodys to the future.

I considered the major challenge of my last two years, a "rebalancing" of the faculty. I knew that iconic members, Len Reid and Dean Krugman in Advertising and Horace Newcomb in Telecom, were on schedule to retire, and that health challenges for Conrad Fink measured his time. When such a convergence occurs, an institution cannot replace the loss, but it can mitigate it through strategic hiring initiatives—a senior professor, may become two associate professors or one associate and an assistant professor. All is based on the overall assessment of how many assistants, associates and full professors populate not only each department but also the college. Owing to the careful planning of department heads Kent Middleton, Ann Hollifield, and Tom Reichert, and with Senior Associate Dean for Academic Affairs, Alison Alexander, and Associate Dean for Graduate Studies and Research, Jeff Springston also involved, plans evolved and were executed with impressive results.

In 2012–13, the college launched yet another strategic planning initiative that built on a successful re-accreditation review in 2012 that Senior Associate Dean Alison Alexander engineered, as well as a university program review that praised the college for its accomplishments, also spearheaded by

**ABOVE:** Alison Alexander as recent arrival, 1991. As Senior Associate Dean she is a mainstay of the college. *Grady College Archives;* **BELOW:** Jeff Jowdy. *Grady College Archives, courtesy Jeff Jowdy*

Alexander. Among other things the college considered merging Journalism and Telecommunication to build on their allied interests in storytelling, which also implies the inter-relatedness of all its disciplines as communications, again echoing conversations from the fifties. At its end-of-year meeting in 2014 and from the planning initiative inaugurated by my successor, Dean Charles Davis, the college did merge Digital Broadcast News and Journalism, a development that holds great promise for the future of journalism at Grady. Mass Media Arts will remain a discreet unit, which makes sense, although I believed that a full merger of Journalism and Telecommunication would have made for a more robust integration of fiction and nonfiction storytelling as each informs the other. That said, the college is making great progress as it corrals and thereby enhances its digital assets for the future.

Also in my final year, I outsourced the public relations function in a successful arrangement with Jackson-Spalding, an Atlanta-Athens-Dallas agency with close ties to the college. Hugely important in that relationship were Brian Brodrick, Suzanne Rutledge (ABJ 97), and Bryan Harris (MA 2003). Their contributions improved the college's messaging and outreach measurably. Also stepping up was Jeff Jowdy (ABJ 83) whose Nashville-based Lighthouse Counsel advises nonprofits on communication strategies. Jowdy undertook a year-long study that led in turn to a set of internal and external engagement strategies for the college that it continues to implement. I especially enjoyed breakfasts at the Mayflower with Jowdy, where the two of us, most often joined by Parker Middleton, thought aloud about where to and what next. (Sarah Freeman who now leads the college's public relations initiatives at its centennial is doing a superb job.)

In November 2012, I announced my pending retirement effective June 30, 2013, saying, "In June of 2013 you (faculty and staff) will find me celebrating 48 years of teaching, observing my 70th birthday, and shredding

Jackson-Spalding team, Bryan Harris (MA 2002), Hannah Groseclose (ABJ 2012) Johnathon McGinty (ABJ 2000) Alicin Henricks (ABJ 2008), Brian Brodrick (member Board of Trust), Suzanne Rutledge (ABJ 1997), Cody Nichelson (ABJ 2014). *Courtesy Jackson-Spalding*

documents." However, the decision was not motivated by age, rather by my belief that leadership positions like being a dean are best served in seven-year stints, although I also believed that principle applied only to me. A memorandum, one month into my deanship, declared, "I am also of the opinion that the life of most deanships is or should be a capital campaign, whether it meshes with a Regents' approved campaign cannot always be controlled. Thus, I anticipate our capital development program to peak in about five years, and if I am still welcomed by that time, I'll give the job another two years to fine-tune directions and set the college on cruise control for the next dean."[195] Alas, it turned out that way.

So I dedicated my final year to the theme of storytelling, the feature that unites all communication disciplines, and throughout 2012-13 Grady celebrated the best among its storytellers. My mantra for that year was "always leave a story better than you found it." I considered staying on through the centennial year, 2015, but the wisdom of my decision to step down was confirmed when a search resulted in the appointment of Charles Nelson Davis from the University of Missouri as my successor.

Davis is a native Athenian, whose best growing up friend was Kenneth Russell, son of Dean Tom Russell. As a result, he virtually grew up in Tom and Judy's home. Davis received a master's degree from Grady and a Ph.D. from Florida, the only blot on his escutcheon. He specialized in communication law and, among numerous other leadership roles at Missouri, spearheaded a campus-wide digital initiative for the provost—also a critical need for UGA. Moreover, like his predecessor he found his "dream job."

Selah.

# PAST AS PROLOGUE

*Dean Charles Nelson Davis*

Charles Nelson Davis. *UGA Photographic Services*

FOR 100 YEARS, GRADY COLLEGE HAS DISTINGUISHED ITSELF AS ONE OF THE NATION'S LEADING CENTERS OF EDUCATION AND RESEARCH IN JOURNALISM AND MASS COMMUNICATION. Through the decades, the college has reinvented itself again and again, rising to meet transformational changes in the mass media. Whether technological, cultural or socioeconomic, the one constant through all the years is change.

When Grady College opened its doors, a manual typewriter was state of the art, newspapers and periodicals comprised the entirety of the media universe, and the news cycle was measured in days. Advertising and public relations, emergent practices later to burst forth as disciplines of their own, had yet to take shape, and few could predict that in a such short time wireless telegraphy would give rise to radio, then television, cable telecommunications and eventually, the Internet.

Each successive wave of innovation ushered in seismic changes to journalism and mass communication education, as faculty through the years continually responded to the latest shifts by reconfiguring the curriculum to reflect the times.

No shift in American journalism history rivals the digital transition currently underway. Its effects have restructured entire industries, posed grave challenges to longstanding product distribution models and built a culture of digital innovation and entrepreneurship.

The current digital transformation offers us the unparalleled opportunity to move in concert with the industries we serve, as age-old distinctions based on media distribution platforms yield to digital-first environments in which print, broadcast and online channels serve to complement one another and serve the news consumer wherever they happen to be as news breaks. Advertising and public relations can speak directly to digital audiences and monitor the effectiveness of messages in real time, altering the landscape of persuasive communication and providing rich new career paths for social media mavens.

To capitalize on the moment and to reflect the many conversations we have had with industry professionals, Grady College initiated a yearlong strategic planning exercise in my first year as dean aimed at envisioning the college of the future. We knew we needed to change to better reflect the mass media itself, with its de-emphasis on silos such as broadcast and print journalism. We knew that we needed to maintain a broad footprint, serving our popular advertising and public relations sequences while expanding opportunities in digital storytelling and film production.

So, in April 2014, we voted to fundamentally reorganize the college. The debate was thoughtful and spirited, the outcome a resounding vote for three departments: Advertising and Public Relations, Digital Media Arts, and Journalism. Faculty and staff moved to form the new structure, and our centennial year will see curricular development efforts begin to create wholly new ways of teaching our students.

Several historical features of Grady College animate our efforts and are worth mentioning as we move forward. First, Grady College long has been, and always will be, a professional school steeped in experiential learning. Students at Grady College always have learned by doing, and will continue to, albeit in exciting new ways.

Second, Grady College begins any curricular effort with an unbroken history of excellent teaching dating back to its origins. Grady College teachers long have been known on the campus as master teachers, and have garnered dozens upon dozens of teaching awards at every conceivable level. This emphasis on classroom and laboratory instruction lends dexterity to our curricular conversations, as we find it easier than other institutions to ground change squarely upon improvement of the student experience.

As I write, it is also worth noting that the Grady student has changed noticeably in recent years, as the ever-increasing academic standards of the University of Georgia raise all academic boats. The 2014 incoming first-year class is the strongest in the history of the university with a grade point average of 3.9 on a 4.0 scale in the most challenging courses. The university's incoming students have also earned the highest test scores for entering freshmen and continue the upward trajectory in the academic qualifications of students at the nation's first state-chartered university.

Equally importantly, the 2014 freshman class also is one of the most diverse in UGA history, with more than 28 percent of the entering freshmen self-identifying as other than Caucasian. Grady College exceeded the 22 percent diversity point in 2013, and the years to come will see that percentage climb ever higher.

The academic excellence and diverse backgrounds of our students require us to work much harder at diversifying our faculty to reflect the students we serve, and to engage students in ever more challenging experiential settings. Learning alliances – partnerships developed between Grady faculty and corporations eager to learn from and teach our students in creative ways – are one way in which we are revitalizing the student experience. The addition of a Director of Experiential Learning in 2014 will further expand corporate partnerships as we work to strengthen ties with corporate and institutional alumni and friends. It is not at all surprising to walk by a classroom at Grady to find an industry professional team teaching with a Grady faculty member, and we are limited only by our imaginations when it comes to ways to work together to further enrich the learning environment.

Signaling our interest in fostering even more collaborative projects with industry, the college in 2013 added a new faculty rank—that of clinical faculty—with an eye towards giving us greater flexibility in the years ahead to attract instructors directly from the professions with which we work in tandem.

Willingness to experiment, curiosity, entrepreneurship and the ability to adapt trump in this era of self-publishing, as emergent media technologies reshape the communications field. Each disruptive technology sends shock waves through the industries we serve yet the elemental basics of journalism and mass communication remain inviolate. Teaching by doing—the DNA of Grady College since its founding—remain at the core of the college's teaching mission.

The years ahead will see us working tirelessly to adapt our curriculum and facilities to meet the needs of a digital-first mass communication workplace, creating more opportunities for cross-disciplinary learning and erasing boundaries between skill sets, so our students can become ever more agile and prepared for jobs that do not exist at the moment. Ours is a dynamic, fast-paced college with a direct relationship to the industries we serve, and now, more than ever, we must be eager to play a central role in preparing the next generation of professional communicators amidst the transformational changes reshaping the mass media.

# AUTHOR'S EPILOGUE

I WAS AT HIS BEDSIDE. WE BOTH KNEW ONLY WEEKS, PERHAPS LESS REMAINED. He gave me an hour, which was beyond endurance, but then he had been an armored commander for Patton, a bull of a man who was yet sweet, almost cherubic. We drifted back over the days that had meant so much to me, the sixties, when he carried the mantle of McGill's crusade for reason on the South's racial future. We nodded to our differences over Vietnam, both acknowledging the generational gap. Then toward the end, he launched on the future of journalism. Social media, he said, would tell us the who, what, where and when, leaving space for a dedicated cadre of journalists to advise on the how and why. He restored my soul.

The "black wolf" had Gene Patterson, as it had had Conrad Fink only a year before, but it did not have their future. A month later I would be back in St. Petersburg for memorial services. I had not known him as had Phil Gailey or Howell Raines or Barbara Matusow. I had not had drink with them (well, there was the Sazerac Bar in New Orleans), swapped war stories of the newsroom, or sung the night away. "Danny Boy" was his signature and left no dry eye and no one who heard it will ever forget. But he and I had talked on and off again over the past twenty years, and when I became Grady's dean I told

**ABOVE:** "O Captain! My Captain." *Grady College Archives, photo by Damien Salas*; **BELOW:** Colonel Bryan Salas, escorted to receive his Dean's Medal by Russell Professor and Lt. Commander Kaye Sweetser. She had just returned from a tour in Afghanistan. *Grady College Archives*

him my office trumped George Patton's, because the torch I carried was for war and peace, democracy's succeeding generations. He did not disagree.

By March, 2013, I would walk behind a caisson at Arlington bearing the body of my hero. At my side would be his legion of friends and family, my wife Mary, and Colonel Bryan Salas, recently retired chief public affairs officer for the Marine Corps at the Pentagon and Dean's Medalist. The Dean's Medal is awarded for singular, often unrepeatable acts of communication leadership. Those acts come sometimes in a moment, other times a season, but each captures the essence, the measure of why the Grady College exists.

Salas's moment came on a dreary, soggy day in D.C. It had been intended as a day of celebration for the unveiling of the Martin Luther King, Jr., memorial, but then nature intervened with a threatened hurricane. Earlier Salas had written his dean, saying that he wanted to use the event to inspire his team. He shared several pages of objectives and lessons to engage his staff. I looked at them and awed by its breadth and depth changed not a thing. With the approaching storm, I thought it was all off, but not for the determined colonel. He secured vans, arrived at the site, and engaged his staff in conversations about the meaning of it all. In a detailed follow up, he advised his dean of the experience. In that instant and unbeknownst to him, a Dean's Medal was struck.

As we walked behind the caisson bearing Patterson to a hero's grave, we spoke not a word, but away from the throng was a young man with a camera.

Day is done. *Grady College Archives, photo by Damien Salas*

"Morning at Grady." *photo by Penny Gheesling*

It was Damien Salas, the Colonel's son and now a Grady student arrived from Athens to capture the moment. The dean had not known but was not surprised. I followed young Salas's progress as a way of diverting emotions and observing a student of Mark Johnson's who knew how to get in position—perfectly situated for the final salute, as taps echoed across hallowed ground.

As the service ended, Colonel Salas asked Mary and me to go with him to Section Sixty, where the more recent arrivals were buried. When we got there, we walked to three gravesites for friends with whom Salas had become close while stationed in San Diego—one woman and two men. He talked about each of them as if it were yesterday and in the telling their souls were restored to us.

And so this story ends, borne up by a Grady graduate, his son, and the reason why.

# APPENDIX

## *Drewry Trial*

JOHN ELDRIDGE DREWRY MARRIED KATHLEEN JEANETTE MERRY ON DECEMBER 23, 1926. HE WAS TWENTY-FOUR, SHE TWENTY-TWO. Private correspondence from 1931-1937 in his papers, reveals the relationship to have been stormy from the beginning, she "hating" him at first but eventually acceding to his marriage proposal. (It is the opinion of the author and that of archivist Steven A. Brown and local historian Charlotte Thomas Marshall that John Drewry directed that these papers be included in his collection of papers to demonstrate the mental state of Kathleen Drewry and its effect on his marriage and her subsequent attempt to murder him and his fiancée Miriam Thurmond.)

The "private correspondence" is among Drewry, his wife Kathleen, and another woman with whom Kathleen had an intense personal relationship. The other woman in this triangle descended from a distinguished Georgia family and had a long and successful career on the UGA faculty. The birth of Milton, the Drewry's only child, occurred the year the correspondence begins. Drewry writes regularly to Kathleen and her companion about living with his wife "separately under the same roof" and of "alienation of affection." Kathleen had consulted at least four physicians for mental health issues—she complains of being forced to do so. Her companion accompanied Kathleen on several visits and corresponded with Drewry about others. Citing Kathleen's doctors, Drewry pleaded with the companion to lessen Kathleen's dependency on her. (Several letters from her physicians to John Drewry are also in this file.) Both women disparaged Drewry, from his looks, to manner of speech, to intellectual pursuits. The companions took trips in the Drewry's only car to Atlanta, to the mountains, as well as to the other woman's hometown in West Georgia. The relationship between Kathleen and her companion appears to have ended in 1937 as Kathleen's obsession led to stalking, even threats to kill her, and at least one attempt to ram her with a car. The companion's father pled with one of Kathleen's physicians at the state mental hospital in Milledgeville to intervene before Kathleen ruined his daughter's reputation personally and professionally.

Still, the Drewry's marriage lasted another twelve years before they divorced the summer of 1949, followed by the subsequent shooting on December 23, 1949. All evidence indicates that the verbal abuse from Kathleen Drewry continued throughout their marriage. The wonder is that Drewry could have had such a successful professional life with such a chaotic personal life.

(Evidence of the trial for attempted murder in April 1950 and again on retrial in January 1952 is drawn primarily from newspaper accounts, there being no surviving transcripts or forensic evidence. However, on Defendant's appeal to the Georgia State Court of Appeals, Drewry v. The State, 33271, decided Feb 1, 1951, rulings and findings were summative and dispositive. The Court of Appeals on a split vote denied a retrial thereby sustaining the conviction. The issue was the trial judge's confused ruling on an insanity plea. On a writ of certiorari to the State Supreme Court, it reversed the appellate court, also on a split vote, and remanded it for retrial, Drewry v. The State, 17459, decided July 10, 1951. It also provides much insight into findings and rulings. Finally, a transcript of the original motion for a retrial in Superior Court does include Kathleen Drewry's unsworn testimony, forty-two pages as originally presented, and edited responses from other parties testifying, including John and Miriam Drewry.)

The trials for attempted murder that followed in April 1950 and on retrial in January 1952 were sensational, with newspapers talking about Drewry's "pretty former secretary," now fiancée, twenty years younger. Kathleen's lawyers, very prominent Athenians, tried two approaches: one ground, "delusional insanity," effectively temporary insanity, and the other, use of deadly force to prevent adultery. Both were false to fact, and both contributed to sensationalizing the trial. The facts were these: in July 1949, the Drewrys sought and obtained a divorce in August. In "early fall," Drewry and Miriam Thurmond engaged to marry. Drewry, unwisely, continued to see his former wife and son, likely to placate and mollify the mercurial Kathleen Drewry and see to their son's welfare. (Drewry said his visits were mostly on Sunday nights, she said much more often.) Drewry did stay at their home over Thanksgiving, while their son was in Atlanta. Kathleen said he "consummated" a common-law marriage by sexual intercourse on Thanksgiving night—a necessary condition to prove "common law marriage." He said quite to the contrary, that she threatened to kill him that night, and further testified that he had not had an intimate relationship with her since their son was born eighteen years before. (From the early thirties he complained of living separately under the same roof; moreover, he may have stayed in the garage apartment Milton occupied. Impossible to know.) A month later she did attempt to murder both John and his fiancée Miriam.

On the night of December 23, 1949, Drewry had what he called a "supper conference" with his ex-wife and son to discuss a Christmas present for their son and help with a debt she owed. She said it was a further effort at reconciliation. (In her unsworn testimony at trial, she says that owing to his advances, she had miraculously turned from hate-filled ex-wife to happy common-law wife. If so, it would have been the first evidence of affection in a twenty-three year marriage.) When he left that evening, she suspected he was going to see his fiancée. He was. He had called Miriam Thurmond around 6:00 p.m. to say he was coming over later and did not arrive until around 9:00 p.m. to find Miriam and her mother, with whom she lived along with her grandmother, making Christmas candy. After chatting awhile, Drewry and Miriam went into the living room to talk—he in an easy chair, she on the ottoman in front. By their account, they may have been talking twenty-five minutes or so.

In the meantime, Kathleen, becoming increasingly agitated over the belief that he was seeing Miriam, got dressed, retrieved a loaded, five-chambered Colt .32 revolver, borrowed a neighbor's car, and drove from her home at 1495 S. Milledge Street seven-tenths of a mile to the Thurmond home at 445 Milledge Circle. She claims to have watched them for some time through the living room window (which would have been easy to do), and then, becoming "nauseated" at what she saw, walked in to take their lives. Miriam said she heard the front door open and shut, but thought it was one of her brothers. John Drewry's first awareness of Kathleen's presence was the look of shock on Miriam's face. At that point he turned to see Kathleen, dressed in slacks and a jacket, and holding the gun in both hands. She proceeded to put two bullets in Drewry, then two in Miriam, and finally another in Drewry. All three bullets that struck Drewry entered his chest with the other two hitting Miriam in the stomach. Miriam was the more critically wounded—Drewry by virtue of wearing a wallet in his vest, less seriously. Still, it was a horrific scene that Miriam's mother encountered. When the mother said she was calling the police, Kathleen retorted, "Call whom you please. I'm going to kill them both."

The neighbor from whom she had borrowed the car remembered Kathleen calling "shortly thereafter" to say "I have killed John Drewry, and I am going to kill myself." If so, it casts doubt on Kathleen's watching at the window for some length of time, growing increasingly "nauseated," as an act of adultery was imminent—an imminent act would have required that the adulterers be sufficiently unclothed to consummate such an act. They were fully clothed when shot. Kathleen was taken to St. Mary's hospital (the neighbor had called the police), where her stomach was pumped on the assumption she had tried to kill herself by poison, there being no other apparent injuries to her. Soon thereafter she posted bond.

In April 1950 a jury of the Superior Court of Clarke County convicted Kathleen of the attempted murder of Miriam Thurmond. Her lawyers appealed on grounds that the judge had improperly charged the jury with respect to an insanity plea and had failed to charge the jury with respect to common law marriage as requested by her attorneys. The Georgia Court of Appeals sustained the trial Court, but on a writ of certiorari, the Supreme Court reversed the appellate court on the confused insanity instruction, even as the Supreme Court sustained the trial judge in his unwillingness to instruct the jury on Defense's "common-law" pleading. Thus, in July 1951, the Supreme Court ordered a retrial. In January 1952, Kathleen Drewry was acquitted by a jury of twelve white men, with one juror saying that she had "acted under stress and strain so severe it would have unbalanced the strongest man." It is clear that Kathleen Drewy's unsworn testimony, designed to establish the common-law relationship, established instead circumstantial evidence for "temporary insanity," even if it remained unclear as to whether the state of Georgia recognized that defense. The author learned of one eyewitness to Kathleen Drewry's testimony, Priscilla Arnold Davis, who was a UGA student and later a courageous *Red & Black* editor. She said, "Mrs. Drewry's testimony was not believable, and certainly not evidentiary, consisting of uncorroborated accusations delivered in agitated tones. She was clearly unbalanced." Davis said she "was surprised at the verdict. I didn't see how the jury could be so gullible." (Email exchange with author, 9-25-14.)

The "unsworn testimony" of Kathleen Drewry, which the author recently recovered in the motion for retrial, is an unrelenting assault on the characters of John and Miriam Drewry. It is also a reasonably coherent and detailed account of Kathleen's suspicions of a prior relationship between Drewry and Miriam, dating to her time as his secretary; suspicions that no doubt enlarged in her mind, when soon after the divorce, Drewry proposed marriage to Miriam. Even if the product of febrile imagination, the testimony is crafted in such a way that an unknowing reader today might suspect the worst of Kathleen's ex-husband and his fiancée. (Kathleen Drewry was no doubt a very smart woman, but her testimony would likely also have been coached by her lawyers. Moreover, one manifestation of narcissism can be fabrications in compelling detail.) Still, as the eyewitness to that testimony noted, no corroborating evidence was ever submitted in court and newspaper accounts report no cross examination. Additionally, no one since has ever claimed knowledge of or revealed any inappropriate relationship to have existed. It is reasonable to assume that John and Miriam developed an affection for each other but had it been demonstrably more than that, as Kathleen claimed, more would have been made of it at the time. It lives only in the innuendo of subsequent retellings.

After recovering from their wounds, John Drewry married Miriam on March 16, 1950, and they honeymooned at the Commodore Hotel in New York—where the Peabodys were held. They lived happily and productively together until his death in 1983. At this writing, Miriam is still living in Athens surrounded by friends from a lifetime of service and fellowship. Indeed she is a Fellow of the Grady College. Kathleen and John Drewry's son Milton, who had stood by his mother during the trial, died in 1975 at age 43, a victim of alcoholism. Little is known of Kathleen after the trial. She died in Augusta, her mother's hometown, in April 1977.

This summary is important for two reasons. First, there was no scandal. Although Drewry's efforts to manage his wife's mental illness would never be advised today, he was doing the best he could. (She could be alternately suicidal and homicidal.) He likely had dependency issues of his own, and both he and Kathleen had to navigate the mores of the day with respect to divorce and mental illness. Second, the suggestion that he and Miriam were on the verge of an adulterous encounter resulted from a legal premise used by Kathleen's lawyers. (The law at that time permitted "deadly force" to prevent an imminent act of adultery. Of course, an adulterous act also would presume a marriage, thus the theory that following divorce, John Drewry sought to reconcile and "consummated" said intent on Thanksgiving night. If so, it would have been the only act of intimacy between the two in eighteen years and admitted to only by Kathleen.)

I have put the evidence before an accomplished clinical psychologist, and certain facts of law before a federal judge and a former associate dean of the law school. The psychologist says Kathleen Drewry likely suffered "borderline personality disorder" that led to periodic "narcissistic breaks or cracks." Those cracks so derange perception, that the resulting rage has no counter-balance in reason. She says that John Drewry's life with Kathleen was no doubt a "living hell," and that their son although siding with his mother at trial was also a victim of her delusional world and fear of abandonment. The psychologist believes Milton's untimely death was almost certainly suicide by alcohol. The law dean said that, yes, the Georgia Code in 1950 would have enabled a defense such as that advanced by Kathleen Drewry's counsel; i.e. common-law marriage justifying deadly force to prevent adultery. But, that defense having been effectively overruled by the Supreme Court as per the trial judge's original instructions, it still played out in the final acquittal as the "unsworn testimony" designed to set it up was re-entered in the second trial. In fact, though, it was a judgment of her mental state that eventually gained her acquittal—"stress and strain as would unbalance the strongest man." Still, given statements and arguments in court, it would have been hard for a juror to distinguish between a "common-law marriage" justification and her true unfortunate state of mind. The results are myths that continue to this day of a scandal and a crime of passion. Neither is true. Kathleen Drewry's mental illness made it possible for her to plan and carry out a home invasion with intent to murder. And she did.

Finally, one must concede that standing alone, uncorroborated and without evident cross examination, Kathleen's testimony influenced the second trial, even as it had protracted jury deliberation in the first. That said, when Kathleen Drewry, with intensifying feelings of "abandonment," her divorce notwithstanding, retrieved the loaded gun from her home, borrowed the neighbor's car, invaded a private residence with intent to murder, she came perilously close to succeeding. One should not blame the victims.

# HENRY W. GRADY COLLEGE OF JOURNALISM AND MASS COMMUNICATION FACULTY, 1915–2015

| | |
|---|---|
| Abbey, Richard D. | 1969–73 |
| Abney, George Morris | 1957–93 |
| Acosta-Alzuru, Carolina | 1999– |
| Agee, Warren Kendall | 1969–87 |
| Ahn, Sun Joo (Grace) | 2011– |
| Aldridge, Emuel L. | 2012– |
| Aldridge, James Larry | 1967–76 |
| Alexander, Alison F. | 1991– |
| Andrew, E. William III | 1981– |
| Anservitz, Robert M. | 1968–78 |
| | |
| Baker, Charles Alfred | 1967–74 |
| Bartlett, William Marcus | 1976–81 |
| Baxter, William S. | 1967–81 |
| Becker, Lee B. | 1997– |
| Benjamin, Louise M. | 1993–2008 |
| Bethune, Beverly Moore | 1967–94 |
| Biddle, James J. | 2006– |
| Bishop, Robert L. | 1982–89 |
| Bobren, Howard Mark | 1962–63 |
| Bond, Graeme A. | 1979–81 |
| Boyd, Valerie J. | 2004– |
| Brack, Elliott Earl | 1973–82 |
| Bryans, Raleigh Gee | 1955–56 |
| Bulloch, Richard D. | 1954–56 |
| Butler, Franklin | 1940–53 |
| Butler, Marion Tyus | 1939–82 |
| | |
| Cacciatore, Michael A. | 2013– |
| Callison, Claude Pickens, Jr. | 1963–70 |
| Cameron, Glen | 1989–98 |
| Cantrell-Bickley, Yvonne (Dodie) | 2013– |
| Castengera, Michael J. | 2001– |
| Cheles, Pamela J. | 1973–74 |
| Chess, Shira | 2013– |
| Clark, E. Culpepper | 2006–13 |
| Clark, Jeff | 1968–88 |
| Clavier, David | 1980–82 |
| Cooper, Charles B., Jr. | 1970–76 |
| Crouse, Edward C, | 1930–39 |
| Crow, Robert P. | 1970–81 |
| Cutlip, Scott Munson | 1975–85 |
| | |
| Davidson, Claude, Jr. | 1969–70 |
| Davis, Charles N. | 2013– |
| Dominick, Joseph R., Jr. | 1974–2008 |
| Dozier, George | 1994–99 |
| Drewry, John Eldridge | 1922–69 |
| | |
| Eberhard, Wallace B. | 1970–99 |
| English, John Wesley | 1970–2000 |
| Evans, Nathaniel J. | 2013– |
| | |
| Fink, Conrad C. | 1982–2012 |
| Fletcher, Alan Donald | 1965–69 |
| Fletcher, James Erving | 1974–2003 |
| Fohey, James P. | 1970–82 |
| Foote, Avon Edward | 1974–80 |
| Freimuth, Vicki | 2003–13 |
| Frost, James William | 1979–84 |
| Fudge, William George, Jr. | 1965–72 |
| | |
| Glynn, Carroll J. | 1983–84 |
| Greenman, John F. | 2004–2015 |
| Griffith, Jennifer P. | 2005– |
| Griffith, Louis Turner | 1949–84 |
| Griswold, William F. Jr. | 1988–2008 |
| | |
| Hamilton. James Frederick | 1999– |
| Han, Jeong Yeob | 2008– |

| | |
|---|---|
| Harper, Clifton E. | 1942–49 |
| Harrison, Harry N., Jr. | 1967–72 |
| Hawkins, Frank N. | 1977–82 |
| Hawley, Melinda | 1993–2000 |
| Hayden, Elaine L. | 1976–79 |
| Hazinski, David C. | 1987– |
| Hedgepath, William Bowling | 1974 |
| Hemphill, Paul J. | 1973 |
| Hester, Albert Lee | 1972–97 |
| Hesterman, Vicki | 1987–90 |
| Himelboim, Itai | 2008– |
| Hippchen, Leonard Joseph | 1953–55 |
| Hollander, Barry A. | 1991– |
| Hollifield, Cheryl Ann | 1997– |
| Holmes, Capers Andrews | 1947 |
| Hough, George A., III | 1979–91 |
| Howard, Jane Temple | 1975 |
| Hudson, Thomas David | 2001– |
| Hume, Janice R. | 2001– |
| Hynds, Ernest Culloden | 1956–99 |
| | |
| Inzer, George F., Jr. | 1973–74 |
| | |
| Jamison, Gayla K. | 1975–76 |
| Jin, Yan | 2014– |
| Johnson, Mark E. | 2005– |
| Johnston, Margaret Mims | 1968– |
| Jones, Betty K. | 1998– |
| Jones, Jeffrey P. | 2013– |
| Jones, Warren Lee | 1942–46 |
| | |
| Kalupa, Francis Boniface | 1980–85 |
| Kavoori, Anandam Philip | 1993– |
| Keever, James Daniel III | 2000–11 |
| Kempton, Willett Main | 1936–42 |
| Kim, Joo Young | 2004– |
| King, Karen Whitehill | 1985– |
| Kitchens, Daniel Walton | 1953–94 |

| | |
|---|---|
| Kitson, John William | 1963–64 |
| Klopfenstein, Bruce C. | 2000–11 |
| Koenitz, Hartmut | 2011– |
| Kohn, Nathaniel H. | 1997– |
| Kopp, Charles Benjamin | 1956–82 |
| Kosak, Herman Harry | 1969–79 |
| Krakowski, Paul | 1947–49 |
| Kraps, Rowland Francis | 1952–86 |
| Kreshel, Peggy J. | 1986– |
| Krugman, Dean M. | 1983–2011 |
| | |
| Landrum, Kim | 2014– |
| Lane, Walter Ronald, Jr. | 1966–2006 |
| Lariscy, Ruthann Weaver | 1989–2014 |
| Leckie, George G. | 1956 |
| Lee, William Eyre | 1977– |
| Len–Rios, Maria E. | 2014– |
| Leonard, Earl Truman, Jr. | 1959–61 |
| Lichtenstein, Allen | 1978–79 |
| Lin, Jhih Syuan (Elaine) | 2012– |
| Lowe, Clayton Kent | 1970–72 |
| Lowrey, John Henry | 1964–70 |
| Lubs, Frederick | 1968–77 |
| Lunceford, Alvin Mell, Jr. | 1949–51 |
| Lynch, Edmund Clayton, Jr. | 1967–90 |
| | |
| MacLeod, Allan E. | 1982–2000 |
| Macias, Wendy A. | 2000–10 |
| Mallery, Elizabeth P. | 1935–45 |
| Martin, Charles H. | 1974–78 |
| Martin, Hugh J. | 2000–09 |
| Martin, Raymond William, Jr. | 1968–87 |
| Massey, Dyar E. | 1940s |
| Masters, Judy Jay Alves | 1980–83 |
| Matthews, Denise | 2012– |
| Mcleneghan, Jack | 1971–73 |
| McDougald, William Worth | 1949–91 |
| McKenzie, Barbara | 1968–86 |

| | |
|---|---|
| Meng, Juan | 2012– |
| Michaelis, Vicki S. | 2012– |
| Middleton, Kent Richards | 1980– |
| Miller, Alfred James | 1966–69 |
| Moore, Hamilton Frazier | 1955–81 |
| Morioto, Mariko | 2005–2010 |
| Murray, Diane H. | 2002– |
| | |
| Newcomb, Horace M. | 2001–13 |
| Newsome, Parks Smythe | 1966–70 |
| Nickeson, Richard Sprowls | 1946–47 |
| Nordstrom, Kurt E. | 1982–85 |
| Nowak, Glen | 1990–2000<br>2013– |
| | |
| O'Brien, Richard Eugene | 1964–81 |
| O'Donnell, Casey | 2008–12 |
| Oyedeji, Tayo | 2008–11 |
| | |
| Paek, Hye–Jin | 2005–08 |
| Page, Roland | 1986–93 |
| Parker, Eugene Fletcher, Jr. | 1969–73 |
| Patterson, Ralph David | 1972–79 |
| Peters, John Samuel | 1950–52 |
| Phua, Joe Jin | 2011– |
| Pjesivac, Ivanka | 2014– |
| Poindexter, Paula M. | 1980–81 |
| Powell, Roy Ferdinand | 1952–53 |
| | |
| Quarles, Rebecca C. | 1975–78 |
| | |
| Reber, Bryan H. | 2004– |
| Reichert, William T. | 2004– |
| Reid, John | 1989–93 |
| Reid, Leonard Noyd | 1980–2012 |
| Rember, Lawrence William | 1935–36 |
| Rhodes, Leara | 1994– |
| Robinson, Brett | 2001–02 |
| Roushanzamir, Elli | 1989–2014 |
| Russell, Karen M. | 1993– |
| Russell, John Thomas | 1967–2000 |
| Ryan, William Daniel | 1965–68 |
| | |
| Sallot, Lynne M. | 1993– |
| Sanford, Steadman Vincent | 1903–45 |
| Sasser, Emery Lewis | 1966–73 |
| Scarritt, Charles Wesley | 1942 |
| Shamp, Scott A. | 1987– |
| Sherman, Barry L. | 1981–2000 |
| Shumway, Christopher | 2011– |
| Smith, Jennifer C. | 2005– |
| Smith, Kristen M. | 2008– |
| Smith, Otto W. | 1976–2004 |
| Smith, Stephen A. | 2003–13 |
| Smith, W. Stanford | 1946–53 |
| Soley, Lawrence C. | 1982–83 |
| Soloski, John R. | 2001– |
| Springston, Jeffrey K. | 1998– |
| Stecker, Alan | 2001–05 |
| Stephens, Ralph H. | 1949–78 |
| Stone, Vernon Alfred | 1974–78 |
| Strausbaugh–Hutchinson, Kirsten | 2000– |
| Suggs, David Welch | 2012– |
| Surlin, Stuart H. | 1970–77 |
| Swain, Bruce McArthur | 1980–89 |
| Sweetser, Kathleen D. | 2006–2014 |
| Swenson, Jill | 1988–92 |
| | |
| Talmadge, John E. | 1940–53 |
| Thomas, Patricia J. | 2005– |
| Tinkham, Spencer Felton | 1981– |
| Tress, Wallace G. | 1968–74 |
| | |
| Virga, James | 2001–05 |
| Vlad, Tudor | 2005– |
| | |
| Ward, Christa J. | 2005–09 |

| | |
|---|---|
| Weatherford, John | 2014– |
| Wenthe, Leila Skidmere | 1977–2000 |
| West, Katherine E. | 2012–13 |
| Whitten, Pamela S. | 2014– |
| Willett, Robert W. | 1982–2008 |
| Wimmer, Roger David | 1979–82 |
| Wise, Alfred Paul | 1969–97 |
| Wolter, Louis John | 1968–69 |
| Wojdynski, Bartosz | 2013– |
| Wright, Donald K. | 1977–83 |
| Wurtzel, Alan | 1975–79 |
| Zellner, Carlos Lawrence | 1967–68 |

## GEORGE FOSTER PEABODY AWARDS BOARD, 1940–2015

| | |
|---|---|
| Elizabeth Ames | 1944–1969 |
| Neil L Aronstam<br>*Chair, 1997–1998* | 1993–2000 |
| Ed Bark | 1995–2002 |
| Joyce J. Bartell | 1980–1988 |
| Bruce Barton | 1940–1942 |
| Dr. Lionel C. Barrow Jr. | 1977–1980 |
| John H. Benson | 1940–1960 |
| Eugene R. Black<br>*Chair, 1967–1977* | 1967–1977 |
| Dr. Gertrude B. Broderick | 1968–1978 |
| Tim Brooks | 2006–2013 |
| Les Brown | 1982–1988 |
| Merrill Brown | 1988–1991 |
| Steve Bryant | 2010– |
| Dr. James Carey | 1995–2002 |
| John Carman | 1984–1991 |
| Elizabeth S. Carpenter | 1977–1983 |
| Dr. Ralph Casey | 1942–1946 |
| Bennett A. Cerf<br>*Chair, 1954–1967* | 1946–1967<br><br>1970–1971 |
| Yuen–Ying Chan | 2003–2009 |
| Sir Michael Checkland | 1994–2000 |
| Peggy Mobley Childs | 1978–1984 |
| Barbara Cochran | 2003–2010 |
| Edward M. Cramer | 1984–1991 |
| John Crosby | 1947–1962 |
| Elizabeth Crow | 1991–1996 |
| Virginius Dabney | 1940–1942 |
| John Charles Daly | 1966–1982 |
| Jonathan Daniels | 1940–1950 |
| Dr. Jannette Dates | 1995–2002 |
| Norman H. Davis | 1940–1942 |
| Eric Deggans | 2013– |
| Helen DeMichiel | 2001–2007 |
| Susan Douglas<br>*Chair, 2010* | 2004–2010 |
| Thomas C. Dowden<br>*Chair, 1991–1993* | 1988–1994 |
| Bruce DuMont<br>*Chair, 1995–1997* | 1992–1998 |
| Holly (Houston) Echols | 1991–1997 |
| Dwight Ellis | 2006–2008 |
| Marcie Ersoff | 1996–2003<br>2008 |
| Jonathan Estrin | 2004–2009 |
| Mark F. Ethridge | 1940–1954 |
| Danforth P. Fales | 2000–2006 |
| Peter Fiddick<br>*Chair, 2006* | 2000–2006 |
| Jean Firstenberg<br>*Chair, 1989–1991* | 1985–1991 |
| Sterling Fisher | 1962–1963 |
| Don Freeman | 1966–1984 |
| Frank–Dieter Freiling | 2006–2008 |
| Arlene Francis Gabel | 1980–1982 |
| Eddie Garrett | 2011– |

| | |
|---|---|
| Raúl Garza<br>*Chair, 2011* | 2004–2011 |
| Earl Glade | 1942–1966 |
| Lamond Godwin | 1987–1989 |
| Julian Goodwin | 1986–1992 |
| Jonathan Gray | 2014– |
| Dr. Elizabeth Guider | 2008–2014 |
| Philip Hamburger | 1950–1952<br>1953–1959<br>1966–1971 |
| Dr. William Harley | 1976–1985 |
| Kitty Carlisle Hart | 1977–1983 |
| Bel Hernandez<br>*Chair, 2008* | 2002–2008 |
| Dr. James Hindman | 1995–2002 |
| Betty J. Hudson<br>*Chair, 2002* | 1996–2003 |
| Robert Hudson | 1977–1979 |
| John Huey | 2013– |
| Edward W. Hummers, Jr.<br>*Chair, 1987–1989* | 1983–1989 |
| Charlayne Hunter–Gault | 2009– |
| Doris Indyke | 1991–1996<br>2002–2003 |
| Joseph Henry Jackson | 1942–1952 |
| Sidney L. James<br>*Chair, 1977–1979* | 1975–1979 |
| Dr. Henry Jenkins | 2013– |
| Harry Jessell | 2006–2011 |
| W. Thomas Johnson | 1976–1980 |
| Dr. Barbara Jordan | 1978–1980 |
| Waldemar Kaempffert | 1940–2956 |
| Alfred A. Knopf | 1940–1946 |
| Edgar Kobak | 1958–1968 |
| Sheldon Krys<br>*Chair, 1993–1995* | 1989–1995 |
| | 1996–1997 |
| Sonia Landau | 1984–1991 |
| John Lardner | 1959–1960 |
| Rebecca Leet | 2003–2007 |
| Robert H. Levi | 2002–2003 |

| | |
|---|---|
| Dorothy Lewis | 1948–1951<br>1952–1977 |
| Dr. Frank Manchel<br>*Chair, 1985–1987* | 1982–1989 |
| Sonia Manzano | 1997–2001 |
| Meryl Marshall–Daniels<br>*Chair, 2007* | 2001–2007 |
| Tom Mattia | 2008– |
| Barbara Matusow | 1983–1988 |
| Ralph McGill | 1945–1968 |
| Melanie McFarland | 2005–2011 |
| Dr. Karl E. Meyer | 1977–1983 |
| Mrs. Harold V. Milligan | 1955–1967 |
| Newton N. Minow | 1963–1976 |
| Grace Moore | 1940–1942 |
| Frazier Moore | 2004–2010 |
| Wade H. Mosby | 1977–1983 |
| Dr. Janet Murray | 2006–2013 |
| Martha Nelson | 2014– |
| Ron Nessen<br>*Chair, 2004* | 1996–2004 |
| | 2009 |
| Dr. Horace Newcomb | 1989–1995 |
| Louisa A. Nielsen | 1989–1995 |
| Dr. Harold Niven | 1967–1984 |
| Terrence O'Flaherty | 1952–1963<br>1964–1965<br>1966–1984 |
| Joanne Ostrow | 2002–2004 |
| Marquita Pool–Eckert | 2011– |
| Clark Pollock | 1989–1994 |
| Paul Porter | 1947–1963 |
| Frances Preston | 1989–1995 |
| Henry Pringle | 1954–1956 |
| John E. Reinhardt | 1980–1987 |
| J. Leonard Reinsch | 1979–1985 |
| Regina Resnik | 1991–1996 |
| Stuart Revill | 1996–2003 |
| Naibe Reynoso | 2014– |
| Doreen Ringer–Ross | 2010– |

| | |
|---|---|
| Johnathan Rodgers | 2002–2003 |
| David Roland<br>*Chair, 2000–2002* | 1995–2002 |
| Howard Rosenberg | 1996–2004 |
| Beatrice Sawyer Rossell | 1943–1944 |
| Jill S. Ruckelshaus | 1985–1991 |
| N. Bird Runningwater | 2011– |
| Maureen Ryan | 2010– |
| Allen Sabinson | 2009– |
| Ernest Sanchez | 1991–1996<br>2007 |
| Marlene Sanders<br>*Chair, 2005* | 1998–2005 |
| Tom Shales | 1991–1996 |
| Ron Simon<br>*Chair, 2009* | 2003–2009 |
| Susan Stewart | 1988–1994<br>2005 |
| John W. Studebaker | 1940–1942 |
| Lawrence B Taishoff | 1984–1991 |
| Dr. I. Keith Tyler | 1942–1952,<br>1953–1978 |
| Harriet Van Horne | 1958–1967 |
| F. Glenn Verrill | 1983–1989 |
| Joe Urschel<br>*Chair, 2012–2013* | 2006–2013 |
| Marjorie Peabody Waite | 1940–1944 |
| Pamela Wallin | 2008–2009 |
| Larry Walters | 1958–1968 |
| Abbott Washburn | 1983–1989 |
| Dr. Dixon Wechter | 1945–1947 |
| Edward Weeks<br>*Chair, 1940–1954* | 1940–1954 |
| Margita E. White | 1979–1985 |
| William F. Woo | 1997–2004 |
| Nancy Woodhull<br>*Chair, 1995–1997* | 1991–1997 |
| Fred Young | 2009– |
| Barbie Zelizer | 2010– |

## HENRY W. GRADY COLLEGE OF JOURNALISM AND MASS COMMUNICATION ALUMI AWARD RECIPENTS

### DISTINGUISHED ALUMNI SCHOLAR AWARD

*The Distinguished Alumni Scholar Award honors Grady graduates who have demonstrated excellence and sustained contributions to scholarship in journalism and mass communication education.*

| | |
|---|---|
| 2006 | J. Thomas Russell |
| 2007 | Jack Lule |
| 2010 | Carol Pardun |
| 2013 | Marie Hardin |
| 2014 | Kathy Richardson |
| 2015 | Denise DeLorme |

### JOHN HOLLIMAN AWARD

*The John Holliman, Jr. Lifetime Achievement Award honors a graduate for sustained contributions to the profession throughout a career.*

| | |
|---|---|
| 1975 | Tom Johnson |
| 1976 | Jasper Dorsey |
| 1977 | Don Carter |
| 1978 | Eugene Patterson |
| 1979 | Bill Ray |
| 1980 | Aubrey Morris |
| 1981 | Frank Hawkins |
| 1982 | William Ott |
| 1983 | William S. Morris, III |

| | |
|---|---|
| 1984 | James G. Minter, Jr. |
| 1985 | Powell A. Moore |
| 1986 | Eugene H. Methvin |
| 1987 | Robert Sherrod |
| 1988 | C. Richard Yarbrough |
| 1989 | Randall E. Savage |
| 1990 | Thomas C. Dowden |
| 1991 | Willie K. Thrower Friar |
| 1992 | Billy Watson |
| 1993 | Connie Stewart |
| 1994 | J. Carrol Dadisman |
| 1995 | Harley Bowers |
| 1996 | James P. Wooten |
| 1997 | Jack Avrett |
| 1998 | Earl Leonard |
| 1999 | John Holliman, Jr. |
| 2000 | Willis Johnson |
| 2001 | Edwin Pope |
| 2002 | Neil Aronstam |
| 2003 | Dennis Berry |
| 2004 | Harry Chapman |
| 2005 | Dan Magill |
| 2006 | Donald Perry |
| 2007 | Millard Grimes |
| 2008 | Carolyn Tieger |
| 2009 | Judge R. Alex Crumbley |
| 2010 | W.H. "Dink" NeSmith, Jr. |
| 2011 | Roger Strauss |
| 2012 | Edward Ingles |
| 2013 | Claude Felton |
| 2014 | Alan Griggs |
| 2015 | Joel Babbit |

### HENRY W. GRADY AWARD

*The Henry W. Grady Award honors a mid-career graduate who has been successful and influential during his/her career.*

| | |
|---|---|
| 1995 | Deborah L. Blum |
| 1996 | Michelle Green |
| 1997 | Bonnie Arnold |
| 1998 | Bill Mattox |
| 1999 | Dan Gearino |
| 2000 | Walt Lloyd |
| 2001 | Dawn McCall |
| 2002 | Betty Hudson |
| 2003 | Brenda Hampton |
| 2004 | Lee Duffey |
| 2005 | Randy Travis |
| 2006 | Bill Dean |
| 2007 | Jennifer Sloan |
| 2008 | Gene Colter |
| 2009 | Josh Jackson |
| 2010 | Justin Gillis |
| 2011 | Col. Bryan Salas |
| 2012 | Lisa Ryan Howard |
| 2013 | William Ostick |
| 2014 | Amy Glennon |
| 2015 | Michael Giarrusso |

### JOHN E. DREWRY AWARD

*The John E. Drewry Award honors a graduate with 10 years or less of experience who has seen exciting and productive career developments in the years closely following graduation.*

| | |
|---|---|
| 1977 | Rex Granum |
| 1978 | Roger Ann Jones |
| 1979 | Rodney Allen Smith |
| 1980 | Frank Compton |
| 1981 | W.H. (Dink) Nesmith, Jr. |
| 1982 | Betty Johnson Hudson |
| 1983 | Dennis McClain |
| 1984 | Mary Jo West |
| 1985 | Ernest T. Johnson, Jr. |
| 1986 | Deborah A. Norville |
| 1987 | Lewis Grizzard |
| 1988 | William R. Jones |
| 1989 | Mary Anne Hill |
| 1990 | Carolyn Carlson |

| | |
|---|---|
| 1991 | Joel Babbit |
| 1992 | Condace Pressley |
| 1993 | Deborah Roberts |
| 1994 | Hanna Ledford |
| 1995 | Julie Bryan Moran |
| 1996 | Timothy W. Mapes |
| 1997 | Lauran Neergaard |
| 1998 | Chip Caray |
| 1999 | Chris Decherd |
| 2000 | Michael Giarrusso |
| 2001 | Todd Fantz |
| 2002 | Amanda Rosseter |
| 2003 | Christopher Grimes |
| 2004 | Erin McClam |
| 2005 | Tom Lasseter |
| 2006 | Kyle Wingfield |
| 2007 | Jon Gallo |
| 2008 | Jessica Foster Bonner |
| 2009 | Jennifer Rainey Marquez |
| 2010 | Lynssey Gardner |
| 2011 | Kelly Hornbuckle |
| 2012 | Alex Wallace |
| 2013 | Ben Mayer |
| 2014 | Greg Bluestein |
| 2015 | Dawn Brun |

## HENRY W. GRADY COLLEGE OF JOURNALISM AND MASS COMMUNICATION FELLOWSHIP

(FELLOW BY YEAR INDUCTED)

INAUGURAL CLASS, 2008

John G. "Jimmy" Alston, ABJ '66
Bill Anderson, ABJ '59
Neil L. Aronstam, ABJ '65
Dennis Berry, ABJ '66
Conway Broun, ABJ '70
Don Carter, ABJ '38
Maxine Clark, ABJ '71
Frank Compton, ABJ '68
Carlton Curtis, ABJ '72
J. Carrol Dadisman, ABJ '56
Tom Dowden, ABJ '62; MA Political Science '64
Miriam Drewry, BBA '42
Jenny N. Duffey, ABJ '80
Lee Duffey, ABJ '80
Bruce Finland, ABJ '74
Rex Granum, ABJ '72
Millard Grimes, ABJ '51
Bill Hartman, ABJ '70
Charles Hayslett, ABJ '73
Betty J. Hudson, ABJ '71
Charlayne Hunter-Gault, ABJ '63
Tom Johnson, ABJ '63
Brian Johnstone, ABJ '68
W. Chris Jones, ABJ '73
Rev. Warren Jones, ABJ '41; MA '42
Tom S. Landrum, AB '72; MA '87
Rebecca Leet, ABJ '71
Dan Magill, ABJ '42
Michael H. McDougald
Jim Minter, ABJ '51
Pat Mitchell, AB '65; MA '67
Frazier Moore, Jr., ABJ '74
Powell A. Moore, ABJ '59
William S. Morris III, ABJ '56
W. H. "Dink" NeSmith Jr., ABJ '70
Deborah Norville, ABJ '79
Gloria Ricks Taylor, ABJ '66

Richard Riley, ABJ ’67
Deborah Roberts, ABJ ’82
Don Rountree, ABJ ’63
Neva Rountree, ABJ ’64; MA ’79
Dr. J. Thomas Russell, ABJ ’63
Swann Seiler, ABJ ’78
Bill Shipp, 1953–54
A. Mark Smith, ABJ ’66
Jay Smith
Loran Smith, ABJ ’62
Celestia “Lessie” Bailey Smithgall, ABJ ’33
Paul C. Stone, ABJ ’71
Carolyn Caudell Tieger, ABJ ’69
Claude Williams, Jr., AB ’44; ABJ ’48
Robert M. Williams, Jr.
Jim Wooten, ABJ ’68
C. Richard Yarbrough, ABJ ’59
Neely Young, BBA ’66

CLASS OF 2009

Claude Felton, ABJ ’70; MA ’71
Brenda Hampton, ABJ ’73
Ray Jenkins, ABJ ’51
Gordon Smith, ABJ ’75, JD ’78
Ruth Estes Trager, ABJ ‘47

CLASS OF 2010

Carolyn Abney
Randall Abney, BBA ‘63
Phil Gailey, ABJ ‘66
Steve Koonin
Edwin Pope, ABJ ‘48
Bo Spalding, ABJ ’78, MBA ‘79
James H. Tate Jr., ABJ ‘42

CLASS OF 2011

David Adelman, ABJ ‘86
Ed Bastian
Julie Moran, ABJ ‘84
Arnold Punaro, MA ‘76
Bill Simpson, ABJ ‘50
Julie Winskie, ABJ ‘84

CLASS OF 2012

Glen Finland, ABJ ‘74
Henry Grady III, BBA ‘84
Jeff Jowdy, ABJ ‘83
Tim Mapes, ABJ ‘86
Greg McGarity, ABJ ‘76
Horace Newcomb

CLASS OF 2013

Cathy Cox, ABJ ‘80
Ron Lane, ABJ ‘63, MA ‘65
Melissa Libby, ABJ ‘85
Steve Oney, ABJ ‘79
Jennifer Sloan ABJ ‘86
Glenn Vaughn, M ‘53

CLASS OF 2015

Deborah Blum, ABJ ’75
Harry Chapman, ABJ ’67
Jody Danneman, ABJ ’88
Chris Dixon, ABJ ’89, MA ’92
Gretchen Erwin, ABJ ’77
Amy Glennon, ABJ ’90
Earl Leonard, ABJ ’58
Condace Pressley, ABJ ’86
Remer Tyson, ABJ ’56
Philip Lee Williams, ABJ ’72
Scott Williamson, MMC ’92

SANFORD CIRCLE

Jack Avrett, ABJ ‘50
Joe Belew, ABJ ‘72

Furman Bisher
Otis A. Brumby Jr., LLB '65
M. Tyus Butler, ABJ '35
Carolyn McKenzie Carter, ABJ '40
Conrad Fink
Charles Giddens, ABJ '67
Betty Gage Holland
John W. Jacobs Jr.
Claude McBride, ABJ '55
Worth McDougald
Eugene Methvin, ABJ '45
Aubrey Morris, ABJ '45
Jesse Outlar, ABJ '43
Eugene Patterson, ABJ '43
Donald A. Perry, ABJ '74
Lamar Trotti, ABJ '21
Robert VanLandingham, ABJ '42

## RALPH MCGILL LECTURES

| | |
|---|---|
| 1979 | Eugene Patterson, *The St. Petersburg Times* |
| 1980 | Tom Wicker, *The New York Times* |
| 1981 | Anthony Lewis, *The New York Times* |
| 1981 | Tom Johnson, *The Los Angeles Times* |
| 1982 | Robert Maynard, *The Oakland Tribune* |
| 1983 | Katharine Graham, *The Washington Post* |
| 1984 | John Seigenthaler, *The Tennessean* |
| 1985 | Gene Roberts, *The Philadelphia Inquirer* |
| 1986 | Alvah Chapman, Knight Ridder |
| 1988 | Jack Nelson, *The Los Angeles Times* |
| 1989 | Reg Murphy, *The Baltimore Sun* |
| 1990 | Claude Sitton, *The Raleigh News and Observer* |
| 1991 | Celestine Sibley, *The Atlanta Journal-Constitution* |
| 1992 | Richard Oppel, *The Charlotte Observer* |
| 1993 | David Lawrence, Jr., *The Miami Herald* |
| 1994 | Clarence Page, *The Chicago Tribune* |
| 1995 | Helen Thomas, United Press International |
| 1996 | Frank Deford, National Public Radio |
| 1996 | Robin Wright, *The Los Angeles Times* |
| 1997 | Robert J. Danzig, The Hearst Corporation |
| 1998 | Jay Smith, Cox Newspapers, Inc. |
| 1999 | Deborah Roberts, ABC News |
| 2000 | John Egerton, journalist and author |
| 2001 | Cynthia Tucker, *The Atlanta Journal-Constitution* |
| 2002 | Geneva Overholser, University of Missouri |
| 2003 | Hodding Carter, III, John S. and James L. Knight Foundation |
| 2005 | Jerry Ceppos, Knight Ridder |
| 2006 | Leonard Pitts Jr., *The Miami Herald* |
| 2007 | Julia Wallace, *The Atlanta Journal Constitution* |
| 2008 | Hannah Allam, McClatchy Newspapers |
| 2009 | Martin Kaiser, *Milwaukee Journal Sentinel* |

2010 Paul Steiger, editor in chief, ProPublica
2011 Jan Schaffer, executive director of J-Lab: The Institute for Interactive Journalism
2012 Bill Adair, editor of PolitiFact
2013 Christine Brennan, sports columnist for *USA Today*
2014 Antonio Mora, host of Al Jazeera America's "Consider This"

## MCGILL MEDAL FOR JOURNALISTIC COURAGE RECIPIENTS

2009 Jerry Mitchell
2010 Chauncey Bailey
*Project reporters:*
Thomas Peele
Josh Richman
Mary Fricker
Bob Butler
2011 Laura Ling
Euna Lee
2012 Rukmini Callimachi
2013 Dorothy Parvaz
2014 Glenn Greenwald
2015 Kathy Gannon

## GRADY COLLEGE OF JOURNALISM AND MASS COMMUNICATION DIGAMMA KAPPA HONOREES

1974 J. Leonard Reinsch
1975 Barbara Walters
1976 Arthur Godfrey
1977 Eric Sevareid
1978 Bob Keeshan
1979 Mark Goodson and Bill Todman
1980 Charles Kuralt
1981 Keith Jackson
1982 Douglas Edwards
1983 John Chancellor
1984 Ed Bradley
1985 R. E. "Ted" Turner
1986 Julian Goodman
1987 Marvin Kalb
1988 Ted Koppel
1989 Monica Kaufman
1990 John Palmer
1991 Walter "Red" Barber
1992 John Holliman
1993 Himan Brown
1994 Bob Costas
1995 Brandon Tartikoff
1996 Robin Roberts
1997 Bud Greenspan
1998 Marlene Sanders
1999 Tom Johnson
2000 Linda Ellerbee
2001 Barry Sherman
2002 Bernard Shaw
2003 John Hockenberry
2004 Brian Ross
2005 Pat Mitchell
2006 John Pruitt
2007 Charlayne Hunter-Gault

| | | | |
|---|---|---|---|
| 2008 | Barbara Cochran | 2012 | Monica Pearson |
| 2009 | Bob Furnad | 2013 | Gale Anne Hurd |
| 2010 | Wolf Blitzer | 2014 | Steven R. Koonin |
| 2011 | David J. Barrett | 2015 | Amy Robach |

## UGA ADVERTISING HONOR ROLL: AMERICAN ADVERTISING FEDERATION AIDE AWARD

| | | | |
|---|---|---|---|
| 1979 | F. Glenn Verrill | 1997 | Neil L. Aronstam |
| 1980 | W. Lawrence Weltin | 1999 | David M. Pektas |
| 1981 | A. Neill Cameron | 2000 | Andy Jorishie |
| 1982 | Claude Williams, Jr. | 2001 | Joy Cantilo |
| 1983 | James S. Pollak | 2002 | Carolee Coker |
| 1984 | Morgan McKeown | 2003 | Mark Kooyman |
| 1984 | Ernest R. Anderson | 2004 | Richard Riley |
| 1985 | Thomas N. Lentz | 2005 | Steven Lang |
| 1986 | Mary Adams | 2006 | Jeff Snowden |
| 1987 | Ron Scharbo | 2007 | Suzanne C. Piehl |
| 1990 | Franklin C. Compton | 2009 | Sean Jones |
| 1991 | Tod A. Martin | 2010 | Matt Wilson |
| 1992 | Bradford P. Majors | 2011 | Monique Birkeli |
| 1993 | Eddie Snyder | 2012 | Rob Marbury |
| 1995 | F. Richard Wemmers, Jr. | 2013 | Meghan Ann McMullen |
| 1996 | Norm Grey | 2014 | Jennifer Tullar |

## GEORGIA PRSA PUBLIC RELATIONS HALL OF FAME: THE ORDER OF THE PHOENIX

| | | | |
|---|---|---|---|
| 1986 | Ann Poland Berg | 1987 | Everett A. Hayes |
| 1986 | Richard E. Hodges | 1988 | Celia Cole Boswell |
| 1986 | George Goodwin | 1988 | Ron David |
| 1986 | Paul B. Karelson | 1988 | Felton H. Gordon |
| 1986 | Harry C. Malone | 1988 | J. Phil Harrison |
| 1986 | Al B. Richardson | 1989 | Hugh K. Rickenbaker, Jr. |
| 1986 | A. Lee Rogers | 1990 | Scott M. Cutlip |
| 1986 | Dorotha (Ric) Willix | 1990 | Harry D. Hollingsworth |

| | | | |
|---|---|---|---|
| 1990 | C. Richard Yarbrough | 2000 | James V. Sheahan |
| 1991 | Gene Dyson | 2001 | Mary G. Ackerly |
| 1991 | Robert K. (Rob) Martin | 2002 | Lynne M. Sallot |
| 1992 | Larry Lowenstein | 2003 | Neva Dixon Rountree |
| 1992 | James M. Montgomery | 2003 | Leslie Lamkin |
| 1992 | Gordon Sawyer | 2004 | Nancy Wood |
| 1992 | Mack D. Secord | 2005 | Gary W. McKillips |
| 1993 | Amanda Brown-Olmstead | 2006 | Ellen Weaver Hartman |
| 1993 | Jan Pringle | 2007 | Michael B. Manning |
| 1993 | Jane E. Shivers | 2008 | Sherry Treco-Jones |
| 1994 | Don G. Reichardt | 2008 | Denise Grant (Honorary) |
| 1995 | James J. Wallace | 2009 | Ray A. Crockett |
| 1996 | Willis Johnson | 2010 | Bari Rosenthal Love |
| 1997 | Donald J. Downs | 2011 | Michael G. Nall |
| 1997 | Dwayne Summar | 2012 | Judy DeRango |
| 1998 | Judi B. Borgo | 2013 | Mark Dvorak |
| 1999 | Donald A. Perry | 2014 | Alicia R. Thompson |

## GEORGIA NEWSPAPER HALL OF FAME
### (BY YEAR OF INDUCTION)

1931 Henry W. Grady
*Atlanta Constitution*

Patrick Walsh
*Augusta Chronicle*

Pleasant A. Stovall
*Savannah Evening Press*

Clark Howell Sr.
*Atlanta Constitution*

Bowdre Phinizy
*Augusta Herald*

C. R. Pendleton
*Macon Telegraph*

W. T. Anderson
*Macon Telegraph*

John Sanford Cohen
*Atlanta Journal*

1931 Royal Daniel
*Quitman Free Press*

Dudley Glass
*Atlanta Georgian & Constitution*

Hal M. Stanley
Secretary-Treasurer GPA and editor, *Editors' Forum*

1942 William G. Sutlive
*Savannah Evening Press*

1944 Thomas J. Hamilton
*Augusta Chronicle*

James Williams
*Greensboro Herald-Journal*

1947 Joe Lawrence
*Ashburn Wiregrass Farmer*

1951 James B. Nevin
*Atlanta Georgian*

1956 Albert S. Hardy
*Gainesville News*

Joel Chandler Harris
*Atlanta Constitution*

Louie L. Morris
*Hartwell Sun*

John Paschall
*Atlanta Journal*

Frank L. Stanton
*Atlanta Constitution*

1959 James Johnston
Georgia's first printer, publisher, *The Georgia Gazette*

Mirabeau Bonaparte Lamar
*Columbus Enquirer*

Elian Boudinot
*The Cherokee Phoenix*

1962 Dr. Wightman F. Melton
*Griffin Daily News*

Jack Williams, Sr.
*Waycross Journal-Herald*

Ernest Camp
*The Walton Tribune*

Herschel Jenkins
*Savannah News-Press*

1964 Otis Arnoldus Brumby
*Cobb County Times-Marietta Daily Journal*

Jere N. Moore
*Milledgeville Union-Recorder*

Henry Martyn McIntosh
*Albany Herald*

John L. Herring
*The Tifton Gazette*

1966 Charles Edward Benns
*Butler Herald*

Pleasant T. McCuthen
*Franklin News and Banner*

Theron S. Shope
*Dalton Citizen*

1966 David Benjamin Turner
*Bulloch Times*, Statesboro

1968 William Thomas Bacon
*Madisonian*

Milton L. Fleetwood
*Cartersville Tribune-News*

Thomas W. Loyless
*Augusta Chronicle*

William Alsa Shackelford
*Oglethorpe Echo*, Lexington

1970 John Hicks Hodges
*Houston Home Journal*, Perry

Ralph Emerson McGill
*Atlanta Constitution*

1972 William Ryan Frier
*Bartow Herald*, Cartersville

Ernest Rogers
*Atlanta Journal*

E. M. Turner
*Valdosta Daily Times*

1974 Nora Lawrence Smith
*Wiregrass Farmer*, Ashburn

William R. Smith
*Cochran Journal*

William S. Morris, Jr.
*Augusta Chronicle-Herald*

1976 Charles Durden Tountree
*Wrightsville Headlight*

James Jefferson Thomason
*Carroll County Times*

Emily Woodward
*Vienna News*

1978 Margaret Mitchell Marsh
*Atlanta Journal*

James B. Chism, Sr.
*Pelham Journal*

Paul Talford Harber
*Commerce Observer*

1980 William T. Thompson
*Savannah Morning News*

1982 Albert S. Hardy, Jr.
*Commerce News*
Louis C. Harris
*Augusta Chronicle-Herald*
Carlton M. Johnson
*Columbus Ledger*

1984 Leo Aikman
*Atlanta Constitution*
Sue Myrick
*Macon Telegraph and News*
Edna Cain Daniel
*Quitman Free Press*

1986 Ron Autry
*Associate Press*, Atlanta
John Drewry
Dean, *Grady School of Journalism*, Athens
Marvin Griffin
*Post-Searchlight*, Bainbridge
Joe Parham
*Macon News*

1988 Charles Leroy Black
*Columbus Enquirer*
J. Roy McGinty
*Calhoun Times*
W. H. McWhorter
*DeKalb News Era*

1990 Roscoe Ernest Ledford
*Vidalia Advance*
Jere Neuville Moore
*Union-Recorder*, Milledgeville
William Kirkland Sutlive
*Blackshear Times*

1992 Sarah Hillhouse Porter
*Washington Monitor*
James H. Gray, Sr.
*Albany Herald*
Sanders Camp
*Walton Tribune*

1994 William A. Ott
*Macon Telegraph*
Quimby Melton
*Griffin Daily News*
Madge Hilburn Methvin
*Vienna News*

1996 Julian and Julia Harris
*Columbus Enquirer Sun*
William Alexander Scott, II
*Atlanta Daily World*
Zula Brown Toole
*Miller County Liberal*, Colquitt

2011 Robert D. Fowler
*Gwinnett Daily News*
David Stanley Parkman
*The Times-Georgian*
William Rogers, Sr.
*The Forest-Blade*
Charles A. Smithgall
*Gainesville Daily Times*
James Jefferson Thomasson
*The Newnam Times-Herald*
James W. Watson
*Macon Telegraph & News*
Charles M. Williamson, Jr.
*The Darien News*

## GEORGIA ASSOCIATION OF BROADCASTERS HALL OF FAME

(HONOREES CATEGORIZED BY YEAR OF INDUCTION)

| | |
|---|---|
| 1984 | J. Leonard Reinsch, Cox Broadcasting |
| 1986 | Douglas Edwards, CBS News |
| 1987 | Elmo I. Ellis, WSB Radio |
| | Aubrey Morris,WXB Radio |
| 1988 | Wilton E. Cobb, WMAZ, Macon |
| | Charlayne Hunter-Gault,The MacNeil / Lehrer News Hour |
| | Donald O. McDougald, McDougald Business Brokers |
| | Esther S. Pruett, WTOC AM / FM and Television |
| | James W. Woodruff, Jr., WRBL AM / FM and Television |
| | Marcus Bartlett, WSB AM/FM |
| | Allan MacMillan, WRNG Radio |
| | Jim Owens, Jim Owens Company |
| 1989 | Lambdin Kay, WSB Radio |
| | George Patton, WBML Radio |
| 1990 | Ridley Bell, WRBL Television |
| | Hank Morgan, Voice of Atlanta Crackers |
| 1991 | Tom Lloyd, WLAQ AM, Rome |
| | Robert Pollock, Author-TV Writer-Producer |
| | Worth McDougald, Broadcaster-Educator |
| 1992 | Ernie Harwell, Voice of the Detroit Tigers |
| | George Page, PBS Host-Programming Executive |
| 1993 | Bill Anderson, Composer-Singer-Entertainer |
| | H. Randolph Holder, WGAU/WNGC, Athens |
| 1994 | Mary Betts, WGAU/WNGC, Athens |
| | Larry Munson, Voice of the Georgia Bulldogs |
| 1995 | Ray Moore, WSB TV Atlanta |
| | Hal Suit, WXIA TV Atlanta |
| 1996 | Michael Hall McDougald, WRGA/WQTV, Rome |
| | Charles C. Smith, WDEC AM/FM, Americus |
| 1997 | Don Elliot Heald, WSB TV |
| | Paul Maymon, WAGA TV |
| 1998 | Charles A. McClure, McClure Broadcasting |
| | Ernest Rogers, WSB Radio |
| | John W. Jacobs, Jr., WDUN/WGGA/WMJE-FM |
| 1999 | John Holliman, CNN |
| | Darwin Humphrey, NBC News |
| | George Weiss, WBBQ Augusta |
| 2000 | Frank Gaither, WSB Atlanta |
| | Guy Sharpe, WXIA TV |
| 2001 | Tom Brokaw, NBC News |
| | Don Kennedy, WSB TV |
| | Bill Sanders, Georgia Association of Broadcasters |
| 2002 | Roy Gaines, WNEG, Toccoa |
| | Charles Giddens, Southern Broadcasting |
| | John Palmer, NBC News |
| 2003 | Rhett Turnipseed, Broadcaster/VOA |
| | Judy Woodruff, CNN |
| 2004 | Don McGouirk, WMAZ |

2004 John E. Lauer, WGST/WPCH Radio

2005 Lowell L. Register, Register Communications

2005 Stan Raymond, Sports Broadcaster, WAOK

2006 Donald Barber, Radio and TV

James A. Lee, Georgia Farm Bureau

2007 E. Lanier "Lanny" Finch, Busby, Finch, Latham & Widman, Inc.

Neal Boortz, WSB AM

2008 Bryon L. Dobbs, WLJA FM / WPGY AM, Jasper

Ernie Johnson, Braves Broadcaster

James Brown, WRDW AM/FM

2008 James A. "Jimmy" Bridges, WSB Radio and TV

2010 Don McClellan, WSB TV

2001 David J. Barrett, Heart TV Inc.

2012 Monica Kaufman Pearson, WSB TV

2013 Lee Brantley, WTVM TV/Raycom Media Inc.

Peter Van Wieren, Atlanta Braves Broadcaster

Harry Christopher Caray, Jr. (Skip), Atlanta Braves Broadcaster

2014 William Cathcart, WTOC TV

John Pruitt, WSB TV

Paul Beliveau, Georgia Farm Bureau

2015 John and Bobbie Foster, WCON AM/FM

Ken Cook, WAGA TV

Mike Roberts, WVEE FM,

Bill Stewart, WJBF TV/WAGA TV

## CENTENNIAL EDITORIAL BOARD

# BIBLIOGRAPHY

## WORKS CITED


Anderson, William. *The Wild Man from Sugar Creek: The Political career of Eugene Talmadge*. Baton Rouge: The Louisiana State University Press, 1975.

Bailyn, Bernard. *Ideological Origins of the American Revolution*. Cambridge: Harvard University Press, 1967.

Boney, F.N. *A Pictorial History of the University of Georgia*, second edition. Athens: The University of Georgia Press, 2000.

Brack, Elliott E. *Gwinnett: A Little Above Atlanta*. Norcross, GA: The Brack Group (Ga), Inc., 2008.

Clark, E. Culpepper. *Francis Warrington Dawson and the Politics of Restoration: South Carolina, 1874-1889*. Tuscaloosa: University of Alabama Press, 1980.

Clark, E. Culpepper. *The Schoolhouse Door: Segregation's Last Stand at the University of Alabama*. New York: Oxford University Press, 1993. Reprint edition with new foreword by Dan T. Carter, University of Alabama Press, 2007.

Clark, Roy Peter and Arsenault, Raymond, eds. *The Changing South of Gene Patterson: Journalism and Civil Rights, 1960-1968*, in Southern Dissent, Stanley Harold and Randall Miller, eds. Gainesville: University Press of Florida, 2002.

Coleman, Kenneth, general ed. *A History of Georgia*, second edition. Athens and London: The University of Georgia Press, 1991.

Couch, William Terry, ed. *Culture in the South*. Chapel Hill: University of North Carolina Press, 1934.

Craige, Berry Jean. *Eugene Odum: Ecosystem Ecologist & Environmentalist*. Athens and London: University of Georgia Press, 2002.

Dadisman, Carrol. *Dear Old U-G-A From the Red & Black: Student Life at the University of Georgia, 1893-2013*. Athens: Carrol Dadisman and the Red and Black Publishing Company, 2013.

Davis, Harold E. *Henry Grady's New South: Atlanta, A Brave & Beautiful City*. Tuscaloosa and London: The University of Alabama Press, 1990.

Dendy, Larry B., foreword by F.N. Boney. *Through the Arch: An Illustrated Guide to THE UNIVERSITY OF GEORGIA CAMPUS*. Athens and London: The University of Georgia Press, 2013.

Dooley, Vince, with paintings by Steve Penley. *History and Reminiscences of the University of Georgia*. Looking Glass Books, Inc., 2011.

Dyer, Thomas G. *The University of Georgia: A Bicentennial History, 1785-1985*. Athens: The University of Georgia Press, 1985.

Fawcett, Edmund. *Liberalism: The Life of an Idea*. Princeton and Oxford: Princeton University Press, 2014.

Fite, Gilbert C. *Richard B. Russell, Jr., Senator from Georgia*. The Fred W. Morrison Series in Southern Studies. Chapel Hill & London: The University of North Carolina Press, 1991.

Fitzgerald, F. Scott. *Tender Is the Night*. New York: Charles Scribner's Sons, 1934.

Goodwin, Doris Kearns. *The Bully Pulpit: Theodore Roosevelt, William Howard Taft, and the Golden Age of Journalism*. New York: Simon and Schuster, 2013.

Graves, John Temple, with intro by Fred Hobson. *The Fighting South*. Tuscaloosa: University of Alabama Press, 1985, originally published in 1943 by G.P. Putnam's Sons.

Grimes, Millard B., Chief Editor and Writer. *The Last Linotype: The Story of Georgia and Its Newspapers since World War II*. Macon: Mercer University Press and Georgia Press Association, 1985.

Guelzo, Allen C. *Fateful Lightning: A New History of the Civil War*. New York: Oxford University Press, 2012.

Gurr, Charles Stephen. *The Personal Equation: A Biography of Steadman Vincent Sanford*. Athens and London: The University of Georgia Press, 1999.

Harris, Joel Chandler. *Life of Henry W. Grady Including his Writings and Speeches*. New York: Cassell Publishing Company, 1890.

Hobson, Fred, ed. with intro. *South-Watching: Selected Essays of Gerald W. Johnson*. The Fred W. Morrison Series in Southern Studies. Chapel Hill & London: The University of North Carolina Press. 1983.

Hunter-Gault, Charlayne. *In My Place*. New York: Vintage, 1993.

Kelly, Robert Lloyd. *The Liberal-Democratic Mind in the Age of Gladstone*. New York: Alfred A. Knopf, 1966.

Levine, Bruce C. *Fall of the House of Dixie: The Civil War and the Social Revolution that Transformed the South*. New York: Random House, 2013.

Logan, Rayford. *What the Negro Wants*. Chapel Hill: University of North Carolina Press, 1944.

Martin, Harold H. *Ralph McGill: Reporter*. Boston and Toronto: Atlantic Monthly Press Book; Little Brown and Company, 1973.

Patterson, Eugene. *Patton's Unsung Armor in the Ardennes: The Tenth Armored Division's Secret Dash to Bastogne*. Eugene Patterson, 2008.

Pratt, Robert A. *We Shall Not Be Moved: The Desegregation of the University of Georgia*. Athens: University of Georgia Press, 2002.

Sanders, Lynn Moss. *Howard W. Odum's Folk Odyssey: Transformation to Tolerance through African American Folk Studies*. Athens: University of Georgia Press, 2003.

Smith, Lillian. *Killers of the Dream*. revised ed. New York and London: W.W. Norton & Company, 1978.

Talmadge, John and Griffith, Louis T. *Georgia Journalism, 1733-1950*. Athens: University of Georgia Press, 1950.

Varon, Elizabeth R. *Appomattox: Victory, Defeat and Freedom at the End of the Civil War*. New York: Oxford University Press, 2013.

Waldorf, Gwendolyn Brock. *The Genesis of Grady County, Georgia*. Tallahassee, FL: Sentry Press, 2006.

Ware, Louise. *George Foster Peabody: Banker, Philanthropist, Publicist*. Athens: The University of Georgia Press, 1951.

Whitt, Rich. *Behind the Hedges: Big Money and Power Politics at the University of Georgia*. Montgomery, Alabama: New South Books, 2008.

Williams, Susan Millar and Hoffius, Stephen G. *Upheaval in Charleston: Earthquake and Murder on the Eve of Jim Crow*. Athens: The University of Georgia Press, 2011.

Wilson, E.O. *Consilience: The Unity of Knowledge*. New York: Knopf, 1998.

Winfield, Betty Houchin, ed. *Journalism 1908: Birth of a Profession*. Columbia and London: University of Missouri Press, 2008.

Yarbrough, C. Richard. *And They Called Them Games*. Macon: Mercer University Press, 2000.

## HARGRETT RARE BOOK & MANUSCRIPT LIBRARY, UNIVERSITY OF GEORGIA

Adams, Michael F., Papers.

Agee, Warren K., Papers.

Davison, Fred, Papers.

Drewry, John E., Papers.

Drewry, John E. and Kathleen Drewry, Letters.

Pelletier, S. William, Papers.

## HENRY W. GRADY COLLEGE OF JOURNALISM AND MASS COMMUNICATION ARCHIVES, UNIVERSITY OF GEORGIA

# ENDNOTES

### CHAPTER I

1 "In Plain Black and White—A Reply to Mr. Cable," Joel Chandler Harris, *Life of Henry W. Grady Including His Writings and Speeches* (New York: Cassell Publishing Company, 1890), 285-308.

2 Allen C. Guelzo, *Fateful Lightning: A New History of the Civil War* (New York: Oxford University Press, 2012), 370-72. For other recent single volume treatments see Bruce C. Levine, *Fall of the House of Dixie: The Civil War and the Social Revolution that Transformed the South* (New York: Random House, 2013) and Elizabeth R. Varon, *Appomattox: Victory. Defeat and Freedom at the End of the Civil War* (New York: Oxford University Press, 2013).

3 Harris, *Life*, "At the Boston Banquet," 180-99.

4 Lillian Smith, *Killers of the Dream* (New York: W. W. Norton, 1949), 72.

5 *American Historical Review* 34, (October, 1928): 30-43.

6 Charles Stephen Gurr, *The Personal Equation: A Biography of Steadman Vincent Sanford* (Athens and London: University of Georgia Press, 1999), 19.

7 Ibid., 32.

8 F. Scott Fitzgerald, *Tender Is the Night* (New York: Charles Scribner's Sons, 1934), 68.

9 Dorris Kearns Goodwin, *The Bully Pulpit: Theodore Roosevelt, William Howard Taft, and the Golden Age of Journalism* (New York: Simon and Schuster, 2013).

10 The National Amateur Press Association, 1876, was first. The United Amateur Press Association, 1895, would have been active in Sanford's time. Amateur associations have continued to this day.

11 Greg Lisby, *New Georgia Encyclopedia*, online edition, and Charles Glover, *Journey Through Our Years* (Atlanta: Longstreet Press, 1999). See also http://www.georgiaencyclopedia.org/articles/arts-culture/cox-enterprises.

12 The thought is owed to Carrol Dadisman, author of *Dear Old U-G-A (From the Red and Black: Student Life at the University of Georgia, 1893-2013)* (Athens: Red & Black Publishing Company, 2013).

13 Gwendolyn Brock Waldorf, *The Genesis of Grady County, Georgia* (Tallahassee, Florida: Sentry Press, 2006) 84-85.

14 George Morris Abney, Jr., "Forty Years of Communications Education at the Oldest Chartered State University, 1915-55," M.A. thesis, University of Georgia, 1959; Frank N. Hawkins, Jr. unpublished and untitled manuscript on history of Grady College, chapt. 1, Grady College Archives.

15 Abney, "Forty Years," 22.

16 F. N. Boney, *A Pictorial History of the University of Georgia* (Athens: University of Georgia Press, 1984), 94; Thomas G. Dyer, *The University of Georgia: A Bicentennial History* (Athens: The University of Georgia Press, 1985), 137-38.

17 Harold E. Davis, *Henry W. Grady's New South: Atlanta: A Brave and Beautiful City* (Tuscaloosa and London: University of Alabama Press, 1990), 227.

18 Abney, "Forty Years," 17.

19 Ibid.

20 Dyer, *University of Georgia,* 175-76; Bony, *Pictorial,* 106 and 123.

21 See Gurr, *Personal Equation*, Chapter 6, "The Decade of Sports," 74-96. All accounts of UGA's history covering the twenties tell this story.

22 Smith, *Killers*, 67-68.

23 Gilbert C. Fite, *Richard B. Russell, Jr., Senator from Georgia* (Chapel Hill: University of North Carolina Press, 1991), 88-89.

24 Dyer, *University of Georgia*, 185.

25 Ibid., 187

26 William Terry Couch, ed., *Culture in the South* (Chapel Hill: University of North Carolina Press, 1934), 234.

27 Ibid., 244.

28 Email exchanges between Benjamin Hill Hardy, III, and the author, April 3-4, 2014.

29 Matilda Callaway, May 5, 1924, UGA 04-026, f 18. Hargrett Rare Books & Manuscript Library, University of Georgia.

30 Various Google searches led to the anecdotal information about Matilda Callaway, most centering on the College of Family and Consumer Science's centennial.

### CHAPTER 2

31 Brochure in UGA 85-036:1, Hargrett Rare Books and Manuscript Library.

32 Betty Jean Craige, *Eugene Odum: Ecosystem Ecologist & Environmentalist* (Athens and London: The University of Georgia Press, 2002) 3-5; Lynn Moss Sanders, *Howard Odum's Folklore Odyssey:_Transformation to Tolerance through African-American Folk Studies* (Athens: University of Georgia Press, 2003), 2.

33 Rayford Logan, *What the Negro Wants* (Chapel Hill: University of North Carolina Press, 1944), publisher's introduction, unnumbered.

34 John Talmadge and Louis T. Griffith, *Georgia Journalism, 1763-1950* (Athens: University of Georgia Press, 1950) 147.

35 Fred Hobson, ed. with intro., *South Watching: Selected Essays by Gerald W. Johnson* (Chapel Hill: University of North Carolina Press, 1983) 76.

36 John Eldridge Drewry and Kathleen Drewry letters, Hargrett Rare Books & Manuscript Library, UGA 04-026:6, folder 2.

37 William Terry Couch, ed., *Culture in the South* (Chapel Hill University of North Carolina Press, 1934) 126-58.

38 What follows is from a keynote address by the author for a gathering of university press publishers in Tuscaloosa, Alabama, Feb. 19, 1995, and is taken from Graves' own words as re-printed in John Temple Graves, *The Fighting South*, originally published in 1943, with intro by Fred Hobson (Tuscaloosa: University of Alabama Press, 1985).

39 Thomas G. Dyer, *The University of Georgia: A Bicentennial History* (Athens: University of Georgia Press, 1985) 218-21.

40 Talmadge and Griffith, *Georgia Journalism*, 239.

41 Boney, *Pictorial History*, 156-57.

42 Frank N. Hawkins unpublished and untitled history of the Grady College, "Drewry insert B." Grady College archives.

43 The following account of Peabody is drawn principally from biographer Louise Ware, *George Foster Peabody: Banker, Philanthropist, Publicist* (Athens: The University of Georgia Press, 1951) and supplemented by various publications, such as anniversary programs of the Peabody Awards scattered throughout the Grady College Archives.

44 There was one exception. The German U-boat campaign was more effective off the U.S. Atlantic coast in the first six months of 1942 than in any other theatre in which their wolf packs operated. The Golden Isles of Georgia were no exception. See Michael Gannon, *Operation Drumbeat: Germany's U-boat Attacks on America's Atlantic Coast* (New York: Harper Perennial, 1991).

45 The following stories of this friendship are based on a full-length memoir by Harold E. Davis, volume one of which, "World Enough: A Memoir," covers his first twenty-three years, and a ten page reminiscence by Arthur B. Darwin that covers his UGA and Grady years. Both are in the author's possession.

46 Davis, "World Enough," 72.

47 William Anderson, *The Wild Man from Sugar Creek: The Political Career of Eugene Talmadge* (Baton Rouge: Louisiana State University Press, 1975) 196.

48 Ibid.

49 Carrol Dadisman, *Dear old U-G-A, From the Red and Black at the University of Georgia, 1893-2013* (Athens: Red and Black Publishing Company, 2013) 125.

50 Anderson, *Wild Man*, 197-200.

51 Talmadge and Griffiths, *Georgia Journalism,* 295-96.

52 Darwin, "World Enough," 3.

53 Virginia Deekle Moore, interview with author, November 28, 2012.

54 Russell interview with author, 1-23-14, and Drewry papers, Hargrett Rare Book & Manuscript Library.

55 Manuscript by Sharon Chickering, in Drewry Papers, Hargrett.

56 Drewry letters, Hargrett, box 1.

57 Ibid. State of Georgia v. Kathleen Drewry, 4328, April Term, 1950, Clarke Superior Court, Motion for New Trial, July 22, 1950; Drewry v. The State, Georgia Court of Appeals, 33271, Feb 1, 1951; Drewry v. The State, Georgia Supreme Court, 17459, July 10, 1951.

58 Millard Grimes, chief editor and writer, *The Last Linotype: The Story of Georgia Journalism and Its Newspapers Since World War II* (Macon: Mercer University Press and the Georgia Press Association, 1985) p. 457.

59 Davis, "World Enough," 55.

60 Grimes, *The Last Linotype*, 458.

61 Drewry papers, Hargrett.

62 Talmadge and Griffiths, *Georgia Journalism,* 242.

## CHAPTER 3

63 "The Editor's Forum," Georgia Press Association Bulletin, Feb 1950, 7-9.

64 Grady College Annual Report, 1954, 20-21.

65 David Brooks, *Atlanta Journal-Constitution*, May19, 2014.

66 E. O. Wilson, *Consilience: The Unity of Knowledge* (New York: Knopf, 1998).

67 Peabody 50th Anniversary Edition, 53.

68 Grady College Annual Report, 1949, 20, Grady College archives.

69 Wallace Eberhard interview with author, February 3, 2014.

70 Thomas Russell interview with author, January 23, 2014.

71 Harold Earl Davis, "World Enough: A Memoir," 70.

72 Ibid. 72.

73 Charlotte Thomas Marshall interview, July 29, 2014.

74 Eberhard interview, February 3, 2014.

75 Russell interview, January 2, 2014.

76 Ibid.

77 Eberhard interview, February 3, 2014.

78 John Talmadge and Louis T. Griffith, *Georgia Journalism: 1763-1950* (Athens: University of Georgia Press, 1950) 274

79 Bill Shipp interview, July 28, 2014.

80 Dadisman, *Dear Old U-G-A, From the Read and Black at the University of Georgia, 1893-2013* (Athens: Red and Black Publishing Company, 2013) 281-82.

81 Robert A. Pratt, *We Shall Not be Moved: The Desegregation of the University of Georgia* (Athens and London: The University of Georgia Press, 2002) 30-40.

82 Grady College Annual Report 1954.

83 Walter A. Lundy phone conversation and email exchange with author, July 31, 2014.

84 Bill Shipp interview, July 28, 2014. Shipp came back with a Sudeten German bride and had to have full employment to qualify her under the Eisenhower Refugee Act.

85 Priscilla Arnold and Patricia Templeton interview with author, February 11, 2014.

86 Lundy email to author, July 31, 2014.

87 Grimes, *The Last Linotype,* 156-58.

88 Russell interview, January 23, 2014

89 Grady College Annual Report, 1963, 14.

90 Conversation between Cecil Bentley and author, May 8, 2014.

91 *UGAzine*, Winter 1991, 19.

92 A degree that was awarded by UGA, although he lacked one course when he left in the late sixties, *Atlanta Journal-Constitution,* obit, March 21, 1994.

### CHAPTER 4

93 Thomas G. Dyer, *The University of Georgia: A Bicentennial History, 1785-1985* (Athens: The University of Georgia Press, 1985) 352.

94 Dorris Kearns Goodwin, *The Bully Pulpit: Theodore Roosevelt, William Howard Taft, and the Golden Age of Journalism* (New York: Simon & Schuster) 11-12.

95 Warren K. Agee Papers, box 4, folder 3, Hargrett Rare Books & Manuscript Library.

96 John English interview with author, January 22, 2014, also Thomas Russell interview same date, as well as Al Hester and Ernie Hynds, April 24, 2014.

97 O. C. Aderhold to Dewitt Reddick, chair accrediting committee, February 25, 1963, Aderhold to Baskett Mosse, ACEJ, March 13, 1963, John E. Drewry to Aderhold, March 7, 1963, Drewry to Aderhold, March 18, 1963, Aderhold to John E. Stempel, ACEJ, July 3, 1963. John E. Drewry papers, Hargrett.

98 Hynds interview with author, April 24, 2014

99 Frank N. Hawkins, unpublished manuscript, history of Grady College, 39, Grady College archives.

100 Hynds interview, April 24, 2014.

101 Warren Agee to Scott Pelletier, March 2, 1970, Agee papers, box 4, folder 7.

102 Journalism Accreditation Report, Accrediting Committee, American Council on Education for Journalism, Evaluation, March 26-27, 1970, Grady College archives.

103 Hester interview, April 24, 2014.

104 Hawkins, 39-40, and Grady College archives.

105 Grady College Annual Report, June 30, 1971, 2.

106 Davison papers, Hargett, and Grady College archives.

107 Jim Minter to Warren Agee, May 3, 1972, Minter to Fred Davison, February 14, 1973, Agee to Davison, February 27, 1973, Grady College archives and Agee papers, Hargrett.

108 Ibid.

109 Eberhard to Agee, November 18, 1974, and Hester to Agee, November 20, 1974, Agee papers, box 4, Hargrett.

110 Davison papers, box 34, Hargrett and Grady College archives.

111 Hester interview, April 24, 2014.

112 Ibid.

113 Hawkins, 43.

114 Russell interview, January 23, 2014.

115 Press release, no doubt written by Barry Wood, Davison's PR advisor and speechwriter, Davison papers, Hargrett.

116 Hawkins.

117 Russell interview, January 23, 2014.

118 Davison papers, box 34, Hargrett Rare Books & Manuscript Library, UGA

119 Russell interview, January 23, 2014.

120 Davison to faculty, Oct 10, 1973, box 34, Hargrett.

121 Pelletier papers, Hargrett.

122 Grady College archives.

123 Russell interview, January 23, 2014.

124 Agee file, Grady College archives.

125 Landrum interview, April 1, 2014

126 Claude L. Williams, Jr., interview, July 16, 2014.

127 Annual Report, '74-'75, and Hynds interview, April 24, 2014.

128 Landrum interview, April 1, 2014.

129 Russell interview, January 23, 2014.

130 Karen Miller Russell interview, August 14, 2014.

131 Interviews with emeriti faculty members of the period.

132 The term used by Landrum in April 1, 2014 interview with author.

133 Ibid.

134 Ibid.

135 Eberhard interview, February 4, 2014.

136 Hawkins ms, unnumbered pages on the Cutlip years, Grady College archives.

137 Davison papers, box 34, Hargrett.

138 Hester interview, April 24, 2014.

139 Davison papers, box 34, Hargrett.

140 Cutlip to Bill Sanders, February 10, 1982, Davison papers, Hargrett.

141 Davison papers include a number of letters about the contretemps.

142 Ibid.

143 Carrol Dadisman, *Dear Old U-G-A* (Athens: Red and Black Publishing Company, 2013) 115.

144 Landrum interview 4-1-14.

145 Cutlip to Leonard Reinsch President Cox Broadcasting, 2-28-78, Grady College archives.

146 *Red & Black*, April 25, 1978.

147 Eberhard interview, February 4, 2014.

148 Email exchange with Templeton, February 12, 2014 and interview March 11, 2014.

149 Donnel Carter to Cutlip, April 27, 1978, Carrol Dadisman to Cutlip, April 27, 1978, Eugene Patterson to Cutlip, April 26, 1978, and Thomas Wood to Cutlip, May 10, 1978, Davison papers, Hargrett.

150 Thomas Wood interview with author, May 23, 2014.

151 Charlotte Thomas Marshall interview, July 29, 2014.

152 Millard Grimes, *The Last Linotype: The Story of Georgia and Its Newspapers since World War II* (Macon: Mercer University Press and Georgia Press Association, 1985) 433.

153 *Savannah Morning News*, February 12, 2001.

154 Pelletier to Cutlip, March 18, 1976, Agee files, Grady College archives.

155 Cutlip to Agee, July 13, 1981, Ibid.

156 *Athens Banner-Herald*, June 15, 2005.

157 Email exchange with Steve Oney, September 2, 2014

158 Karen Russell interview, August 14, 2014.

159 William E. Lee interview, September 16, 2014.

### CHAPTER 5

160 Vince Dooley, with paintings by Steve Penley, *History and Reminiscences of the University of Georgia* (Looking Glass Books, 2011) 86.

161 Wallace B. Eberhard interview, February 4, 2014.

162 Landrum says Beaird was the one, as de facto "in-house" legal counsel, who advised "stonewalling," but Cutlip would have assented to the strategy. Dooley also uses the term "stonewall" and attributed it to unfortunate advice from Davison's "advisers," Dooley, *History and Reminisces*, 85.

163 Cutlip to Karl E. Meyer, April 10-86, Davison papers, box 25, Hargrett Rare Books & Manuscript Library, UGA.

164 Charlotte Thomas Marshall interview, July 29, 2014.

165 Middleton to Journalism Faculty, April 1986, Davison Papers, box 25, Hargrett Rare Books and Manuscript Library.

166 Jerrold K. Footlick, Chapt. 3, "Bulldog Determination," *Truth and Consequences: How Colleges and Universities Meet Public Relations Crises* (ACE/Oryx Press, 1997) 56 and 69; and Landrum interview April 1, 2014.

167 *Red & Black*, February 24, 1981, see also *Red & Black*, February 19, 1981 for report.

168 Grady College Annual Report, 1985.

169 Philip Lane Gailey interview, August 14, 2014.

170 See *Southern Changes: The Journal of the Southern Regional Council*, 10 number 6, 1988, 8-10, by Eric Guthey, a graduate student in the Graduate Institute of Liberal Arts at Emory University. For a different and more balanced discussion, see Richard Shumate, "Life after Kovach," *Atlanta Magazine* in *American Journalism Review*, September 1992.

171 Ibid., and Jay R. Smith interview with author, May 15, 2014.

172 Ibid., and follow-up email, 5-16-14.

173 By memo to staff from Patterson, September 27, 1968, he denied that either the "rate increase" story or his relationship to Tarver, whom he described as supportive, had anything to do with his resignation. The author has a copy of the memo courtesy of Tom Wood, who at the time, 1968, was assuming ever-increasing responsibility with the Atlanta papers, eventually as President of Atlanta Newspapers, Inc.

174 See also Millard Grimes, *The Last Linotype*, 78-122. In these pages Calvin Cox, no relation to the James M. Cox family, a 37-year veteran of the Cox Atlanta papers, furnishes a complete and convincing essay on Cox involvement in Atlanta.

175 Harold H. Martin, *Ralph McGill: Reporter* (Boston, Toronto: Atlantic Monthly Press Book; Little, Brown and Company, 1973) 236-45.

176 Ibid. and Gailey interview, August 14, 2014.

177 Elliott E. Brack, *Gwinnett: A Little above Atlanta* (Norcross, Ga: The Brack Group, Inc., 2008), 242-44.

178 "Betty Gage Holland 1914-2004, Memories of Betty," memorial booklet, Grady College archives.

179 Hester interview, April 24, 2014.

180 Grimes, *The Last Linotype*, 119-20. Jay Smith says the company's reputation for management turn-over is undeserved, and to be sure there are numerous long-termers, Smith interview, May 15, 2014, and Thomas H. Wood says he does not deserve credit for the newsroom merger, but he did announce it and as he notes, "It was long overdue." Wood interview, May 23, 2014.

181 Minter interview, July 8, 2014.

182 Grady College Annual Report, 1993.

183 C. Richard Yarbrough, *And They Called Them Games* (Macon: Mercer University Press, 2000) 69. See also *Saporta Report*, May 6, 2014 for a retrospective on the Atlanta Olympics.

184 David Hazinski to Senator Paul Broun, Mr. Carl Swearingen, Ms. Melita Hayes, and Mr. Claude Williams, May 7, 1998, Claude L. Williams, Jr., papers, Grady College Archives.

185 Scaife obituary, *Atlanta Journal-Constitution*, July 6, 2014

## CHAPTER 6

186 At the author's request, Dean Soloski constructed a nineteen-page narrative of his time in office. Much of what follows derives from this valuable contribution.

187 Leonard Reid interview, July 9, 2014.

188 Soloski to Adams, June 17, 2003, Grady College archives and Michael F. Adams papers, Hargrett Rare Books & Manuscript Library, UGA, UA 05-034, box 9.

189 Soloski interview with author, March 17, 2014.

190 John Soloski, plaintiff, v. Michael Adams, et al, defendants, U.S. District Court, N.D. Georgia, Atlanta Division, March 2, 2009 is summative and dispositive of the facts, findings, and rulings in the case. Soloski narrative follows the contours. Also helpful is an article in *Daily Report*, the official legal organ of Fulton County, by R. Robin McDonald, "UGA settles federal suit with professor," Feb 8, 2010.

191 Soloski narrative.

192 Carolyn Crist interview with Soloski, *Red & Black*, posted February 14, 2010, and Soloski narrative.

193 Rich Whitt, *Behind the Hedges: Big Money and Power Politics at the University of Georgia* (Montgomery, Alabama: New South Books, 2008), and Vince Dooley, *History and Reminiscences of the University of Georgia* (Looking Glass Books, Inc., 2011) Chapt. 6. See also Bob Ryan, *Boston Globe*, March 28, 2010, whose column obviously aimed at sabotaging any chance President Adams may have had to succeed Myles Brand as head of the NCAA. In his copy of the Whitt book, Conrad Fink wrote on the title page, "A Curious book. . . . It re-hashes old quarrels and arrives at no new interpretation of interest to discerning readers." April 4, 2009. Although New South Books apparently received no subvention to publish it, this author did learn from reliable sources that Whitt may have received as much as $50,000. He died right after its publication. Although no new ground was plowed, the appendices do contain: The Deloitte & Touche Audit; Regents' Response; Adams' Response; and other relevant correspondence and letters. As such, it is as complete an accounting of who found and said "what."

194 *Atlanta Journal-Constitution*, May 15, 2014, D-1.

195 "Grady College: A One Month Report," 2006 Administrators Retreat, Clark Files, Grady College archives.

# INDEX